Library of
Davidson College

MUSICAL LIFE IN POLAND

MUSICOLOGY: A BOOK SERIES
edited by F. Joseph Smith

Volume 1 THE EXPERIENCING OF MUSICAL SOUND
Prelude to a Phenomenology of Music
F. Joseph Smith

Volume 2 MUSIC AND ITS SOCIAL MEANINGS
Christopher Ballantine

Volume 3 MUSIC, FILM, AND ART
Haig Khatchadourian

Volume 4 LATE RENAISSANCE MUSIC AT THE HABSBURG COURT
Polyphonic Settings of the Mass Ordinary at the Court of Rudolf II (1576–1612)
Carmelo P. Comberiati

Volume 5 WITNESSES AND SCHOLARS: STUDIES IN MUSICAL BIOGRAPHY
Hans Lenneberg

Volume 6 THE TROMBONE: ITS HISTORY AND MUSIC, 1697–1811
David M. Guion

Volume 7 MUSIC FROM THE MIDDLE AGES THROUGH THE TWENTIETH CENTURY: ESSAYS IN HONOR OF GWYNN S. McPEEK
edited by Carmelo P. Comberiati and Matthew C. Steel

Volume 8 UNDERSTANDING THE MUSICAL EXPERIENCE
edited by F. Joseph Smith

Volume 9 STRAVINSKY
The Music Box and the Nightingale
Daniel Albright

Volume 10 MUSICAL LIFE IN POLAND
The Postwar Years 1945–1977
Lidia Rappoport-Gelfand

This book is part of a series. The publisher will accept continuation orders which may be cancelled at any time and which provide for automatic billing and shipping of each title in the series upon publication. Please write for details.

MUSICAL LIFE IN POLAND
The Postwar Years
1945–1977

Lidia Rappoport-Gelfand

Translated from the Russian by
Irina Lasoff

Gordon and Breach
New York Philadelphia London Paris Montreux Tokyo Melbourne

Copyright © 1991 by OPA (Amsterdam) B.V. All rights reserved. Published under license by Gordon and Breach Science Publishers S.A.

Gordon and Breach Science Publishers

Post Office Box 786
Cooper Station
New York, New York 10276
United States of America

5301 Tacony Street, Drawer 330
Philadelphia, Pennsylvania 19137
United States of America

Post Office Box 197
London WC2E 9PX
United Kingdom

58, rue Lhomond
75005 Paris
France

Post Office Box 161
1820 Montreux 2
Switzerland

3-14-9, Okubo
Shinjuku-ku, Tokyo 169
Japan

Private Bag 8
Camberwell, Victoria 3124
Australia

Library of Congress Cataloging-in-Publication Data

Rappoport-Gelfand, Lidia.
  Musical life in Poland: the postwar years 1945–1977.
  (Musicology ; v. 10)
  Translated from the Russian.
  Bibliography: p.
  Includes index.
  1. Music—Poland—20th century—History and criticism.
I. Title. II. Series: Musicology (New York, N.Y.) ;
v. 10.
ML297.5.R313 1991   781.7438   88-25950
ISBN 2-88124-319-3
ISSN 0275-5866

Cover: From the XIX International Festival of Contemporary Music, Warsaw Autumn 1986.

No part of this book may be reproduced or utilized in any form or by any means, electronic or mechanical, including photocopying and recording, or by any information storage or retrieval system, without permission in writing from the publishers. Printed in the United States of America.

CONTENTS

Introduction to the Series	vii
Introduction	ix
List of Photographs	xvii
Chapter I. Music of the First Postwar Decade (1945–1956)	1
Notes to Chapter I	40
Chapter II. Music of the Second Postwar Decade (1956–1965)	44
Notes to Chapter II	90
Chapter III. Music of the Third Postwar Decade (1965–1977)	93
1. G. Bacewicz	104
2. T. Baird	111
3. H. M. Górecki	117
3.1. The Second Symphony: "Copernican"	121
3.2. The Third Symphony of Sad Songs	126
4. K. Meyer. Symphonies	133
5. K. Serocki. Compositions 1965–1970	142
6. B. Szabelski. Fifth Symphony	150
7. K. Penderecki. St. Luke Passion	154
8. K. Penderecki. Dies Irae	168
9. K. Penderecki. Cosmogony	173
10. W. Lutoslawski. Preludia i Fuga	178
Notes to Chapter III	194

Appendix I. Music and Musical Life in Contemporary Poland:
        Musical Examples   197
Appendix II. List of the Works of the Polish Composers   200
Footnotes for Appendix II   218
Bibliography   219
Footnotes for Bibliography   241
Index   243

INTRODUCTION TO THE SERIES

The Gordon and Breach *Musicology* series, a companion to the *Journal of Musicological Research*, covers a creative range of musical topics, from historical and theoretical subjects to social and philosophical studies. Volumes thus far published show the extent of this broad spectrum, from *Music and Its Social Meanings*, *Music from the Middle Ages through the Twentieth Century: Essays in Honor of Gwynn S. McPeek,* and *Understanding the Musical Experience*, to *Musical Life in Poland: The Postwar Years 1945–1977*. The editor also welcomes interdisciplinary studies, ethnomusicological works, and performance analyses. With this series, it is our aim to expand the field and definition of musical exploration and research.

INTRODUCTION

Never in the history of Polish music had there been a period like the one which followed the Second World War. No other period gave the world so many outstanding composers, so many talented works in all kinds of genres, or saw such a flowering of musical culture. Polish music asserted itself on the world scene as an independent, distinct and creatively important phenomenon.

Much of the destiny of Polish music was determined by the innovative experimentation which took place under the influence of the social and spiritual changes that occurred in Poland. At the same time, progressive national musical traditions were also quite significant. The music of the 1900s played a special role in the development of the contemporary symphony, for it was then, at the junction of the two centuries, that the influential musical association Young Poland began its activities. Following the example of two organizations that were formed at that time in other arts, young musicians strove to renew radically expressive means, perfect techniques of composition, and raise the general level of culture.

Young Poland's outstanding contribution was the creation of a national symphonic school. Composers endeavored to introduce into Polish music the great achievements of contemporary European musical art. The compositions of the late romantics (Wagner, R. Strauss, Reger, Bruckner), as well as those of Debussy and the Russian music of the turn at the century, all served as models for the young composers. For the first time in the history of Polish music, a national symphonic art attained a high aesthetic and creative level.[1]

The most eminent members representing Young Poland were M. Karlowicz and K. Szymanowski. Karlowicz, in many ways a follower of R. Strauss, successfully introduced the symphonic poem into Polish music. Many of his poems, such as *Stanislaw and Anna Oświecimowie*, *The Sad Story*, *The Returning Waves*, *The Lithuanian Rhapsody*, *Episode at a Masquerade*, and the triptych *Three Ancient Songs*, have great artistic merit. A master of orchestral color and a gifted symphonic composer, Karlowicz preserved a national, distinctly Slavic, quality in his music.

K. Szymanowski's compositions are more universal and comprehensive in scope. He composed piano, violin, symphonic, operatic, and ballet music and received international recognition. His art was nurtured by the various artistic tendencies of the age. At different stages of his development, Szymanowski absorbed and reinterpreted the influences of late romanticism, especially of R. Strauss and Wagner, and at a later date, of Debussy, Scriabin, Bartok, and Stravinsky. These influences surface in the fine nuances, the chromaticism of Szymanowski's harmonic and melodic language. While utilizing Debussy and Ravel's innovative coloristics, he created his own colorful style in which exotic Eastern elements were also assimilated. Throughout his life, Szymanowski attempted to create a new, specifically national style, which, in the composer's opinion, would reflect the spiritual life of the Polish people, and in a musical sense, embody the highest level of compositional mastery. His ballet *Harnasie*, his song cycles *Slopewne* and *The Kurpiowskie Songs* provided models for the artistic rendering of folklore. Polish highland folklore, with its archaic modalities, was merged with contemporary harmony through orchestral color. In taking this direction, Szymanowski was not alone, for Bartok and Stravinsky travelled along paths parallel to his.

Szymanowski's works had a great influence on the various trends of the Polish music of our own time. Thus, Szymanowski's folkloric methods were taken up by S. Wiechowicz, A. Malawski, W. Rudziński, W. Poźniak, S. Poradowski, J. Mlodziejowski, J. Maklakiewicz, M. Kondracki, and others, while T. Baird's music has a close affinity to the romantic elements of Szymanowski's works.

Great mastery, perfection of compositional technique, and an ability to interpret and transfer to his native soil the progressive achievements in contemporary music of other countries are all attributes of Szymanowski's music, which served as an example for the postwar generation of musicians.

Neoclassicism was another musical tendency in Poland. In the 1930s there were a number of composers exploring this direction, and many of the young ones were aided in their work by contacts with French composers and with Stravinsky. Polish musicians living in Paris at that time organized the Society of Young Polish Musicians (Stowarzyszenie Mlodych Muzyków Polaków;

SMMP), with P. Perkowski as its first chairman. The primary goals of the SMMP were to make known in France outstanding Polish compositions of various periods, to acquaint the Polish public with French music, and also to work toward perfecting the contemporary manner of composition. A renewed interest in old Polish music proved to be a worthwhile initiative. The *Overture* by A. Szalowski, written in 1936, led to a number of imitations in subsequent years. A. Malawski, B. Szabelski, J. Maklakiewicz, T. Szeligowski, P. Perkowski, G. Bacewicz, and at times W. Lutoslawski, Z. Mycielski, and S. Kisielewski all continued to work in the sphere of neo-classicism.

The patriotic tradition stemming from Polish history of the 18th and 19th centuries had a special significance in establishing a new cultural trend in Poland. Despite repeated geographic and political divisions and the loss of their own government, the Polish people retained their spiritual and national values in folk and professional art. It is generally recognized that patriotism became the main theme of Polish romanticism in the art of Mickiewicz, Slowacki, and Chopin. In the 20th century, the generation of composers calling themselves Young Poland was brought up in this romantic tradition.

The Second World War abruptly curtailed the development of Polish culture. Under the German occupation, all manifestations of national art were suppressed. Musicians, like other artists, went underground. They composed antifascist songs and organized illegal concerts of works by Polish composers.

With the liberation came a rapid growth in all spheres of Polish culture, including music. Conditions for composers in postwar Poland were remarkably different from those in other countries of the Soviet bloc. While in the first postwar decade the communist powers of Poland blindly copied Soviet methods of leadership and held art under rigid control, by the middle 1950s increasing pressure by artists for a renewal of Polish national artistic traditions forced Gomulka's regime to relax its ideological control and cease its official support for any particular stylistic trend. Mistakes made during the era of the Cult of Personality were publically admitted, and twists and turns on the part of the leadership of culture were condemned. From that moment began the real rebirth of artistic life in Poland.

In the course of this book the specifics of national traditions of Polish culture and music will be discussed in detail, for there everything is unusual, beginning with the purely Polish romantic and expressive tradition and ending with the powerful influence of Catholicism on Polish art. We will outline the general trend of the evolution of postwar music by periods.

In 1974, the Polish people celebrated the 30th anniversary of the liberation. Although in the history of an entire culture such a span of time seems brief, scholars attempted to sum up accomplishments of that 30-year period in the various areas of cultural life. Attempts were also made to categorize the music of the last 30 years into periods. The evolution of the music can be conditionally divided into stages also, and each stage basically corresponds to one of the three postwar decades. This division is neither superficial nor arbitrary, but is determined by social, historical, and aesthetic criteria.

During the first decade, the period of restoring a destroyed economy coincided with the period of the formation of a new culture. At the same time, acting under the influence of the U.S.S.R., the Polish government demanded that the principles of so-called socialist realism be reflected in art. In conjunction with the general social task mentioned, a process was underway to bring artistic works within reach of mass audiences.

Oversimplified ideas became evident about the potentials inherent in various musical genres, about the directions and boundaries of musical experimentation, and about the correlation of individual features of art and its basic problems.

When the Second World War ended, the generation of composers who had begun their work during the years between the two great wars had many artistic problems to solve. Among these musicians were such major figures as K. Sikorski, W. Rudziński, S. Wiechowicz, W. Lutoslawski, G. Bacewicz, and B. Szabelski. After the war, they saw their mission as one of reviving the progressive foundations of national music, renewing the palette of expressive means and creating a new musical art. The leading pre-World War II artistic trends of neoclassicism and the use of folklore were further developed in their works. These experiments encompassed, in essence, all musical genres.

The creative character of the period proved to be the determining factor in opening new possibilities for the development of musical culture. A number of musical societies and artistic unions were organized. The Union of Polish Composers (ZKP) was established in 1945, with P. Perkowski as its first chairman. In the same year, musical education was revised at all levels in conservatories and musical schools. A number of journals appeared, such as *Muzyka* (dedicated to the problems of musical scholarship), and *Ruch Muzyczny*, a bimonthly periodical covering a broad range of issues in Polish musical life. The work of various musical institutions grew to such an extent that it greatly exceeded the activity level of prewar organizations. Many opera theaters and philharmonic halls were built or restored, and symphony orchestras and choruses were organized. The professional level of performance was improved, and much attention was given to the formation of new national artistic groups.

Another new organization, the Polish Music Publishing House (PWM), was highly influential in the development of the country's musical culture. This organization was directed by the well-known scholar T. Ochlewski, who saw its main task to be the publication of materials on the history of Polish music and of collections of works by the most eminent composers of the past and present.[2] Publications of the works of Chopin, sponsored by the First International Congress of Musicologists, contributed to the study of Chopin throughout the world. Later monographs appeared on Moniuszko, Szymanowski, the composers of Young Poland, and on the contemporary works of Z. Lissa, S. Lobaczewska, J. M. Chomiński, B. Schäffer, S. Jarociński, and others.

This was the period when the study of folklore in both its theoretical and practical aspects truly flowered. Field expeditions to collect folkloric materials and the deciphering of collected records increased. Song and dance groups proliferated and among them were the well-known Mazowsze and Śląsk ensembles. Publication of the complete 70-volume collection of works, begun in 1857 by the prominent national ethnographer O. Kolberg, was resumed. The well-known scholars A. Chybiński, M. and J. Sobieski, J. Ligęza, and L. Bielawski were involved in the study of problems connected with folklore. A search for new means of expression was energetically pursued in all spheres of artistic endeavor during the first decade. In music this involved literally all genres, though development was especially intense in symphonic music.

Significant changes in the political, social, and cultural life of Poland in the middle of the 1950s determined the next stage in the evolution of Polish musical art. The year 1956 marks the first year of the Warsaw Autumn festivals. The Polish people consider this to be the beginning of the second decade. From that year on, music developed in different directions, which occasionally led to a polarization of artistic tendencies. During this second half of the 1950s, a broad use of new compositional techniques, primarily dodecaphonic and serial, may be observed. These systems, however, soon became for Polish composers one of the means to develop so-called sonorism, an area in which Polish composers appeared in the vanguard. As early as the beginning of the 1960s there appeared, along with experimental opuses, the highly artistic and conceptually significant compositions by composers such as Lutoslawski, Baird, Penderecki, and others.

The cultural life of the country grew even richer and more active. The number of festivals increased, allowing music lovers to enjoy performances of music of different periods and genres from Renaissance organ music to jazz and popular songs.[3] Various state institutions organized competitions in composition. For example, the Union of Polish Composers and the Ministry of Culture, working together, sponsored the Fitelberg and the Malawski composers' competitions, as well as some others. Often a competition was limited to works in a single genre with the goal of strengthening that particular area (for example, the All-Poland A Cappella Song Competition in 1961).

Towards the end of this second decade, a striving towards the fusion of new techniques with tradition can be seen in the works of leading composers. The third decade appears as a period of relative stabilization. It is characterized by the heightened interest in traditional, large instrumental and vocal-instrumental forms, in which contemporary expressive means often led to new readings of traditional subjects and genres.

We must ask the reader's indulgence for a certain inexactness in the dating of the new phase. It is not easy to separate it from the preceding period. As early as 1962 and 1963 there appeared such significant works, in both the conceptual and stylistic sense, as Penderecki's *Stabat Mater* and Lutoslawski's *Three Poems of Henri Michaux*. Yet the break between the periods was to appear somewhat later, after the first performance of Penderecki's *St. Luke Passion*, for it was at that particular time that the essence of the new period was manifested: the increasingly organic connection between the composer's conception and the principles of expression. In the 1970s, experimentation was directed towards a broad synthesis of different elements. This was the time when numerous outstanding operas, oratorios, symphonies, and chamber works appeared and gained worldwide recognition.

The author admits that a comprehensive view of Polish music in all of its manifestations cannot be given in this limited study. The problems connected with contemporary Polish music are complicated and have not been sufficiently researched. In a comparatively short book such as this, it is impossible to answer all the questions which may arise in the process of attentive listening and close study of numerous scores by Polish masters. The aim of this work is to acquaint the reader with the development of Polish music during the three decades following the Second World War. A number of aesthetic and stylistic questions will be touched upon by analyzing specific compositions.

As can be seen when the music in the three periods is examined, individual developmental stages of music did not resemble each other. With each decade, new questions and new problems arose. Because of this, different approaches have been used to study the different phenomena. Therefore, appropriate types of exposition were chosen. In some cases, it seemed expedient to give a historic survey of music in terms of genres, thus painting a general picture of Polish musical art (Chapter I, and the introductory sections of Chapters II and III). Here the discussion about compositions is often informational and annotational. But individual problems required theoretical treatment, as in the body of Chapter II. A more detailed stylistic aspect of Polish music is revealed in concrete examples; therefore Chapter III is composed of a series of sketches and portraits of leading composers in which their most significant works are analyzed.

The American musical public is, for the most part, aware of only two contemporary Polish composers—Lutoslawski and Penderecki. In this book I have set myself the task of introducing a large group of talented composers and their artistically valuable works to the English-speaking reader.

I express my gratitude to the Directorate of the Union of Polish Composers (ZKP) and to the composers and musicologists of Warsaw and Cracow, who rendered great help by presenting me with music, books, and records. My special appreciation goes to the Polish composer and musicologist Krzysztof Meyer, who read the individual sketches at an early stage of my work, and to Dr. Kornel Michalowski who sent me important bibliographic materials.

My thanks also go to my American colleagues: composers Paul Fetler and Alexander Lubet, composer and conductor Stanislaw Skrowaczewski, musicologist Johannes Riedel, and literature professor James Walker for their help, advice, and moral support.

Steven Stucky was especially helpful as an advisor. His knowledge of contemporary Polish music and his comments were invaluable.

My thanks go to Irina Lasoff for her enthusiasm and unlagging interest in the translation of this book.

LIST OF PHOTOGRAPHS

1. Zygmunt Mycielski, after the concert at the Warsaw Autumn 1980. P. 20
2. Wojciech Kilar, 1971. P. 46
3. Zbigniew Bujarski, 1974. P. 47
4. Wlodzimierz Kotoński, 1974. P. 49
5. During the performance of a piece by François-Bernard Mâche. Performers: Eugeniusz Knapik, Krzysztof Meyer, Andrzej Dutkiewicz, and Szabolcs Esztényi (the Hungarian composer and pianist). "W.A." 1985. P. 50
6. Zygmunt Mycielski, 1977. P. 51
7. Marta Ptaszyńska with Józef Patkowski, director of the Polish Radio Experimental Studio. "W.A." 1979. P. 52
8. Andrzej Dobrowolski with members of the Warsaw Accordion Trio (Jerzy Lukaszewicz, Jerzy Kaszuba, Krzysztof Olczak). "W.A." 1979. P. 53
9. K. Penderecki, 1978. P. 67
10. Tomasz Sikorski and Jerzy Maksymiuk, the conductor of the Warsaw Philharmonic Orchestra. "W.A." 1983. P. 71
11. Witold Lutoslawski during a rehearsal at the 10th Festival of Polish Contemporary Music in Wroclaw, 1974. P. 83
12. Maniola Kowalczyk (alto) and Bernadetta Matuszczak after a performance *Canticum per Voci ed Orchestra*. "W.A." 1981. P. 100
13. Edward Pallasz, Boguslaw Schäffer. "W.A." 1981. P. 103
14. Grażyna Bacewicz. P. 105

15. Tadeusz Baird at the General Convention of the Union of Polish Composers, 1979. P. 112
16. Henrik M. Górecki, 1975. P. 118
17. Krzysztof Meyer. P. 135
18. K. Meyer with members of the Wilanów String Quartet—Tadeusz Gadzina (violin), Pawel Losakiewicz (violin), Ryszard Duź (viola), Marian Wasiolka (cello). "W.A." 1983. P. 140
19. Kazimierz Serocki, 1968. P. 143
20. Boleslaw Szabelski, "W.A." 1969. P. 151
21. Krzysztof Penderecki conducting of his opera *Paradise Lost. Sacra rappresentazione*. "W.A." 1979. P. 156
22. Witold Lutoslawski conducting his *Double Concerto for Oboe, Harp and Chamber Orchestra*. "W.A." 1980. P. 179
23. K. Meyer after the 1st performance of the opera *The Gamblers*. Wuppertal, West Germany, 1983. P. 195

I
Music of the First Postwar Decade (1945–1956)

Poland bore the first blow delivered by the Nazi war machine. The war destroyed one-fifth of the country's population. Warsaw, the nation's capital, was almost wiped off the face of the earth. No other European country suffered a catastrophe of such proportions.

The tragic experiences of war, as well as class dissensions which tore Poland apart during and after the liberation were all reflected in post-war art. This was the time when new works in theater, literature and cinema first made their appearances. The generation of Andrzej Wajda and Andrzej Munk, Tadeusz Różewicz and Tadeusz Borowski, Roman Bratny and Tadeusz Goluj, Andrzej Wróblewski and Konrad Swinarski had arrived.

The annexation of Poland into the Soviet East European bloc put a specific stamp on the thematic material and character of artistic work produced during the first decade after the war. For some time, the arts found themselves under pressure imposed by communist ideology and slogans of socialist realism. Art was forced to become the mouthpiece for certain ideas, while the artists had to become the "educators of society." This was the time when the question was often posed, both in articles by Polish musicologists and at public appearances of composers, about the role of the "addressee" of the arts—the public—the "consumers of art" ("odbiorca").

The question "What ideological and stylistic direction should Polish music take?" became the subject of numerous discussions, conferences and conventions. In 1949 the national convention of Polish composers met in Lagów. It reflected the ideology of the Stalinist era. A platform of aesthetics was adopted that called for the extensive use of national traditions in professional music of all types, for accessibility in musical language, for connections between music and actual contemporary problems. But composers tried to impose their own interpretations on these slogans. Ignoring their negative aspects, they adopted, whenever possible, what was positive to their music. "Group 49" formed by Tadeusz Baird, Jan Krenz and Kazimierz Serocki, may serve as an example of how composers were able to survive the transitional difficult period of government pressure on the arts. The convention's declarations became the base of the group's platform. In the program printed on the occasion of the first joint concert by the group (January, 1950), Stefan Jarociński edited its credo: "Three young composers have come together in 'Group 49,'* joined by their intention to support each other in solving problems—problems, which, in their opinion, are posited by a new social reality in Poland. . . . The young musicians ardently desire to re-establish contact with that listener, who, today, is becoming the chief consumer of culture. Their music, anti-elitist in spirit, is not meant to flatter cheap bourgeois taste. Therefore, in the pursuit of their goals, the young musicians do not wish to forego the use of any of the innovations of modern harmony."[4]

Meanwhile, the ZKP (Związek Kompozytorów Polskich—Union of Polish Composers) convention of 1950 emphasized the need to strengthen ideological work. This convention represented the quintessential cultural policy of that time. The ZKP took and approved the position that national traditions, above all those of folklore, should constitute the base on which composers structure their work. Directives were formulated—preferences voiced for programmatic, vocal and all forms of popular music. The convention demanded major simplifications in musical means. Any complexity whatsoever in the realm of professional technique was looked upon as "bourgeois influence" and labelled "formalism." The battle against "formalism" was a typical progeny of socialist realism. In this, Polish ideologists followed the lead set by Soviet cultural policies during the era of the "personality cult."

Rigidity, one-sideness, the absence of sensible objective criteria accompanied subsequent discussions during the hearings of new works: mass-song, "club music" (music intended for use by community centers), and chamber music. These events took place at various sessions of the ZKP (Union of Polish Composers).

The convention culminated in a "festival of Polish Music," where the greatest attention was devoted to a competition in mass-song.

However, crude pressure exerted by official circles on arts organizations in Poland was a temporary phenomenon; the spirit of independence had long been ingrained in Polish artists. Nevertheless, the liberation of art from ideology was to be a long, gradual process.

---

*Referring to the year the group was formed.

The Sixth Convention of ZKP (1953) was the first one to witness some initial changes in what was then the prevalent dogmatic atmosphere. Thoughts were clearly formulated on the need to broaden the scope of expressive means, and on the necessity of looking for new solutions.

In the Seventh Convention of ZKP (1954), governmental cultural policy in regard to music came under frank criticism for the first time. A new directorate of ZKP, under the guiding hand of K. Sikorski, worked out a fresh concept for a festival of Polish music, with attention focused on high professional standards.

During discussions at the Eighth Convention of ZKP (1955), which evaluated the results of the second festival, a resolution was passed to hold periodic international festivals. This led to cultural exchanges with the West, and artistic isolationism came to an end.

With the birth of the "Warsaw Autumn" festivals (the first was held in 1956), the influence of governmental cultural policy waned. Polish art now entered its second phase of post-war development.

In spite of all the difficulties of the first decade, a significant development could be observed in all branches of music: in opera, ballet, and symphonic composition; in vocal-instrumental and choral works; and in the broad areas of popular song and lyric theater. True, not all branches of musical endeavor were successful. Thus, political song, a genre new to Poland, never became assimilated in that country, although some Polish songs did receive general acclaim, and a whole rank of composers specializing in song did come to the fore, among them E. Olearczyk, A. Gradstein, W. Szpilman, and T. Sygietyński.

Polish post-war mass-song (or state authorized popular song) drew its material from native sources arising out of Kościuszko revolutionary songs and marches. Its prototypes were May First songs, songs of insurgence, campaign marches, and other revolutionary songs: *Warszawianka* by K. Kurpiński dating back to the uprising of 1830; *When the People Rose in Battle (Gdy naród do boju)*, text by G. Erenberg, 1836; and also some workers' revolutionary songs: *Warszawianka* by W. Święcicki, *Red Banner* by B. Czerwieński; *The Convinct's Mazurka (Mazurka Kajdaniarski)* by L. Waryński, the founder of the first Marxist Party in Poland; and many others. It is known that the Polish songs, *When the People Rose in Battle, Warszawianka,* and *Red Banner* served as models for songs of the 1905 Russian Revolution. Their most distinctive feature is the triple meter, mazurka rhythm.

Now the agenda of the day called for the creation of a new type Polish mass-song, one which would fulfill a specific educational purpose. Inevitably, the influence of Soviet compositions was felt, especially as contemporary Russian, Ukrainian, and Byelorussian songs were all familiar to Poles. Thus appeared songs by W. Szpilman and others, their melodic and rhythmic elements modeled on Soviet examples.

In songs of this genre, collaboration between composer and poet was very important, especially since the objective was to focus attention on native poetic folk imagery. Among poets working in this genre were: K. Gruszczyński, G. Kolaczkowska, K. Winkler, and S. Wygodzki. The last was especially popular. In the structure of a song, composers relied on rhythmic formulas and melodic motifs characteristic of national dances (*The Rowan Tree* by K. Serocki, *A New Mazurka* by J. Mklakiewicz, *Not Far Away from Cracow* by Gradstein, and *Mary, Little Mary* by W. Rudziński).

Among the most beloved compositions in Poland were: *Millions of Hands* by the talented composer Olearcyzk (words by K. Gruszczyński), *Wind of Freedom* by Szpilman (words by K. Winkler), and *Song of the Six Year Plan* by T. Sygietyński (words by S. Wygodzki).

Composers aimed to give the melodic content of these songs either an impetuous, dynamic quality, or else a march-like character as in Tadeusz Sygietyński's *March of Peace* (words by Edward Fiszer). Ex. 1.

Example 1

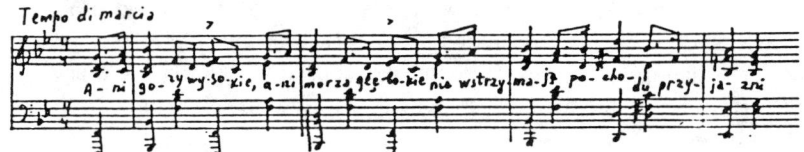

State-authorized popular songs as a new form of post-war art attracted not only those composers who specialized in this type of work, but also those whose interests normally lay in serious music. Note the following examples: a song about Nowa Huta**, *A Splendid Dream*, music by W. Lutoslawski (words by S. Wygodzki), and *The Rowan Tree*, music by K. Serocki (words by T. Urgacz).

The best of these songs by Sygietyński, Gradstein, Olearczyk, Lutoslawski, Serocki, Turski, Szpilman et al, won wide acclaim and many of them entered the repertory of the *Mazowsze Ensemble* which was formed during this period by Sygietyński. An energetic man, a talented composer and conductor, Tadeusz Sygietyński had dreamt of creating a large folkloric ensemble of singers and dancers as far back as the 1920's. Now, at last, with government support and subsidy, he was able to realize his dream. By a painstaking selection process, performers were chosen from hundreds and thousands of young village girls and youths. The *Mazowsze Ensemble* came

---

**Nowa Huta—New Huta is the name of a recently built large metallurgical combine.

into being. Such splendid compositions as Sygietyński's *Beloved Land* (words by Galczyński), Szpilman's *Sea Eagles* (words by Urgacz), Olearczyk's *At the Frontier's Barrier* (words by M. Lebkowski), Gradstein's *Not Far Away from Cracóv* (words by Kolaczkowska), and other songs were all performed by the *Mazowsze Ensemble* and became known far beyond the borders of Poland.

In evaluating mass-song of the first post-war decade, we come to the conclusion that it was a genre that did not "take" in Poland. Artificially grafted onto Polish culture by govermental policy "from above," taking for its models compositions from the neighboring "Big Brother," this type of song was foreign to the traditions of Poland. The unfortunate effects of arbitrary ideological governmental interference in the arts became clear. It was hardly surprising that the most successful efforts took the form of lyric song, in which the composers could be sincere and express their individuality (songs by Lutoslawski, Serocki, Sygietyński, et al). In contrast to these songs, workers' songs were colorless. Their gray dullness was stupifying. Influenced to a great extent by Soviet songs, their artistic failings were obvious: cliches, formalistic designs, sameness in rhythmic patterns, lack of originality in structural and melodic solutions.

The mass-song genre did not last long. It outlived itself on the threshold of the second post-war decade, which marked a turning point in art in response to changes in internal politics.

Similar processes were taking place in the sphere of choral forms: in cantata and oratorio. A widespread interest in choral song appeared during the first post-war decade.

In the development of this particular genre, two government-sponsored ensembles of signers and dancers were instrumental: Śląsk*** under the artistic direction of S. Hadyna, and the above-mentioned Mazowsze*** under the direction of T. Sygietyński.

Composers working in the field of choral music turned their attention toward the development and adaptation of folklore material. They looked to authentic folk songs still heard in our own times, or else found material in the classic collections of O. Kolberg, W. Skierkowski, J. Ligęza et al. Among composers workin in this genre were: T. Baird, M. Dziewulska, J. Krenz, J. Maklakiewicz, T. Paciorkiewicz, K. Serocki, K. Sikorski, T. Szeligowski, S. Wiechowicz. Besides arranging existing songs, composers also wrote original compositions in the style of folk songs. Outstanding composers in this field, such as K. Sikorski and S. Wiechowicz, exhibited a high level of craftsmanship. Choral compositions in this genre ranged from simple songs written in couplets to large works in extended forms, such as the broadly developed *Ballade-Kujawiak* by S. Wiechowicz.

***Śląsk (Silesia) and Mazowsze (Mazowia) are two historical regions in Poland.

Some composers used innovative means to enhance expressive possibilities of choral music. Thus *Small Songs* by K. Serocki is such a work. Polytonality, a fine contrapuntal technique, sinuous melodic design, all make this work accessible for performance only to professional groups. W. Lutoslawski's *Ten Folk Songs on Soldiers' Themes* is another composition of great interest. Here, the composer relied on multi-voice national folk practices to evoke specific sound colors.[5]

Some compositions reflect a composer's personal style. An individual approach marks A. Panufnik's *Five Polish Songs*. This piece was composed in 1940 and then revised in 1945. Panufnik is known for his involvement with problems of expanding the formal means and sound color in Polish music. In this rather small composition, the treatment of folk melodies is achieved by means of an impressionistic color palette, not only from the point of view of the musical texture (an original polyphonic fabric), but also in its instrumentation (a boys' choir and a transparent chamber ensemble).

From an artistic point of view, the more substantive works are those in which folk traditions and principles of composition are united into an organic whole. In *Carols (Kolędziolki beskidzkie)*, written for women's chorus, Wiechowicz achieves this goal. Wiechowicz's individual style rises spontaneously out of folk melody types, characterized by dotted rhythms and modal-harmonic alteration. The composer's experience in choral music was put to good use in his cantata and oratorio compositions. An interesting crossing of two genres (the choral song and cantata) is to be found in Wiechowicz's *On a Clay Vase* for à capella chorus.

Skillful thematic development, complex choral techniques, a wide range of polyphonic devices, original monumental concepts—such are the means that transform choral song into cantata.

The cantata-oratorio genre was relatively new to Poland with no deep roots in the traditions of the 19th Century. Such work as existed in these forms developed within the framework of church traditions, and few compositions had any outstanding artistic merit. Among the exception is Szymanowski's *Stabat Mater*. Now a new interest in the cantata genre put a burden of responsibility on composers. Necessity forced them into founding a new tradition. As some of the work that emerged had definite artistic value, we will pause briefly to examine developments in this field of musical endeavor.

The widespread interest in oratorios and cantatas during the 40's and 50's can be attributed to certain specific features typical of the genre: monumental forms, large choruses, a general treatment of the form which, in its boldness, could be likened to poster-art. All these distinctive traits of the genre lent themselves well to the expression of ideological problems that were dic-

I. Music of the First Postwar Decade (1945-1956)   7

tated by political reality. The imprint of ideology was most visible in the types of texts and subjects that were chosen for cantatas. These were: Revolution (*Revolutionary Song* by T. Baird); Peace (*Cantata in Praise of Peace* by A. Dobrowolski, and *Peace Cantata* by S. Skrowaczewski); War and victory over Nazism and glorification of the native land (*Victory* by W. Lachman, *Grenada* by J. Maklakiewicz, *Cantata on Greatness* and *Vistula* by J. Mlodziejowski, *Heroic Poem* by B. Szabelski, *Land* by Z. Turski, et al.)

A mood of enthusiasm for reconstruction had gripped the whole country, and composers reflected it in their cantatas. The building of new cities and the rebuilding of those ruined by the war became the thematic material of a particular group of compositions which were closely modeled on the thematic structure of the Soviet cantata. In these compositions, the influence of mass-song was stronger than in other works written in the same genre (*Two Cities* by J. Krenz; *Silesia Works and Plays* by J. Maklakiewicz; *Warsaw Stonemason* by K. Serocki; *The Old City—Stare miasto* by A. Swierzyński; *Cantata in Praise of Labor* by B. Woytowicz, et al.)

Some cantatas were composed for special occasions to commemorate a particular day or mark an event: thus, on the occasion of Chopin's jubilee, F. Dąbrowski wrote *The Passing of Fryderick* (1949). Pushkin's anniversary was marked by Woytowicz's *The Prophet*; the Polish poet Mickiewicz's by two compositions—S. Wiechowicz's *Romantic Cantata* and Paciorkiewicz's *Ode to Youth*. Many cantatas were dedicated to the memory of fallen heroes.

A specific group of cantatas arose connected to the folkloric trend. Composers recreated folk rituals. In this category, we find: *An Old Tale* by A. Malawski, *The Wedding* by H. Czyż, *Lublin Wedding* by T. Szeligowski, *The Harvest Cantata* by S. Wiechowicz, etc. Sometimes composers would highlight some particular aspect of regional folklore, as in J. Maklakiewicz's *Lowicka Suite* and K. Serocki's *Mazowsze*.

While some compositions were inspired by musical folklore, others used actual folk texts, and they too were a part of this trend (Lutoslawski's *Silesian Triptych*). Compositions which bear the characteristics of ballads have much in common with national folk traditions and must also be included: *Ballad of Soldier's Mug* by T. Baird, *Pomorski Ballad* by P. Perkowski, *Man and Maid* by T. Szeligowski, *The Peasant's Road* by W. Rudziński. All are set to texts by well-known poets (Lenartowicz, Konopnicka, Wolski, et al).

During the first post-war decade, the cantata appeared mostly in the form of a choral or solo suite, and as a one-part vocal-instrumental composition. Many cantatas were written with amateur performances in mind; hence the lack of an orchestral accompaniment. In the more extended cantata cycles, the most popular form followed the principle of the suite. This was especially true of those cantatas which dealt with folk life (*Lowicka Suite* by J. Maklakiewicz, *Lublin Wedding* by T. Szeligowski). From the artistic standpoint, the most interesting works are the ones in which different "borderline" types of cantata genres intersect. Thus, in Malawski's *An Old Tale*, the subject of folk rites is an essential element, yet it is but a part of a broader oratorio conception. *An Old Tale* is an extended composition in six movements with an introduction. Each movement, in accordance with oratorio tradition, is divided into separate numbered sections. At the same time, there is a pull towards the through-development of an extended form. In the fourth movement the center of the composition stands a large independent section—a scene depicting the feast day of John the Baptist.

The extended vocal solo part and chorus in the pantomime-ballet *The Mountain Tops* clearly indicates Malawski's desire to broaden the framework of the cantata form. Here, the composer relied on traditions started by Szymanowski in *Harnasie*. *The Mountain Tops* is sub-titled *Góralski Rhapsody*, thus pointing to the ballet's origins.

The composer makes much use of melodic turns, rhythms and modalities peculiar to Góralski songs and dances. But the character of the transformation of this material, when compared to Szymanowski's treatment, is more superficial and tends to be over-stylized. In *The Mountain Tops*, Malawski used folk modes, particularly the Lydian and Mixolydian (Podhalski); syncopated rhythms typical of this region; alternating meters; original melismatics; sudden shouts—often heard in Goralski singing—and other specific features of Goralski multi-voice style: bourdon counterpoints, tritones, bitonality, and "exotic" devices in instrumentation (for instance, bells of different pitches which the native mountaineers hang around their sheep's necks). Taken as a whole, *The Mountain Tops* is an original, poetic composition combining ballet and oratorio. Created in 1951, it was frequently performed on the concert stage. In 1961, in keeping with the composer's original idea, it was staged by the Warsaw Opera.

The search for vivid and rewarding ways to enhance expressivity led composers to create parts for narrators in cantatas (*Ballad of the Soldier's Mug* by T. Baird, *The Song of Songs* by S. Skrowaczewski, *Portrait of a Muse* by Z. Mycielski, *Weeping Odysseus* by T. Szeligowski.) At times, however, an exaggerated highlighting of the text led to a disruption of musical development. The balance in the relationship between musical and textual elements was lost. In the *Cantata in Honor of Peace* by A. Dobrowolski, and in *Chart of the Heart (Karta Serc)* by T. Szeligowski, whole sections are written as recitatives or choral "pseudo-recitatives" (the definition is Chomiński's). Obviously they suffer musically.[6]

Two compositions, *The Prophet* by B. Woytowicz, and *Silesian Triptych* by W. Lutoslawski must be included as works that attained a high degree of excellence among cantata art of the first ten post-war years.

The cantata *The Prophet* by T. Woytowicz (set to Pushkin's verse and translated from Russian into Polish by Julian Tuwim), was written for the 150th anniversary of Pushkin's birth. This event was celebrated in 1949, not only in the USSR, but also in Poland. The poetry selected, in which an idea is expressed through allegory, dictated the choice of the musical genre: the traditional lyrico-philosophical cantata. The composer consciously turned to Russian traditions in this form (Rimsky-Korsakov's *The Prophet* and S. Taneiev's *John of Damascus*). Woytowicz borrowed from the Russian cantata its epic sweep and pictorial quality, as well as the cantilena in the orchestral-choral episode, where an image of a land of boundless distances is evoked. This romantic music makes one aware not only of its pan-slavic sources, but also of its national origins, and above all, of the influence of the composers of *Young Poland*—Szymanowski and Karlowicz.

The music in Woytowicz's cantata is distinguished by its Polish broad emotional scope, epic images, and a contemplative lyricism that alternates with highly dramatic moments.

In this one-movement composition, whose prototype is a poem with introductory and concluding sections, the single line of a through development is drawn. A tendency towards symphonic development is clearly expressed. The principle on which a poem is constructed is combined here with some sonata features.

A juxtaposition of sharply contrasting themes lies at the very base of the form. Each section clearly fulfills its function of exposition, development, and recapitulation.

The choral part fulfills many functions. The chorus adds supplementary tone color to the orchestral timbre in the introduction and recapitulation. The chorus often takes on the role of the crowd (in the dialogue with the bass soloist). At times, the chorus becomes a commentator through whom we hear the author's voice, and then again it becomes a crowd reacting with animation to the events of the drama. This variety of aspects and functions results in a richness of choral texture. It encompasses song-like chorale, recitatival repliques, and a speaking chorus shouting out key words or phrases at climactic moments. One of the basic means of the symphonic development is polyphonic technique: fugal structures, imitations, and stretti. The composer also often employs a method which calls for the use of easily recognizable musical formulas that can evoke certain associations in the minds of the public.[7] At such moments, when literal meaning is important, a march or a song-like theme appears. The coda—a summation of the whole com-

Example 2

position—is modeled on traditional codas of cantatas written in praise and celebration of some event. As a result of symphonic development throughout the length of the composition, song is transformed into majestic hymn. Let us compare the lyrical cantilena of the introduction with the hymn-like march of the coda. Ex. 2.

Such affirmative, powerful concluding sections are typical of Russian cantatas in general, and of Soviet cantatas in particular. Woytowicz may well have heard such endings in Prokofiev's *oratorios*. *The Prophet* is full of vivid imagery, massive symphonic development in the cantata genre, and demonstrates a high level of mastery of the craft of composition. This is an outstanding work in the field of the Polish cantata.

Whereas *The Prophet* represents the "pure" cantata, W. Lutoslawski's *Silesian Triptych* (*Tryptyk Śląski,* 1951) for soprano and orchestra, as a genre, may be placed on the boundary between a cantata and a symphonic cycle with a vocal solo. In *Silesian Triptych*, Lutoslawski eschewed using literal quotations from folkloric sources. Such quotations had lowered the artistic worth of many compositions of that time, making them imitative and faceless. In working with folkloric themes Lutoslawski's methods were different. And although he, himself, emphasized that these pieces were of secondary importance, yet the force of his talent is such that they stand out amid the general folkloric compositions written during this time in Poland. The craftsmanship and originality of Lutoslawski's pieces place them outside the framework of functional music. In the *Little Suite* for orchestra (1950), Lutoslawski had demonstrated his ability to utilize folk materials within a large form. *Silesian Triptych* represented the next step on the same path. The composer had been diligent in his study of little-known Silesian songs collected by J. Bystroń and J. Ligęza. Now he boldly took and developed those typical turns of phrase and rhythms found in national folk melodies. The authentic poetic text, however, he used in its entire original form. The subject is a traditional one in folk poetry: a maiden is deceived and deserted.

Proud and strong, she finds resources within herself to forget her worthless lover.

In this work, the composer was able to achieve an organic unity of content, conveying the particular way in which a folk perceives the world and responds to it. The cycle is ternary. A dramatic line runs steadily from the objective narrative in the first movement through the deepening drama of the second (the lyrico-philosophic center of the piece), and on to the finale (life-affirming, dance-like and virtuoso in character). *Silesian Triptych* is an example of the symphonic development of a miniature vocal work. The composer's mastery over his craft is shown in the balance between the objective tone of the composition, evinced in its narrative manner, as well as by its whole thematic system, and the meticulous attention given to each one of the musical elements: refinement and polish in harmonization, instrumentation, etc. In the Polish art of the first post-war decade, *Silesian Triptych* pointed the way toward the synthesis of inividualistic and national tendencies in art.

A considerable amount of attention was devoted to opera and ballet during this first post-war decade. In spite of some achievements it must be said that Polish composers did not attain the high level of artistry in these genres that they attained in symphonic and chamber music of the same period. The cause for this failure cannot be ascribed solely to performance or production difficulties. Rather, the chief complication arose from ideological and aesthetic considerations. In choosing an outline and a genre for an opera, composers found themselves facing a whole set of problems, solutions to which demanded time. Questions were posed: "Should social changes and reforms occurring in the nation influence an opera's subject matter?" "Is opera in need of reform?" At times, composers took a somewhat doctrinaire approach to these problems.

Opera and ballet, as two big genres which synthesize several different art forms and are tied directly to dramatic action, were more affected by governmental ideology than other types of music. The example set by the Russians of sleepless vigilance and interference in musical and theatrical affairs loomed large before the eyes of the Poles. Two notorious instances of fulminations by the Central Committee of the Communist Party come to mind. One was a resolution directed against Dmitri Shostakovich's opera "Lady Macbeth of Mtsensk." It read, "Muddle instead of music" (1936); the other against Vano Muradeli was simply headed, "On the opera 'The Great Friendship' by V. Muradeli" (1948).

The problem of content, however, was not the only one facing Polish composers. Their difficulties were increased by lack of serious national traditions in the operatic field. Only the operas of Stanislaw Moniuszko and Ludomir Różycki could serve as models. Traditions stemming from the period between the two great wars were discounted and considered to be irrelevant to present day problems as defined by the new cultural policies of Poland. Operas of Feliks Nowowiejski, Boleslaw Wallek-Walewski, and even Karol Szymanowski were considered to deflect attention from contemporary problems. Thus, a short-lived yet very real national tradition had to be rejected, for now it was looked upon as the progeny of a decadent culture. Of necessity, composers turned to well-known models of heroic folk and lyric opera. Unfortunately, operatic stereotypes were hard to avoid, and so opera became one of the least productive of musical genres. Many composers attempted to write operas, but not many were able to bring their work to full fruition. Only a few of the best compositions were ever produced, or remained for however short a time, in repertory. (*The Students' Rebellion* by Tadeusz Szeligowski, *Johnny, The Musician* by Witold Rudziński, *Andrew of Chelmno* by Piotr Rytel, and the children's operas of Mieczyslaw Drobner and Wladyslaw Walentynowicz.)

Prior to starting work on the opera *The Students' Rebellion***** (*Bunt Żakow*), T. Szeligowski had already composed many symphonic and vocal works. The most notable were a piano concerto, the cantata *Lublin Wedding*, and a ballet *The Peacock and the Maiden*. In *The Students' Rebellion*, Szeligowski chose to work in the historical opera genre.[8]

This opera shows, to some extent, how Polish composers and authors interpreted Polish socialistic realism. In this case, that interpretation concerned itself with the opera's subject (libretto by Roman Brandstaetter) and with the choice of genre. But, drawing on so many different types of sources (national folk, historical drama, lyric opera, oratorios, etc.) led to an eclectic and imitative style.

The moving force that propels the action in *The Students' Rebellion* is class conflict, the battle between a community of poverty-stricken students (the common people), and the ruling powers of the city in conjunction with the king's court. In spite of the fact that the conflict unfolds in a rather simplistic fashion, some unquestionably successful solutions to both musical and dramatic problems were found.

The authors were most successful in their handling of mass choral scenes. Written with a broad sweep, they carry the opera's dramatic line of action.

The opera is unified via a wide system of leit-motifs. The Cracow heinal[†]

Example 3

*****The Students' Rebellion* is also translated as *The Scholars' Revolt*.
[†]The Cracow heinal is an historical fanfare of national origin.

signals the coming of dawn. It stands as a symbol of the students' love of freedom. The sound of fanfares opens and closes the opera and is repeatedly heard throughout the mass scenes. Ex. 3.

Among other leit-motif themes is a students' song which serves to create a group portrait. "Gregorianka" is a song connected with St. Gregory's day—a holiday. Ritualistic in character, the song is stylized. The melody is archaic in tone color, narrow in diapason, of a diatonic structure with parallel fourths in the vertical. Rather unexpectedly, the refrain of the song "modulates" into a different style of complex modal turns reminiscent of Moussorgsky. Ex. 4.

The very first couplet of the students' song in the opera is repeated again and again. It embodies the spirit of battle which has gripped the rebellious students. A many-sided image of the student body emerges, and in the development section acquires a vivid ethnic individuality. A characteristic dialogue takes place in the second act between the students and the professors. The students sing a four-part chorale. Its melodic structure indicates its national folk origin. The chorus of conforming professors, on the other hand, appears to have no national origin. It has been stylized in the 12th century by a medieval organum in parallel fourths.

The scene of the students' procession to the court of Wawel (Act III) makes the strongest musical impression. The powerful melody of a protestant chorale serves as a foundation from which dynamic variations evolve. A unison theme is gradually interwoven with orchestral counterpoint. An image arises of a mighty power approaching. Unfortunately, Szeligowski was less successful in his handling of scenes of conflict, battles and collisions. In Act IV, superficial illustrative devices prevail: galloping rhythms, chromatic passages, trumpets signalling unrest.

Example 4

Example 5

Far more convincing is the musical solution in the scene where the students first appear. Here the composer is aided by the use of recognizable generic rhythmic and melodic formulas: lively, dance-like songs of a national character in mazurka and kujawiak rhythms.[a] Ex. 5.

The numerous and varied mass scenes provide a historical and ethnic background for the opera's action. Szeligowski shows himself to be a master of this genre, capable of sketching a character in quick, revealing strokes. Not only the students, but a colorful crowd of Cracow natives is depicted (lively dialogue in Scene 5), a company of revellers in a wine cellar (drinking song in Scene 2), a group of professors, conservative and obdurate in their opinions (Scene 3), and a crowd of courtiers (ensemble in Scene 6), whose musical characteristics are contrasted to those of the students.

From the standpoint of musical dramatization, a weakness becomes apparent in the treatment of individual roles. The composer was unable to rise above operatic stereotypes. An absence of individuality in the character portrayals of the protagonists, sentimentality and an over-strained emotionalism in love scenes all lower the artistic worth of the opera. The musical language of the different characters lacks variety. It is recitatival and declamatory, and only occasionally melodic. These are the factors which lead to blurred characterizations which resemble each other. True, the composer did make some attempt to individualize roles through identifying thematic devices. Thus, the entrances of the hostess of the tavern (Katarzyna) are frequently accompanied by the sound of the krakowiak[b]; those of Konopny by a bracing fanfare. But, in the love scenes, Konopny is in no way distinguishable from other lovers in opera. Like them, he is over-emotional, over-enthusiastic,

---

[a] Kujawiak: A Polish folk dance in triple meter, named after the province of its origin, Kujawy. The dance is related to a rapid mazurka, but unlike the latter, its accents fall with strict symmetry. As a rule, every fourth measure is accented.

[b] Krakowiak: A Polish dance named after the city of Cracow (Kraków). The music is in 2/4 time and employs simple syncopated patterns.

and melodramatic. The same criticisms hold true for Anna's character. Closely allied to Puccini's lyrical heroines, the melodramatic nature of her musical pronouncements obviously fails to blend into the epic structure of the opera. Furthermore, a dramaturgic error was committed here, for the lyric scenes are static and suffer from their similarity to each other. Long duets are inappropriately placed in the action, slowing it down and impeding dramatic development.

The Students' Rebellion leaves us with contradictory impressions. Dramatic solutions may be considered to be successful. The greatest weakness of the opera is in its style. Eclectic, it draws on too many variegated genres. Nevertheless, the shortcomings of this work do not outweigh its positive qualities. *The Students' Rebellion* is an example of a national folk drama. It is by this standard that its significance in the music of the first post-war decade must be measured. Still, with the passing of time, this opera was to disappear from the stage.[9]

The other significant achievement of this ten-year period is W. Rudziński's opera, *Johnny, The Musician* (Janko muzykant) (1951—2nd edition 1953), libretto by Stanislaw Wygodzki and Tadeusz Borowski, based on the novel of Henryk Sienkiewicz. Rudziński was a composer of instrumental and vocal music, with two symphonies, a piano concerto, and chamber works to his name. Like Szeligowski he was making his debut in opera. At the start of work on *Johnny, The Musician*, a major decision had to be made as to what kind of genre would answer adequately to the demands placed on it by the content of Sienkiewicz's novel. The composer and librettist rejected the social realistic genre, and decided instead to work along three parallel lines of dramatic development: realistic, folkloric, and grotesque. Realistic scenes of folk life alternate with scenes of fantasy. Massive choral scenes exist side by side with ballet-pantomime, as, for instance, in a scene in which Johnny, as if in a half dream, succumbs to temptation and steals a violin. Sharp and grotesque means portray the members of the ruling class, contrasting them to the simple, common people. By means of this contrast, the authors brought class conflict into the opera and paid tribute to the aesthetic demands of socialist realism.

In this opera, also, as in *The Students' Rebellion*, the most successful scenes are choral. Their liveliness and dynamism make some of them equal to the classics of Polish operatic literature (S. Moniuszko's *The Haunted Manor—Straszny dwór*).

Masterly writing gives sparkle to the brilliant finale of Act I, in which two choruses and five soloists perform in complex polyphony. The final choruses are also effective. Although the style of the opening acts are alien to Poland, the music of the finale, *Glory to Italy*, flows out of the fable of the opera and justifies itself.

Too many different styles and insufficient dramatic cohesiveness in the opera proved to be detrimental and prevented *Johnny, The Musician* from remaining on the boards. It failed to enter the repertory of an opera house. In spite of the relevance of its theme, Rudziński's other opera, *The Commandant of Paris* (dedicated to J. Dąbrowski; libretto by T. Marek, 1960), met with the same failure.

The operas of Piotr Rytel also proved to be short-lived. His career as an opera composer had begun in the period between the two great wars (*Iola, Introduction to Drama*). During the occupation, Rytel composed *Knights of the Cross*, based on Sienkiewicz's novel, and *Andrew of Chelmna—Andrzej z Chelmna*. Destroyed during the Warsaw uprising, the latter score was reconstructed through memory. The opera's style is derived from late romanticism and is reminiscent of Wagnerian and Italian dramas of the 19th century. Alien to Polish national opera, neither of these works were able to survive.

Operatic art provoked some radical criticism from Polish musicologists, while at the same time, they admitted that during a period of establishment of a new musical culture, a time of exploration, discovery and failures, the search for new solutions to the complex problems that attend the creation of operas of divergent types deserved encouragement and recognition.

For all of the above-stated reasons, operatic art of the 1940's–1950's holds a considerable historical interest.

The development of ballet in the first post-war decade aimed to expand its circle of themes, and to find ways to create a new national ballet.

Polish ballet tradition was very modest. There were only two important works in its history: Szymanowski's *Harnasie* and L. Różycki's *Pan Twardowski*. Both belonged to the period between the two wars. The first ballets appearing after World War II carried on the traditions of the 1920's and 1930's with fairy-tale fantasy and folkloric themes setting the scene for the performance of numerous national dances.

Besides full-scale ballet productions, a group of choreographic suites "without libretto" was created. Some of them enjoyed a long life on the stages of the lyric theater. Small one-act ballets intended for production by amateur collectives were also popular. Some ballets written before 1939 were re-constructed and produced; for instance the one-act *Cagliostro in Warsaw (Cagliostro w Warszawie)* by J. Maklakiewicz and the three-act *Swantewit* by P. Perkowski.

Cagliostro in Warsaw, a "light" ballet full of humorous incidents, tells the well-known story about Count Cagliostro's rejuvenation and about his many disguises. In the post-war period, some choreographers transposed the action of this ballet to modern Poland. Scenes of Warsaw in flames and allegorical images of class conflict were, however, at variance with the character of the music. Such an artificial approach to ballet music proved to be unsound.

The other pre-war ballet, *Swantewit* by P. Perkowski, already completed and then reconstructed by 1948, underwent considerable revisions by the composer and the librettist (T. Marek). Because of the symphonic treatment accorded to ballet forms, the only dance music that remained was a waltz. The composer aimed to give an old slavic color to the ballet, but music typical of the 1920's and 1930's, influences of romanticism, impressionism, early Stravinsky and Szymanowski, and, above all, echoes of *The Rite of Spring* rob the music of any specific individual national character.

Well worth mentioning is *The Golden Duck* ballet by J. Maklakiewicz (libretto by J. Rey). Its subject is an old Warsaw legend found in the *Or-Ot* collection of tales. A contrast between the real and the fantasy world is expressed through images of the life of a poor populace on the one side, and an underground kingdom on the other. The first is characterized by national dances: mazurkas, kujawiak and oberek[c]; the second by court and classical dances: quadrille, polka, polonaise and waltz. The pivotal point in the musical development of the ballet is a leit-motif; its melody is borrowed from a children's song, *The Duck Has Little Golden Feet*. Richness of dance elements and visual effects all contributed to the success of this production, mounted not only in Poland, but also in other countries.

The year 1954 saw the production of Grażyna Bacewicz's ballet *From Peasant to King (Z chlopa król)*, libretto by A. Swinarski. Having shown herself to be a talented artist in the sphere of symphonic music, Bacewicz now proved her exceptional gifts in the ballet sphere, as well. *From Peasant to King* recounts the adventures of a drunken peasant dressed up as the king by some pranksters. This ballet, too, makes room for contrasting juxtapositions of national folk and courtly dances. But the ballet's special quality stems from the many characteristic ways that Bacewicz uses parody and grotesquery, which create endless possibilities for misunderstandings. The music of the ballet fits into the stylistic framework of neo-classicism. Particularly well-realized is the stylization of ancient courtly dances: gaillard, passepied, and siciliana. The sound of Poland's own national dances, the oberek and the mazurka, is heard as a contrast. Special effects, such as: parody, displaced accents, polytonal collisions, sharply marked rhythms, all

---

[c]Oberek: A variant of a Kujawiak, characterized by a quicker tempo, and often performed after a kujawiak. The accent usually falls on the third beat of every other measure.

create great dynamism and expressivity. It should be emphasized that the specifics of the ballet genre have been carefully retained in this work.

The King's Jester (Królewski blazeń), a ballet by T. Kiesewetter (libretto by I. Turska), touches on historical themes. Its hero, the jester Stanczyk, is characterized as an intelligent, clear-thinking advisor to the king. Like Bacewicz, Kiesewetter chose to write in the style of ancient dances. As material, he took old Polish dance music for the lute: goniony, chodzony, pavane, and others; however, chromatized in a contemporary manner, the melodies are deprived of their archaic flavor. The music of the ballet retains the late romantic traditions.

Z. Turski, who composed *Warsaw Legend*, and K. Wilkomirski, composer of *Kaszubski Ballet (Balet Kaszubski)* both looked for material in folk life. In their ballets, the artistic tendencies of the first post-war decade continue to be evident: folklore used as a means to democratize ballet and to draw professional music closer to its national and folk origins.

The first post-war decade saw the production of a considerable number of ballets, and although none could be called outstanding, yet the lively and, in many ways, fruitful beginnings of activity in this field played a positive role in the cultural life of Poland, a country which previously had had but few traditions in this type of art.

Following the war, the most interesting work in music took the form of symphonic compositions. It was the period when the works of such major composers as G. Bacewicz, W. Lutoslawski, A. Malawski, A. Panufnik, B. Woytowicz and B. Szabelski first appeared. Towards the end of the 1940's and the beginning of the 1950's, a new group of talented young composers were to come on the scene (T. Baird, K. Serocki, et al.).

Symphonic music, more than any other genre, called forth a multiplicity of compositional approaches. An abundance of theme and concepts appeared.

In symphonic and chamber music forms, demands imposed by socialist realism were easier to avoid than in music tied to the poetic word or dramatic action. Yet, some compromises were inevitable. Usually, they took place in the area of subject matter. As could be expected, there was a trend of writing programmatic music—music accessible to a broad mass of listeners. Works of this sort were dedicated to historical events, national heroes, and revolutionary subjects.

Programmatic symphonic music came in a variety of forms beginning with overtures, poems, and suites, and ending with large symphonies. To cite some examples: *Grunwald*, a symphonic poem by J.A. Maklakiewicz (1946); *Revolutionary Overture (Uvertura rewolucyjna)* by S. Prószyński (1950); *Symphony No. 2 (II Symfonia) Mickiewiczowska* (1949) and the

I. Music of the First Postwar Decade (1945–1956)   19

poem *Żelazowa Wola* (1950) by P. Rytel. Some compositions drew on literature for material. For instance, T. Baird's *Colas Breugnon* was inspired by Romain Rolland's narrative.

Contemporary themes were reflected in: *The Festive Overture* (*Uwertura uroczysta*) by B. Szabelski (1953); *Overture for the 10-Year Anniversary— Uwertura Dziesięciolecie* by K. Sikorski (1954); *The Staromiejski Concert* (dedicated to an old walled city) by S. Wiechowicz (1955); *The Victory Symphony* (*Symfonia zwyviestwa*) by S. Skrowaczewski (1954), et al. As we have mentioned, many compositions were based on folkloric material. Besides those already named, the following works also fall into this category: *Goralski Dances* (*Tańce góralskie*) by W. Kotoński; *Goralski Triptych* (*Tryptyk góralski*) (podhalanski) by A. Malawski (1950); *The Second Symphony* by T. Kiesewetter (filled with elements from Góralski mountain songs and dances); the suite *Kasia* by S. Wiechowicz; *The Dance Symphony* (*Symfonia o tańcu*) by S. Wislocki. Folkloric elements also permeate both symphonies by K. Serocki, the second is known as *The Symphony of Songs* (*Symfonia pieśni*), and the *Polish Symphony* (*Symfonia polska*) by Z. Mycielski.

In some compositions the folkloric traits are rather remote. A very interesting synthesis of folkloric material and complex coloristic sound appears

Example 6

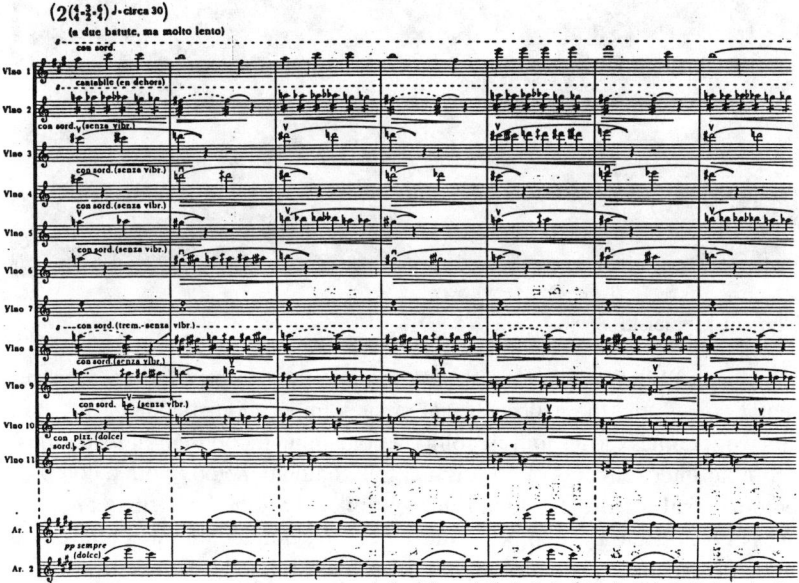

Zygmunt Mycielski, 1980

in A. Panufnik's *Sinfonia Rustica*. Woven into the complex fabric of instrumental voices, the thematic material creates impressionistic spots of color. This work comes closer to folk compositions in its mood than in its themes.

Similar interweavings of an original folk diatonic melody with a complex compositional texture are found in Panufnik's *Lullaby* for strings and two harps (1947). Here the composer introduces a technique that was innovative for that time: quarter-tone intervals in a most refined network of voices.

Thus he anticipated the findings of the sonoristic tendencies that were to come into Polish music during the late 50's and 60's. Ex. 6.

Thus, folkloric elements appear in the most diverse kinds of genres, and with no reference to stylistic orientations. The basic stylistic tendencies in symphonic music of the first decade leaned toward neo-Classicism and toward traditions of late romanticism, including the traditions of Szymanowski and Karlowicz.

Symphonic works of this period reflect one other aim that composers held in common: they tried to create a national version of a contemporary symphony, while still depending on the traditions of the European classic symphonies.

Not only did classical legacy play its part in the formation of the Polish symphony, but Soviet symphonic music played a role of equal importance. Examples of various approaches to genre types of big symphonies could be found in classical Soviet works by Prokofiev and Shostakovich; works that presented monumental forms, large symphonic concepts, and masterly craftsmanship.

The type of extended symphonic composition that arose in Poland after 1945 was closely tied to dramatic subjects portraying the heroic struggle of the Polish people in the Second World War. In symphonic cycles the new heroic genre of the Polish symphony of this era is established. In some instances, the war theme is reflected directly (*The Warsaw Symphony* by Woytowicz, *Peace Symphony* and *Tragic Overture* by Panufnik).

Desiring to expand expressivity, composers would, at times, add a chorus to the symphony. A Panufnik's *Symphony of Peace* belongs to this category of symphony-cantata. The combination of a symphony with an oratorio gives the work its monumental dimensions. A chorus is introduced in the outer movements of the symphony: in the first it performs without a text, while in the finale Iwaszkiewicz's texts are used. The first movement is written in the style of a litany. The dramatic expression deepens in the purely orchestral second movement.

The *Tragic Overture* which belongs in the same rank of Polish compositions, is also outstanding in its expressive power.

In other instances, representation of war themes is accomplished indirectly via a thematic system of evocative imagery. Many variants of the so-called "war symphony" were composed,[10] among them: *Olympic Symphony*—Olimpijska, by Z. Turski; *Symphony No. 1* by J. Krenz; *Symphonies Nos. 1 and 2*, by T. Baird; *Symphony No. 2* by A. Malawski; *Symphony No. 1* by W. Lutoslawski; *Symphonies Nos. 3 and 4* by G. Bacewicz.

Not without reasons did T. Marek call these compositions "The Combat Symphonies."[11] Drama, expressive and explosive at climactic moments, marches, evocative of invading forces; funeral marches, all put these compositions into the same category as other European "war" symphonies. Certain recognizable specific features give the Polish symphonies their distinctive national character. Musical material that has acquired a symbolic meaning and is familiar to every Pole from childhood days, is to be found here: well-known songs of uprisings and revolution, church chorales, melodic turns and rhythmic patterns characteristic of folk music, modal peculiarities, etc.

Nationalistic interpretations of anti-war themes were to be found in postwar Poland, not only in music, but in other arts as well. The Polish art historian, A. Wojciechowski, in coming out against widely held views on the prevailing influence of foreign art on Polish painting, remarked that the importance of the European influence is "exaggerated and diverts attention away from the study of those uniquely Polish traits that are characteristic of the generation which entered the field of art immediately after the war."[12]

The "war" symphonies were mostly written by composers of an older generation, whose style in many ways depended on late romanticism. Its legacy to composers was a thick texture, numerous climaxes, mixed instrumentation with a heavily weighted brass section.

B. Woytowicz's Second Symphony, *The Warsaw Symphony* (1945), is typical of this group of compositions. On its title page is a dedication, "To Andrew—killed in the Warsaw Uprising." The whole concept of this work, from its opening movements saturated in drama to its affirmative finale, is characteristic of "war" symphonies.

Woytowicz's music, during these years, bears witness to the many-sided interests of the artist. The palette of techniques used in the symphony is strikingly different from the cantata, which was written shortly thereafter, *The Prophet*, with its lyric over-flow of feeling.

Now, Woytowicz combines a romantic emotionalism with certain elements of classical structures. The resultant fusion is original and gives to the romantically expressive character of his music its unique quality. Strict polyphonic forms have the effect of creating both a measure of control and a universality of expression. Classical forms served as specific models in the first movement (Sinfonia) and the third movement (Fuga).

Sinfonia, a mighty preamble to the cycle, is of utmost importance as a philosophical postulate. Written in a developed form, it is presented as a large epitaph—the last words in memory of a friend (Moderato, lugubre). The basic thematic material crystallizes in the introduction to the Sinfonia.

An especially important role in the work is assigned to the primary motif—a fanfare by a horn in a sharp dotted rhythm. The main theme (Moderato) grows out of this particular motif. It is a marching theme, restrained in feeling, based on a *trichord diatonic turns*.

The great cumulative power, generated in the first movement, is held in check by the firm measured pace of a mass procession. We are reminded of

Example 7

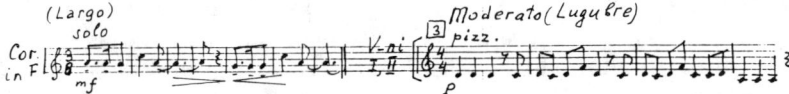

similar processions in Honegger's symphonies. In its structure, this music also has an affinity to another composer, N. Miaskovsky.

A lament—a burial song—that is the second theme (Lamento, recitativo). Like the first, it, too, is developed. At times darkly sorrowful, at times brightening, at times ceremonial and austere, it has intense pathos at the climax.

The main theme in the development becomes a typical "march of invasion"[††] (mechanized rhythms, hoarse timbre of muted brasses). However, in the midst of the unfolding what is heard is not the ominous "invasion" theme, but the lament. Gaining strength and courage in its movement towards the climax, it stands—a symbol of passionate protest.

The dramatic conflict of the first movement continues to develop in the second (Scherzo). The Scherzo is a fast purposeful march—a "march of invasion." In the irresistible torrent of its movement, fragments of both basic themes appear, only to be drowned.

The slow third movement takes an unexpected turn, for here a song-like fugue is heard. Its theme is an expressive melody, slavic in color. Endowed with the character of a "Romanze" by reason of its background (a sway in a 2nd to 4th figuration), this melodic fragment is allied to the subordinate theme of the first movement. In an endless unfolding, this swaying motion accumulates an affirmative power as it climbs toward a heroic climax. Here is the turning point of the development. A triumphant fanfare theme takes on the character of a victorious march in the recapitulation. An organic preparation has been made for the finale—spontaneous, lively and festive. Out of the kaleidoscopically quick-changing themes of the finale, a scene of life in a time of peace emerges. Similar finales in Lutoslawski's *First Symphony*, Honegger's *Second,* Shostakovich's *Sixth*, Prokofiev's *Sixth*, come to mind.

In other symphonies, form based on a cardinal transformation of themes is treated differently. A significant example that demonstrates this point is another "war symphony," Z. Turski's *Second.* Known as *The Olympic*, it received the gold medal at the International Composers Competition in London at the time of the 14th Olympic Games (1948), hence the symphony's sub-title. In Turski's art, two traditions converge: that of Polish romanticism (with Szymanowski's influence in the forefront), and French neo-Classi-

---

[††]"Theme" or "March of Invasion" is a term that came into use in connection with Shostakovich's "War Symphonies."

cism. Such original neo-Classicism, with its highly dramatic moments of incandescent emotion, is found in other works of Turski as well; for instance, in *Sinfonia da Camera* (1947), and in the well-known *Concerto for Violin and Orchestra* (1951). The dramatic conflict in the *Olympic Symphony* is based on the gradual transformation of romantic themes, which acquire a highly dramatic emotional tone in the energetic, joyfully affirmative march of the finale. The principal theme in the first movement is sounded by a summoning fanfare. Endowed with a dense polyphonic texture, this theme undergoes a powerful development. It unfolds freely, like a ballad. Expressive melodies follow each other: stately and heroic (in the introduction), energetically march-like (in the main theme), taking on a cantilena character—transparent soli (in the subordinate theme). Sharp contrasts, dramatic conflicts, emotional tension, all these late romantic features of symphonic writing have their place in Turski's work. The steady formation of life-asserting ideas in the symphony is reaffirmed by the direction that the developing marching theme takes in the finale. From scherzo-like grotesqueries, through various types of marches in the development, to a gigantic epic coda: such is the way in which the basic theme of the symphony is transformed.

Another composer who merits serious attention is Stanislaw Skrowaczewski. The work of this master is distinguished by a high degree of professionalism, a classical kind of discipline in his thinking, and also an interest in coloristically combined sounds.

Symphony No. 3,—Symphony for Strings,—written in 1947, reflects the orbit of the composer's interests. The influence of post-romanticism (in part his beloved Bruckner's, in part Berg's, especially in the contours of his thematics) shows itself in the strong dramatic imagery, in the neo-romantic type of expression, in the prevailing polyphonic texture, and in the tense build-ups of the pre-climactic and climactic sections.

The other area of interest for the composer is the color of sound. It flows out of a typically national tradition in art: Polish colorism. The beautiful, muted, impressionistic sound, the development of the instruments' distinctive timbres, the delicate nocturnal imagery are characteristic of another composition of those years, *Music at Night*, based on the material of the ballet *Ugo and Parisina*.

Both these tendencies, neo-romantic and impressionistic (coloristic) are fancifully combined in the later work of Skrowaczewski. Refracted through the prism of his own musical language, they constitute his own musical style.

Panufnik, one of the most prolific Polish contemporary composers, had a strong and original musical personality. He was an innovator in the area of means. His compositions, no matter of what form or genre, were distinguished by their individuality, and, quite often, bold experimentation. Among his symphonic works of that period the *Nocturne for Orchestra* was most interesting. It received the first prize at the Szymanowski Composers' Competition of 1948. In it Panufnik's stylistic traits were already clearly evident: the original treatment of rhythm and sense of time—unhurried, measured movement in even durations giving weight to each sound; the masterfully executed dynamic plan in the unfolding of the whole form; the subtle colors of an impressionistic orchestral palette; the clearly audible layered polyphony; the unstandardized harmonic language. A choral type of diatonic is alternated with a chromatization that comes close to atonality.

In the future stylistic innovations of the early creative period would be firmly established in large symphonic cycles (*Sinfonia elegiaca, Rhapsody for Orchestra*, etc.). The slower movements of Panufnik's cycles are the more original. The focus of attention is on the song-like themes of choral and recitatival character, on free, broad rhythms, on slow development of form. In fast movements, the active, motoric rhythms, driving dynamics and figurative fabrics stemming from the neo-classic style, seem less original.

The most widespread tendency of the first post-war decade was toward neo-Classicism, although examples of stylization of actual forms and genres are rather rare (*Colas Breugnon* by T. Baird). Much oftener, one sees fairly free transformations of the styles and genres of the Baroque period. Repeatedly, one observes a fascination with concerto forms: concerto grosso, polyphonic forms, passacaglia, and fugue. A special interest was evoked by certain types of motoric movement; for instance, by the toccata, etc. Some musicologists have called this tendency "neo-Baroque," or "Baroquism."[13]

One of the major composers to actively exploit the genres and form of Baroque and early classic periods was B. Szabelski (*Toccata*, 1946; *Third Symphony*, 1951; *Concerto Grosso*, 1954). In his compositions, the particular elements of form-building, thematic development, and some toccata features (all typical of neo-Classicism) are combined with a treatment of the orchestra that belongs to the late romantic period. Bruckner's influence is felt in the way the brass section is brought out, Mahler's in the expansion of massed sound, etc. Concerto Grossi was written not only by Szabelski, but also by Kazimierz Sikorski and Andrzej Koszewski. Concertos for orchestra were written by Lutoslawski, Bacewicz, Baird, and Stefan Kisielewski; Concertos for strings by Bacewicz and Michal Spisak.

One of the significant neo-classic works is the *Third Symphony* in the form of a *Concerto Grosso* by K. Sikorski (1953). In this eight-part cycle, the monumental symphonic forms are combined with a specifical concerto treatment of the orchestra. The names of the different movements stem from the musical practices of the Baroque period; i.e. Preludio, Fuga I, Recitativo and Chorale I, Aria, Fuga II, Recitativo and Chorale II, and Postlude. Unity in Sikorski's symphonic cycle is achieved through an extensive system of thematic ties and elements of concentric construction of forms. Furthermore, another device appears which cements the form: the cyclic theme. First heard in the introduction to the cycle, the Preludio, this austere theme in the bass clarinet maintains an epic character. Narrational and balladic in style, based on diatonic 2nd figures and assertive tonic turns, it endows the symphony with its basic national character. Ex. 8.

An essential feature of the opening theme, as indeed of all the material in the composition, be it fugal or arioso, is its melodic character.

The basic line of development is connected to the various transformations of the leit-motif. It appears at key points in each movement of the cycle, at times like a lament, at times in a mood of heroic celebration.

K. Sikorski also worked in the form of the solo concerto, composing many instrumental works for clarinet and orchestra, for horn, for trumpet, for bassoon, and for flute.[14]

The solo concerto was one of the most popular forms in the first post-war decade. Concertos were written for piano and orchestra (Grażyna Bacewicz, Stanislaw Wislocki, Jan Krenz, Tadeusz Paciorkiewicz, Kazimierz Serocki, Michal Spisak, Tadeusz Szeligowski, et al.), violin and orchestra (G. Bacewicz, Jan Maklakiewicz, Piotr Perkowski, Adam Świerzyński, Zbigniew Turski), cello and orchestra (G. Bacewicz and K. Wilkomirski).

A new phenomenon in Polish music appeared in the form of concertos for wind instruments. The appearance of musical literature for winds turned out to be very timely. The rise of many new orchestras created a demand for a more extensive and varied concert repertory, and the training of young wind instrument performers further increased the need for new repertory. During these years, concertos were written for horn and orchestra (Kazimierz Sikorski), for bassoon and orchestra (Tadeusz Baird, Michal Spisak, Andrzej Dobrowolski), for trumpet and orchestra (K. Sikorski and Andrzej Panufnik). In the *Gothic Concerto* for trumpet and orchestra, Panufnik took music of the Polish Renaissance and Baroque periods and set it in an interesting contemporary stylization. The composer made use of material by Waclaw from Szamotuly and Adam Jarzębski.

Example 8

However generally the folkloric trend, the use of Góralski, Mazowiecki and Kurpiowski regional elements continued to appear not only in symphonic music but in the concerto genre as well. They can be seen in the piano concertos by Baird and Sikorski, in the *Second Concerto for Violin* by Maklakiewicz, in the *Third Concerto for Violin* by Bacewicz, and in the *Concerto for Horn* by Sikorski. The first composer to use and transform elements of Góralski and Mazowiecki folklore was G. Bacewicz. This she did in a highly original fashion in her *Third Violin Concerto* (1948).

The music of G. Bacewicz, who was the brightest and most talented representative of neo-Classicism in Poland is firmly tied to the forms of "pure" instrumental music. During the first post-war decade, she wrote (besides the solo concertos already mentioned) a *Concerto for String Orchestra*, three symphonies, and four quartets. An earlier work, *Overture for Orchestra* (1943), still showed strong traces of the influence of French music. Bacewicz had studied with Nadia Boulanger in the 1930's. The *Overture* is a small, one-part composition in which classic forms and motor movement are combined with a heightened romantic expressivity close to Szymanowski in tone.

During the following decade, Bacewicz would continue to develop the same qualities in her symphonic and chamber works.

In his book, Tadeusz Zieliński sets forth some thoughts about Bacewicz's symphonic style which, in the opinion of this author, are both true and interesting. Since her symphonies are the least known part of her legacy (Bacewicz died in 1969), we will permit ourselves to quote Zieliński on this subject. "In the post-war years, Bacewicz leaves strict neo-Classicism . . . her style wavers between sharply pulsating rhythms and soft romantic phrases. . . . On the other hand, Bacewicz treats this romanticism in a classic manner. The outward contours of her composition present a type of symphony that is close to Prokofiev's and closer still to Roussel's. This music is massive in texture, monumental and energetic, with dramatic accents used in moderation. The instrumentation is somewhat undifferentiated, with the chief role assigned to the strings. . . . These remarks also apply to the lyric *Second Symphony* (1950), and to the more dynamic *Fourth*. Only in the *Third Symphony*, pathetic, loud, and monumental, do the brasses play an important role. All these symphonies contain splendid scherzo episodes. There, the individual traits of Bacewicz's style can be easily perceived: a playful, lively flow of sound in a three-quarter meter; a rhythmically angular spinning and turning melody, most often in an oberek style."[15]

The Concerto for String Orchestra (1948) stands up not only as a significant example of Bacewicz's works, but also as an important example of the Polish neo-classic style during the late 1940's and early 1950's. A three-movement cycle, the *Concerto* has much in common with the three-movement symphonic concept of contemporary French neo-Classicism: Allegro, Andante, Vivo. The composer turns to the Baroque style, using polyphonic-harmonic types of texture freely. The main theme of the first movement is maintained in a toccata-like motion, which dissolves the framework of the theme, and transforms it into a thematic figuration. The motoric motion gives the main theme a certain objective character, reminiscent of the energetic ostinato rhythm formulas in Bach concertos and cello sonatas.

The subordinate theme is structurally formed, full of active march rhythms. It appears in a unison-tutti. Its sonorous power recalls the epic quality in Borodin's music. Subsequent transformations of the theme take it far from its original forms, and in the recapitulation bring it close to the main theme. In the development of themes, Bacewicz attaches great importance to the role of rhythmic variations. Increase and decrease in the rate of motion, and alteration of motoric formulas (a typically classic manner of thinking!) not only fill the texture with internal breath, but also provide the impulse for the development of form.

In the second movement, *Andante*, cantilena comes to the forefront. The main theme, with its constant rocking in its background, recalls a lullaby. As the theme develops, its mood changes from elegiac lyricism to pathos. The genre also changes from song to ballad-narrative to epos. Thus, in the second movement, lyricism becomes more objective and is woven into the main dramatic line.

The Third Movement, *Vivo*, is a sparkling, impetuous finale. Here, the rules governing the concerto form are consistently observed. There is a play of counterposed timbres, and more broadly, of themes. The tense first theme (tutti) is contrasted to the romantic second one. In the recapitulation, motor movement once more gains the upper hand. The affirmative coda is written in the tradition of the classical concerto and symphonic cycles.

Bacewicz's *Concerto* stands out among other compositions written in this form because of its unusual richness of timbres.

She, herself, was a fine performer on both violin and viola, and had complete mastery over the string section of the orchestra. The division of the ensemble into groups, the counterposing of solo voices to those groups, extreme registers, and various means of articulation, all were used to obtain a multiplicity of coloristic effects.

In summation, let us underline that, although Bacewicz turned toward the classical cycle and preserved its essential structural concept, still she treated it in her own individual manner.

The Concerto for String Orchestra pointed the way toward the development of this genre in Poland. In her future works, Bacewicz was to take her findings and develop them in larger forms (*Music for Strings, Trumpets and*

Percussion, 1958). But that was to be a new stage in the work of this composer.

For Tadeusz Baird, the first decade was a period of search to establish his own manner in writing. He first appeared in connection with *Group 49*. At that time, Baird's work bore the mark of his war-time experiences. At an early age he had been sent to a concentration camp, condemned to be executed by the Gestapo, and twice miraculously escaped death. The Liberation found him seriously ill.

Baird's compositions of the 1950's bear witness to his close ties to Polish and European romantic music. These compositions included: a *Piano Concerto* and *Symphonietta*, two symphonies, and a *Concerto for Orchestra*. The *Piano Concerto* (1949), not yet self-standing, comes close in style to the light, refined and witty music of the French *Six*. At the same time, some of its themes are almost folkloric. An individual feature of the *Concerto* is its harmonic language (soft, whimsical dissonant chords in the second movement).

More in keeping with the declarations of *Group 49* is the *Symphonietta* (1949). Open-hearted, youthfully fresh, it nevertheless remains close to French neo-Classicism (Ravel, Poulenc). At times, it even comes close to Soviet "msuci for youth" (Dmitri Kabalevsky), possessing the same ease and natural flow in the impetuous first movement and finale, where a melodic, playfully gay theme dominates (soli of piano and winds).

Quite different in feeling is the middle movement, a kind of passacaglia built on a short theme in the basses. Chorale-like and somber, it is, in its measured unrelenting pace, reminiscent of a mournful procession. This episode is, to some extent, alien to the character of the exterior movements. But it is powerful, "speaks" expressively, and thus becomes associated with the theme of sufferings in the war.

Baird's symphonies establish him as a disciple of late romanticism. His individuality is revealed most fully in intensely concentrated lyricism, which is found side by side with outbursts of pathos. Fascination with the big "Mahler" orchestra is revealed in *The First Symphony* (1950), a monumental five-movement cycle. Here, critics have discerned Shostakovich's influence.[16] Baird's stylistic realization demonstrates that he had absorbed some elements of the expressive symphonic tendencies of Bartók, Honegger and Shostakovich (first movement). Contrasting movements: the third (a brilliant, witty scherzo) and the calm, translucent finale in a march rhythm speak of a different influence—that of Prokofiev.

A pull toward monumental symphonic writing was also evident in the three-movement *Second Symphony, Quasi Una Fantasia* (1952). According to the testimony of his contemporaries, this work, full of contrasting sonorities and changes of mood, was the one in which the Mahler tendencies were most evident. Regrettably, Baird destroyed this composition. The only existing record of it is a recording made during the broadcast of its only performance.

Baird's development followed two parallel lines. Not only was he writing monumental symphonic works, but he was also developing the neo-classic side of his music. *Concerto for Orchestra* appeared in 1953, as well as several stylized compositions: the suite *Colas Breugnon* (1951), *Four Love Sonnets* from music written for a production based on Shakespeare's *Romeo and Juliet* (1956), and *Songs of the Trouvères* (1963).

Colas Breugnon, a suite for strings and flute, came into being as music for a radio play. Elements of the instrumental style of late Renaissance, two authentic galliards from the collection *Quartorze Gaillardes*, 1570 (14 galliards) are artfully realized in Baird's unique manner. Here, lyricism, melody, simplicity and Baird's own characteristic harmonic color are dominant. The means by which this stylization is attained are: polyphony in texture, transparent instrumentation, segmentation of melody into short phrases, and binary forms in the dances.

Similar methods were used by Baird in the Shakespearean *Love Sonnets* for baritone and chamber orchestra, a lovely poetic work. Unusually colorful are the *Songs of Trouvères (Pieśni Truwerów)* for the viola, two flutes and cello, a poetic cycle in an old style. Baird took the texts and melodies from a work by P. Aubris, *Trouvères et Troubadoures*. Artful use of timbres, translucent harmonic colors, and an ability to feel his way into the style of another epoch, allow the composer to capture the ambience of music from a distant past.

The culmination of this given line of artistic development was reached in the *Concerto for Orchestra*. In it, the composer made broad use of musical forms and devices of the middle ages, and Renaissance period, as well as Greek modes (Dorian, Phrygian, etc.), faux-bourdon techniques, and Palestrina's nota contra notam. He also employed some forms of the Baroque era in the *Grave e Fugato* in the first movements, and in the *Toccata* in the finale.

Yet, the composer did not limit himself to these means. In this monumental *Concerto*, the type of development obviously stems from a "romantic" origin. An austere Gregorian chant at the opening is expounded through heavy octaves played by trombones and trumpets. Later, it sounds forth solemnly in a call to arms, a war signal. A declarative fanfare fugato theme in the trumpets and an hymn-like chorale appear in the first movement and in the finale.

Epos and lyricism, a tale of the heroic past, an ode to man and his creative energy, such is the framework which contains the thematic content of the *Concerto*. In this composition, Baird showed an extraordinary mastery in his handling of an orchestra. Specifics of the genre appear in the play of orchestral colors, the contrasting juxtaposition of soli and group timbres to the powerful tutti. Particularly impressive is the augmented brass choir (tripled section). Virtuosity in orchestral treatment, brute strength in climaxes, sharpness and driving intensity in rhythm over large spans of time, a monumental style, objectivity, and a positive outlook on the world: these are the special traits of Baird's early symphonic music.

Kazimierz Serocki's music during the first post-war decade is distinguished by its symphonic monumentality. Serocki had written a cycle, *Three Kurpiowski Melodies (3 Kurpiowski melodie)* for chorus, soprano, tenors, and chamber orchestra (1949), two symphonies (1952 and 1953), concertos for piano (1951), and for trombone and orchestra (1953). A folk song tendency dominates Serocki's music. Folkloric elements pervade almost all of his early symphonic compositions. To an even greater extent than Baird, Serocki followed the precepts of *Group 49*. During an early period of search for his own independent path, Serocki's style was somewhat eclectic and proclamatory. Nevertheless, his early compositions already show him to be a major artist, with his symphonies as the most important part of his work of that time.

The *First Symphony* is a large canvas, painted in broad poster-art strokes. A spirit of battle permeates it: war-like fanfares, marches, dotted rhythms, brass choirs, and martial songs. It was this particular symphony that the Polish musicologist, T. Marek, called "A Symphony of Combat."[10] The aggressive energy of its music, its combative kettle drums and fanfares show clearly that much of its aesthetics stem from the theater. The massive scale of its large fresco style and a particular laconic manner of expression are all close to Prokofiev in style. Yet, not only Prokofiev's influence, but that of the French "Les Six" is evident. Shostakovich's presence, too, can be felt. It shows itself in the incandescent passion and verve of the marching themes, and also in the expressive "speaking" quality of the subordinate themes set against a background of interrupted rhythms in the strings. Frequent use of tutti and an abundance of climactic moments can be related to traditions of late romanticism in symphonic writing (Bruckner, Mahler). Purely national traditions find their way into the vivid pictorialization of a national holiday in the second movement.

At the base of the various movements of this cycle lie traditional classic forms: the sonata allegro in the first and fourth movements; the ternary form in the scherzo of the second, and also in the third slow movement. The cycle is held firmly together by a highly developed system of thematic ties.

The first movement is preceded by a short introduction (Maestoso quasi una fantasia). Its spirit resembles Shostakovich's introductions to the main

Example 9

theme. Massive string unisons make their entrance in a heroic-pathetic theme of an acutely angular melodic design, which changes into the energetic march of the main theme of the symphony. Ex. 9.

A majestic brass choir appears in the subordinate theme, written in the spirit of the old Polish national war songs. The structure of the theme resembles a hymn. Several energetic themes of a march-like character establish the jubilant atmosphere of the concluding section.

A dramatic interpretation of a national dance unfolds in the scherzo. At the base of the fugato lies the theme of an oberek with its cumulative effects and powerful climax. The whole orchestra is gradually involved in this process, and in the reprise, this frolicsome melody comes close to the symphony's march and chorale theme, acquiring a heroic sweep.

Written in the narrative style of a ballad, the theme of the third movement resembles Shostakovich's lyricism. Yet, it bears its own vividly expressed national coloration, especially in the soft roundness of its short phrases with their Dorian and alternating modal turns. Ex. 10.

Aggressive march themes dominate in the Finale (Appassionato). Here, one can observe that familiar phenomenon—exaggerated dynamics. A thunderous orchestra with endless fanfares, is dominated by brass choirs and percussion. The same excess can be observed in the way all themes are brought to a common denominator; in this case, the march. The composer's choice of style calls to mind revolutionary posters and can be faulted for its superficially illustrational elements.

"To use folklore as a technique in a craft is not sufficient. One must seek to deepen folklore's meaning, and then absorb it to the point where it becomes a means of expression for the composer." This precept of Serocki

Example 10

found its application to a large extent in the *Second Symphony (Symfonia pieśni)*, sub-titled a "Symphony of Songs for Soprano, Baritone, Chorus and Orchestra Set to Folk Texts" (1953). *The Second Symphony*, to an even greater degree that the *First*, represents a "song-like symphonic trend," a distinct direction in musical art during the first ten years after the war. Some musicologists, finding it difficult to place the symphony in its proper generic category, mention this composition in relation to the problem of symphonic development in the cantata.[17] Actually, this work stands at the crossroads of the symphonic and cantata-oratorio genres. It also resembles a vocal-instrumental suite in its structure. However, the composer did, indeed, conceive it as a symphony, an extended four-movement cycle, and assigned a key position to the compositional principle of "vocalization" of the genre. Possibly, this problem gave direction to the original treatment of the cycle, with its preponderance of slow tempos: I–Arioso; II–Scherzo; III–Quasi variazioni; IV–Finale (the first and third movements slow and lyric, the other two in quick dance tempos). The music is written in a folk style, but with no direct quotations. Central to the concept of the symphony are the authentic folkloric texts which form the scenes depicting the life of peasants. The content of each text determined the choice of a corresponding genre for each movement: arioso–a lyric song about the sad life of a wretched beggar; scherzo–a depiction of a wedding (here several marriage ritual songs appear); variations—a lullaby; finale—a haymaking and harvest holiday (seasonal work songs). In this way, the cycle of folk life is re-enacted in the symphony: love, marriage, the daily round of work, and the harvest holidays. Undoubtedly, the element of subject matter brings the symphony close to the cantata genre. At the same time, the subject matter here has a general impersonal character, as opposed to Lutoslawski's *Silesian Triptych*, in which the cycle is unified by the consecutive development of a literary subject.

The musical fabric of the *Second Symphony* is permeated by characteristic features of folkloric song: voice-leading, and certain types of structure and form-building. In his organization of metric-rhythmical elements, the composer used the metrical formulas of folk dances. This, however, does not mean that Serocki intentionally simplified symphonic structure. Avoiding classical forms, which would have conflicted with the melodic material, and turning to forms which are more natural to folk art (variations, ternary form, and rondo), the composer nevertheless applied the principles of symphonic development broadly. The basic method here was to employ a wide network of polyphonic devices: imitations, stretti, elongation of voices by means of through development, contrapuntal texture, independent melodic lines. A mobile fabric appears, supple and fluid, made up of a variable number of voices. A choral writing in the tutti is typical of Polish multi-voiced texture.

Example 11

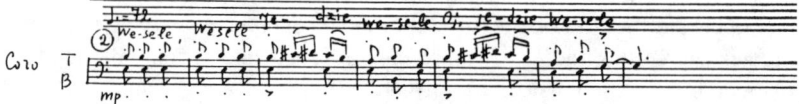

In the scherzo, there is a characteristically kinetic dance movement (oberek, kujawiak). Also characteristic are the syncopated endings, "irregular rhythmic accents"[18] called forth by the displacement of strong beats in an ostinato triple meter. An original technique in development is employed interweaving various rhythms in triple and duple meter, both on the vertical and horizontal, creating great rhythmic variety over long durations. Here, the chorus sings mostly in unison, or else in colorful parallel fifths. In the middle of the scherzo there is a small contrasting scene, resembling a birde's wail (a part of Slavic folk wedding customs). Ex. 11.

In the third movement (Quasi Variazioni), much attention is alloted to the coloristic factor. The orchestra is divided into groups of refined soli. Effective timbres are introduced: harmonies in seconds in the vibraphone, harp harmonics, figurations in the celesta, marimba, etc. The condensing and thinning out of vivid coloristic devices in this movement of the symphony becomes a means of form-building, thus enriching the structure of a "song" symphony.

In the finale, the autumn harvest scene is depicted in bold sweeping strokes and deep colors. The songs and dances are impetuous, fiery, and marked by national traits such as bourdon pedal points, motor ostinati, changing meters, and syncopated rhythms in the cadences as if in imitation of the reapers' movements. The composer achieved great variety by colliding melodies of contrasting modes and metric designs, and by alternating in a lively play of dialogue male and female solo parts with choral tutti.

The search for a synthetic genre in this work, its pictorial quality (based upon analogies drawn from different scenes of peasant life), the masterly transformation of folklore material in a large symphonic form—all this places the *Second Symphony* high in the rank of those compositions which developed folk themes in music during the first post-war decade.

Witold Lutoslawski's works are an outstanding artistic achievement in the music of the first decade. Beginning to compose just before the outbreak of the second world war, Lutoslawski at first seemed to be a disciple of Szymanowski (*Sonata, Symphonic Variations*), but the experiences of the war years impelled him to search for other paths in his art. The extraordinary demands that he placed on himself, his artistic integrity, his constant dissatisfaction with his achievements, plus a desire to be in step with his own times became the cause of repeated changes of direction in his music. For ten years after the war, he was an active figure in many important official organizations: member of the editorial advisory council of the *Polish Music Publishers* (*Polskie Wydawnictwo Muzyczne*—PWM), and member of the *Council of Culture and Music*. He also played an active part in the work of the *Union of Polish Composers* (*Związek Kompozytorów Polskich*—ZKP).

The composer's larger concepts are related to the extended symphonic form. Lutoslawski was always distinguished by his intellectual mathematical turn of mind. It is not surprising then, that the neo-Classical tendency in European music was close to him. Neo-Classicism found its vivid expression in his *First Symphony* (1947), whose style has a certain affinity to Stravinsky's in its type of figurations, and the grotesqueness of some of its imagery. Yet it has an even greater affinity to Prokofiev's in its bubbling pulse, and the buoyant tone in some segments of the first movement and the finale.

Objectivity and neo-Classical balance in the symphonic form in some sections of the symphony are combined with a telling sharpness of expression in other sections, especially in the middle movements.

Unlike Woytowicz's *Warsaw Symphony* (*Warszawska*) or *Symphony of Peace* by Panufnik, Lutoslawski's *First* is not programmatic. Nevertheless, a vivid concrete imagery and generic analogies do evoke definite associations. While some critics have included this symphony in the group of "Symphonies of War and Peace,"[19] other writers (such as S. Stucky) sharply dispute this interpretation. Yet there is a basis for discerning certain analogies between the imagery in Lutoslawski's First Symphony and the so-called "war" symphonies of that time. We do not have in mind a literal narration of a "war libretto" typical of programmatic music, but rather an indirect reflection of emotional states and impressions of actual events. Indeed, nowhere else in Lutoslawski's music is the war experience reflected so spontaneously (the first movement was composed during the occupation, while the others were conceived at the same time). In the first movement, contradictory processes collide. A resonant fanfare in the main theme goes through frequent "modulations of genre," changing from a march to a jocose scherzo, and later acquires a cruel, and grotesque character. Thus, in the first movement, a dramatic line of distortion appears—an ominous beginning.

In the second movement, the composer seems to respond to the tragic events of the recent past. Conflict evolves sharply within the scherzo, where, in the midst of a brutal onslaught by mechanized powers, the lyric strains of a waltz are heard. Entering tentatively, it gains strength until it triumphantly dominates the scene, symbolizing peace. This line of general development determines the resolution of the finale, whose bubbling energy and bright major tone seem to affirm the jubilant approach of victory. Yet, repeated disruptions, incursions of grotesque images inject anxiety, speak of contradictions, and of the difficulty of attaining the ultimate goal.

Lutoslawski's *First Symphony*, when compared to the "War Symphonies" of his contemporaries, comes closer in its imagery and emotional tone to the Sixth, and in part, to the Fifth Symphonies of Prokofiev. It is characteristic of both composers to depict real life in all its diversity and with all its conflicts, and to present them in generic scenes. Both composers enlarge the scope of the content in the middle movements by introducing, on one hand, scherzo episodes into slow lyric movements, and on the other hand, lyric and dance episodes into scherzos. Many images of war (as of peace) are common to both composers: "storm" themes, gloomy and disturbing, original in their tone-color; various grotesque aspects of imagery; fanfares in epigraphic themes in the first and fourth movements; different types of war signals; and the bonds of death. Frozen ostinati in the second movement of Lutoslawski's symphony are similar to Prokofiev's famous "piti-piti."[†††]

Finales, too, are related to each other in character: bubbling, triumphantly exultant, impetuous, full of dance elements. Thus, the most important links in the conceptions of the two composers come in touch, giving voice to optimism, and a healthy positive perception of life.

We should add that some analogies also exist between Lutoslawski's *First* and Stravinsky's *Symphony in Three Movements*, Shostakovich's *Seventh*, and Honegger's *Second*. Furthermore, certain traditions based on Szymanowski's works are developed. Taken as a whole, Lutoslawski's composition is profoundly original and may take its rightful place as a musical classic of our time.

In the 1940's and 1950's, Lutoslawski also showed a considerable interest in Polish folk art. His work on this material bore fruit in the form of cycles of instrumental and vocal miniatures: *Twelve Folk Melodies* (*12 melodii ludowych*), *Bucolics* (*Bukoliki*) for piano, children's songs, 20 Christmas carols for voice and piano, and two original symphonic compositions, *Little Suite* and *Silesian Triptych*.

The largest composition in which Lutoslawski's study of folklore is reflected is the *Concerto for Orchestra*. Here, different folkloric elements are woven into the fabric of the neo-Classic style (forms and textures specific to Baroque music in the concerto genre). In its conception, massive development, and complexity of its structure, the *Concerto* is more like a symphony. The uninterrupted sequence of the last three movements heightens the significance of the second half of the composition. The dramatic climax of the concerto occurs in the *Finale*. Henceforth, this was to become obligatory in most of Lutoslawski's symphonic works.

[†††]"Piti-piti" refers to nonsense syllables insistently repeated in delirium by Count Volkonsky as he lies dying. The scene takes place in Prokofiev's *War and Peace*.

The *Concerto* consists of five movements, the last three are continuous: I–*Intrada*; II–*Capriccio* notturno e *Arioso*; III-V–*Passacaglia, Toccata e Corale*. No stylistic imitations of the Baroque are to be found here. Lutoslawski, like his contemporaries, treated old forms in a modern way. Similar approaches may be seen in the *Third Symphony in the Form of a Concerto Grosso* by K. Sikorski, or in the *Toccata* and *Concerto Grosso* by Szabelski. Lutoslawski's composition is distinguished by its significance and exists on the same artistic level as the concertos of Hindemith, Stravinsky, and Bartók.

S. Stucky once described Lutoslawski's work with folklore thus: "Folk songs and dances are mere raw material from which he fashions not only themes but also the tiny motivic fragments of which to build up an elaborate contrapuntal edifice. Folk tunes are never simply quoted: they are radically transformed, manipulated, made to serve the composer's artistic vision. . . . The composer is master, not slave, of folklore."[20]

The structural material of the *Concerto* is made up of characteristic short motifs.[21] A short syncopated motif at the beginning of the *Intrada*, thanks to its repetitive ostinato and the measured pace in the bass voice, is transformed into a resolute march. Another theme of the *Intrada* bears the character of a summoning fanfare. It reappears in the second movement (Arioso). The stentorian call of its trumpets, resembling signals made by horn instruments, is close to old types of Polish reveilles. Ex. 12.

Pastoral tunes, lyric songs, tunes with bourdon background in "bagpipe" fifths, fanfares, choral singing—these are the sources of the folkloric genre in the thematicism of the *Concerto*.

At the same time, an entirely different type of thematics is also presented here. For example, structural complexes of ornamental or improvisational character, "whirlwind" rotational figurations in the violins lie at the base of the Capriccio nocturne.

Brilliant "finger" technique, open-work "arabesques," transparent in texture, elicit associations with the ornamentations of Baroque texture. Stronger analogies with Baroque music appear on further acquaintances with the Passacaglia. In this movement, the overall character of the distant past contains a plethora of national features. The basso-ostinato theme is an authentic Polish song, a narrative ballad, with a Lydian coloration. Ex. 13.

The dynamic developed in the *Passacaglia* reaches a tremendous intensity and prepares the way for the *Finale: Toccata*. Rising on the crest of a wave,

Example 12

Example 13

the *Finale* gives full play to a dynamic movement which, in its toccata form, acquires a variety of shadings.

In the *Finale*, too, a solution is found which makes it possible to unite both of the main lines of the composition. The motoric theme of the toccata is built on the sound of the basso-ostinato of a folk melody. The whole character of the *Finale* stems from the following: a folkloric theme organically transformed into symphonically interpreted toccata form. In the coda, all themes converge in the unrestrained movement of a dance.

Lutoslawski's *Concerto for Orchestra* showed him to be a major symphonic composer with a bent for strict, logical thinking in the construction of forms. The composition of the *Concerto* is symmetrically balanced. In many sections this is expressed through concentric forms and tonal plans. The dramaturgic concept is directed toward a unification of two interacting and mutually complimentary lines (the neo-Classic and folkloric) which constitute the composer's style. This tendency to synthesize different styles was to remain with Lutoslawski in the 1960's, though it was to take completely different forms.

For the composer, the aesthetic principles formulated during his neo-Classic, folkloric period would always remain inviolable.

The Concerto for Orchestra belongs to the mainstream of musical trends of the first post-war decade. It is renowned as an extraordinary achievement in the music of this time.

SUMMARY

An analysis of musical art in the first post-war decade shows the most successful compositions came from the spheres of symphonic, concerto, and chamber music, the least successful from song and cantata genres, while the value of operatic and balletic works was uneven. The cause of inadequacies lay in ideological pressure from "above." Nevertheless, although surrounded by socialist propaganda, many composers were basically able to preserve an independent artistic spirit. The Party slogan of "building a new socialist culture" was, as far as music was concerned, a declaration that remained on paper. Mostly, its influence was felt in the themes of a rather small group of song and cantata compositions, which ceased to exist toward the end of that period.

Going with the current of reconstruction in cultural life, composers made use, in their own ways, of conditions created by a general cultural and national revival. This was the period of renascence of the traditions of Polish national music of the past. The joining of a romantic, heroic tradition with rediscovered and freely interpreted folklore gave rise to some highly artistic work in professional music. The future would show that here was the turning point on the path of a new search for an original style. Its constructive character defines the significance of the first decade in the evolution of Polish post-war music.

Notes

Chapter I

1. There are several reasons for the late development of symphonic genres in Poland. The lack of regular symphonic concerts, of philharmonic societies, and regularly operating orchestras in the 19th century hindered the development of symphonic music. Only in the 20th century, owing to the activities of "Young Poland," was the first philharmonic society established—the Warsaw Philharmonic, founded in 1901. (The Artistic Director and Conductor was E. Mlynarski.)
2. The attention of music historians was focused on three periods that represented landmarks in the development of Polish national musical culture: the Renaissance, the XIX Century, and contemporary times. Basic reference works, encyclopaedic dictionaries, and historical studies were published. Original works of composers of earlier periods were revived and individual genres incorporating works written before the XIX Century were printed in separate series. For example, "Polish Symphonies" and "Sonatas" have been published, and "Operas" and "Cantatas" are planned. In conjunction with the Frederick Chopin Institute (reorganized in 1945 into the Frederick Chopin Society, TIFC), the publication was begun of a 10-volume series of studies entitled *Analysis and Commentaries to The Complete Collection of Works of Frederick Chopin.*
3. During the second decade, the following events were a regular part of Polish musical life: The International Festival of Song (in Sopot); Song and Dance Ensembles (in Zielona Góra); festivals of jazz music (in Wroclaw, Kraków), symphonic orchestras and ballet (in Lódź); Chopin festivals (in Duszniki), besides the International Chopin competitions; the Wieniawski violin competition (in Poznań); festivals of ancient Slavic music (in Bydgoszcz); and folklore ensembles (in Zakopane).

Yearly festivals were organized to present contemporary Polish music of different regions: Poznań Musical Spring (from 1961); Kraków Spring of Young Composers (from 1962); Competition of Composers of Western Lands in Wroclaw; Lublin Musical September. Festivals and competitions of young talent became famous with The General Competition of Student Choirs, the All-Poland Festival of Young Musicians (from 1964), the Festival of Polish Song in Opole (from 1965), and others.

4 Associations of creative artists sprang up in arts other than music as well. For instance, "Group of Self-Improvement" at the Cracow Academy of Arts (1947), whose members included A. Wróblewski, A. Wajda, A. Strumillo, F. Bunsz, and others. Their program was primarily socio-political.

It is worthwhile noticing the resemblance between the declarations of "Group 49," and the aesthetic platform of "The Six" in France during the 1920's. Both groups address themselves to the need for artists to avoid narrow propagandist objectives, and both set up goals of adhering to general world-wide democratic traditions.

5 During the war years (1943–1944), Lutoslawski also composed *5 pieśni walki podziemnej* (*5 Songs of the Underground*): *Żelazny marsz; Do broni; Przed nami przestrzeń otwarta; Jedno slowo, jeden znak; Wesoly pluton* (*The Iron March*; *To Arms!*; *The Spaces Before Us*; *One Word, One Sign*; *The Merry Platoon*).

6 Jósef Maria Chomiński, "Kantata" in *Kultura muzyczna Polski Ludowej 1944–1945* (Kraków: PWM, 1957), p. 17.

7 Compositional method of musical-associative thinking were fully elucidated by the Soviet musicologist Arnold Alshvang in his theory of "generalization (universalization) via the genre." According to Alshvang, composers desiring to "decipher" the content of music, turn to certain types of genres which have crystallized over centuries of musical practice. These generic types evoke recognizable visual associations in the consciousness of the listener. For instance, a listener may sense the presence of grief or death on hearing the intonation of a moan or the rhythm of a funeral procession. These condensed formulas, conductors of "coded" information, may be certain rhythmo-intonational models, such as a marching song, a ceremonial procession, or a funeral march, or else folk and national dances (mazurka, polka, tarantella, siciliana, gavotte), and songs (lyric, ritual, wedding, choral, etc.) See: Arnold Alshvang, "Opernyie zhanry 'Carmen' " ("Operatic genres in 'Carmen' "); *Sovietskaya muzyka*, No. 12, 1938. The theory of genres was developed by Soviet musicologists: Boris Asafiev, Lev Mazel, Sergei Skrebkov, Arnold Sokhor, Victor Zukkerman.

8 The libretto was based on actual events that took place in sixteenth century Poland. A poor student ("żak" in Polish), Lochmanek is killed for his disobedience to his masters by the Burgomeister's son. In response to this "execution," Konopny, another student, calls on his fellow students to resist. On learning that the king has declared his intention to bring Konopny to trial, the students, headed by their leader, abandon their native town of Cracow in protest.

9 For further information about opera see: Mieczyslaw Drobner, "Opera i balet," in *Kultura muzyczna Polski Ludowej 1944–1945* (Kraków: PWM, 1957).

In 1955 Szeligowski finished an opera for children, *Krakatuk (Nutcracker)*, K. Niżynska's libretto based on *Tales of Hoffman*—a lively fantastic parody.

10 The term was first used by the Soviet musicologist Boris Yarustovsky in his book, *Simfonii vojny i mira (Symphonies of War and Peace)* (Moscow, Nauka, 1966), p. 7.

11 Tadeusz Marek, foreword to score of Serocki's *First Symphony* (Kraków: PWM, 1955), p. VI.

12 Ludmila Tananaeva, *Ocherki polskoj grafiki XX veka (Essays on Polish Graphics of the Twentieth Century)* (Moscow: Iskusstwo, 1972), p. 73.

13 This term appears in many works by Zofia Lissa, especially in her article "Muzyka symfoniczna," in book: *Kultura muzyczna Polski Ludowej 1944–1945*, opus cit., p. 128.

14 Sikorski's contributions to pedagogy were indeed extensive. He was the author of numerous volumes of texts on composition, including various theoretical disciplines: *Harmony, Counterpoint, Instrumentation*. Many young composers studied under him.

15 Tadeusz A. Zieliński, "Grażyna Bacewicz," *Spotkania z muzyką wspólczesną* (Kraków: PWM, 1974), pp. 10–11.

16 Tadeusz A. Zieliński, *Tadeusz Baird* (Kraków: PWM, 1966), p. 23.

17 Józef Maria Chomiński, "Kantata," *Kultura muzyczna Polski Ludowej 1944–1945*, opus cit., p. 187. Chomiński makes an error when he speaks of a five-movement cycle. He separates the exposition of the work from the *arioso*. Actually they form a single movement.

18 The term is Valentina Cholopova's in her book: *Voprosy ritma v tvorchestvie kompozitorov XX vieka (Rhythmic Problems in the Works of Twentieth Century Composers*. Moscow: Muzyka, 1971). p. 194 and further.

19 Galina Taraeva, "Pretvoryaya patrioticheskiye tyemy . . ." ("The Realization of Patriotic Themes"), *Sovietskaya Muzyka*, No. 5, 1977.
Steven Stucky disputes the conception of the Symphony No. 1 as a

"war" symphony. See: S. Stucky, *Lutoslawski and His Music* (Cambridge: Cambridge University Press, 1981), p. 30.
20 S. Stucky, op. cit., p. 49.
21 These motifs have their source in Masovian folklore. The composer made use of an anthology: Oskar Kolberg, *Mazowsze*, vols. 2, 5, 25 (Cracow: Druk Wl. L. Anczyca i Spólki, 1886, 1890). The original songs appear in S. Stucky's book; op.cit., p. 50, examples 2,5.

II
Music of the Second Postwar Decade (1956–1965)

The second post-war decade in the musical culture of Poland was a time of intensive search and experimentation in the area of musical language. Significant changes had taken place in the political life of the country. Weakening governmental pressure had a beneficial effect on art as a whole and on music in particular. The year 1956 saw the first of the international music festivals, "Warsaw Autumn."

The chief initiators of the "Warsaw Autumn" were T. Baird and K. Serocki. "Warsaw Autumn" complemented the only other festival of that period that took place in Eastern Europe, "Prague Spring." Since the latter occurred in spring, the Warsaw festival was scheduled for autumn. The goal of this festival, as defined by its founders, was to present contemporary music. In this "Warsaw Autumn" differed from the Prague festival where modern music occupied a secondary place.

The organizers of "Warsaw Autumn" aimed to re-establish contacts with Western Europe which had been disrupted since 1939. They also wished to introduce their own contributions to European music. They believed that Warsaw could become a center of contemporary music no less important than Darmstadt, Donaueschingen, Köln, Milan or Venice. At the same time the Poles tried to avoid extremes and one-sidedness, presenting music objectively in its broad scope and not only in its avant-garde aspect.

During the very first season, a panorama of 20th century music, covering almost sixty years in chronological order, was presented. Here were heard compositions written at the turn of the century (Richard Strauss); music of the beginning of the new century (Arnold Schoenberg); of the 1920's (Arthur Honegger); and of the 1940's and 1950's. In selecting compositions, the aim was not only to present a historical process of development, but also to show a spectrum of different musical directions: Schoenberg's expressionism, Stravinsky's neo-Classicism, the early works of the French "Les Six," the music of "Young Poland," etc.

Polish music was presented extensively and in all its variety. For the first time it showed itself to be a national school which not only had sources and roots in its own past culture, but was also a composite phenomenon engendered by a variety of European tendencies of this century. A multitude of individual aspirations and directions was displayed by composers: folklore, refracted through the prism of a composer's original vision (*Little Suite* by W. Lutoslawski, *Polish Symphony* by Z. Mycielski); a neo-Classic line presented in multiple aspects (*Concerto for Orchestra* by W. Lutoslawski, *Concerto for Strings* by G. Bacewicz, *Concerto Grosso* by B. Szabelski); the traditions of the Polish Renaissance (*Third Symphony* by K. Sikorski), etc.

1958, the year the second "Warsaw Autumn" took place, is taken as the birth-date of the Polish avant-garde. Two composers, H. M. Górecki and W. Kilar, who for a time were considered the chief representatives of the Polish avant-garde, made their debuts. New works by prominent Polish composers were performed: Lutoslawski's *Musique Funèbre*, Baird's *Four Essays*, Palester's Symphony No. 4. Kotoński also made his debut. Stockhausen, invited from Germany, gave the first concert of electronic music in Warsaw, and John Cage's *Music of Changes* was presented for the first time in Warsaw.

Warsaw Autumn festivals proved to be of great cultural importance to Poland. Taking place every year, they came to be a unique showcase for the ideas and aims of Polish composers, demonstrating processes which had been evolving in Polish music during the last ten years. Not only did the Poles become acquainted with the music of different countries at the *Warsaw Autumn*, but foreign musicians discovered for themselves the art of Poland.

At the first festivals, toward the end of the 1950's, Polish musicians heard what to them had been little known works: masters of the new-Viennese school, the major French composers (O. Messiaen, P. Boulez), the Italians (L. Nono, L. Dallapiccola), Americans (C. Ives, E. Varèse), and others. Accepting the various principles of the new compositional techniques and substantially increasing the musical palette of contemporary means, Polish composers made an important contribution to the music of the 1960's. Creative experiment took the form of an all-encompassing search and touched upon the most diverse areas of music. Some composers' predominant interest was in form (Z. Krauze), others' was in the organization of musical texture (K. Penderecki, K. Serocki). There were also instances of interest in abstract form-building (W. Szalonek, B. Schäffer).

This period saw major achievements. New technical means evolved out of the purely experimental stage into the sphere of expressivity. A productive search for the musical equivalent of contemporaneity was taking place.

Wojciech Kilar, 1971

II. Music of the Second Postwar Decade (1956–1965)

Zbigniew Bujarski, 1974

Thus, already at the beginning of the 1960's, such significant works, as Penderecki's *Threnody*, Górecki's *Genesis*, Lutoslawski's *Venetian Games* appeared.

From the point of view of themes, art in the second decade continued to develop along the lines laid down in the preceding period.* A special emphasis was put on nationalism, a theme that was presented in a variety of guises: as the reflection of a people's historical destiny (T. Szeligowski's cantata about Boleslaw The Brave, *Inditus rex*); as a patriotic theme (W. Rudziński's *Gaude Mater Polonia*, and T. Paciorkiewicz's *Native Land–Ojczyzna*); as an illustration of the life and customs of a people (suites on folkloric themes). Polish composers turned to their own literature, and to their cultural heritage. The art of the great poet and dramatist of the Polish Renaissance, Jan Kochanowski held a special attraction for composers. One of his poetic works (*Tren—Threnody*) became the basis of S. Prószyński's cantata *The Eighth Threnody by Jan Kochanowski* for a men's and boy's à cappella chorus. Another Kochanowski work, the tragedy *The Dismissal of the Greek Envoys (Odprawa posłów greckich)* became the basis for W. Rudziński's opera of the same name.

Polish artists always felt an affinity for universal humanistic problems. Working with such themes, Polish composers found interesting solutions and created more than a few vivid and talented compositions. Deep reflection on existential meaning permeates *Funeral Music* and *Three Poems of Henri Michaux* by W. Lutoslawski and Penderecki's *Strophes*. Universal humanistic themes were of foremost importance in religious genres and forms. Catholicism, an inseparable part of Polish upbringing, was instrumental in inducting certain musical forms, originating in the practices of the church, into the general Polish tradition rooted in ancient past. Repeatedly, the church had taken a part in the country's tragic history, its partitions and struggle for national independence. In this struggle the Polish people steadfastly held onto their national consciousness and cultural values. As far back as the Polish Renaissance, religious content music began to acquire a broad interpretation; one example is the famous *Missa Pulcherrima* composed in the 17th century by Bartlomiej Pękiel. In the 1950's this tradition in Polish art was revived. Compositions were written whose meaning went far beyond the confines of church worship. To cite a few examples: Penderecki's *The Passion According to St. Luke; Requiem* by Z. Rudziński; some part of the mass and psalms (*Laudate Omnes Gentes* by T. Szeligowski, *Stabat Mater* by K. Penderecki, *The Minor Orthodox Liturgy* by R. Twardowski, etc.)

A great variety of genres proliferated in the musical art of the second post-war decade. Traditional forms, opera, ballet, oratorios and choral mu-

---

*Some of these compositions appeared after 1965.

Wlodzimierz Kotoński

sic, all continued to attract composers. Besides the operas and ballets already mentioned, new works appeared based on well-known themes drawn from literary and dramatic sources: T. Szeligowski's ballets *Mazeppa* and *Weeping Odysseus*; R. Twardowski's opera *Cyrano de Bergerac*, and his ballet *The Emperor's New Clothes; Ugo and Parisina* by S. Skrowaczewski, *Titania and the Ass* by Z. Turski; the ballet *Sulamith* by W. Rudziński, based on *The Song of Songs; Niobe*, based on a Greek myth, by J. Łuciuk. An historical revolutionary theme was the basis for W. Rudziński's *Commandant of Paris*.

During the performance of a piece by François-Bernard Mâche. Performers: Eugeniusz Knapik, Krzysztof Meyer, Andrzej Dutkiewicz, and Szabolcs Esztényi (the Hungarian composer and pianist). "W.A." 1985.

A new genre appeared—the radio-opera (*Adventures of King Arthur* by G. Bacewicz, and an eastern tale, *Neffru* by Z. Wiszniewski). In the field of radio genres, composers were to become especially productive as electronic techniques developed in the 1960's and 1970's (B. Schäffer, Z. Wiszniewski, A. Dobrowolski, et al.). In contrast to the first post-war decade, when large scale traditional operas "ruled the day," the second decade saw more and more attempts to go beyond the borders of traditional operatic forms.

Similar transformational processes took place in other genres. Oratorio and symphony, concerto and quartet, small vocal and instrumental pieces, all these forms seemed to exist on two parallel planes: in their traditional guise, and in a new one, often created by a conjunction of different genres, or emerging out of new compositional techniques.

A number of "poem" type of compositions were written with prominent sub-titles, a part of the mainstream of 20th century symphonic and concert music. Here, two tendencies may be observed: one, to bring symphonic forms closer to chamber forms; the other, its reverse: to enlarge the orchestral apparatus in writing of music conceived as a chamber work. These compositions partially displaced the large symphony.

The numerous examples mentioned demonstrate the succession of artistic

II. Music of the Second Postwar Decade (1956–1965)

lines from the first decade to the second, although many of the compositions cited above left no visible trace on the development of Polish music. However from the second half of the 1950's, completely new processes sprang up, gradually blotting out what, up to that point, had been the existent tendencies. These new processes were reflected both in the aspects of compositional forms, and in technical transformations of existing language systems.

As examples we cite the following compositions: *Perpetuum Mobile* by Kisielewski; *Confessions* by Szalonek; *Scontri* for string orchestra and *Diagrams* by Górecki; *Anaklasis, Dimensions of Time* and *Silence, Emanationen, Fluorescences* for Orchestra, *Polymorphia* for 48 strings by Penderecki; *Tertium datur, Music for MI, Little Symphony Scultura* by Schäffer; Four Essays for Orchestra, *Etude* for vocal orchestra, percussion and piano, *Epiphany Music* by Baird; *Musique en relief* by Kotoński; three *Postludium*, and *Jeux vénitiens* by Lutoslawski; *Episodes* for strings and

Zygmunt Mycielski, 1977.

Marta Ptaszyńska with Józef Patkowski, director of the Polish Radio Experimental Studio. "W.A." 1979.

percussions, and *Segmenti* by Serocki; *Herbsttag*, *Riff 62*, *Générique*, and *Diphtongos* by Kilar; *Aphorisms 9* by Szabelski; *Contrasts* by Penherski; *Kinoth* by Bujarski; *Contra fidem* by Z. Rudziński; *Prologues* by T. Sikorski.

No need to continue this list. The reader has probably noticed unusual titles borrowed, at times, from physics or mathematics—a reflection of the musicians' desire to incorporate that new phenomena, the turbulent evolution of scientific-technical thinking. In all of this, one may discern a wish to give new meaning to music as an art that expresses ideas—ideas that formerly had had no part in the musical sphere.

As we examine the music of the second decade, we will pay special attention to techniques. Analysis of actual, specific compositions will help to demonstrate connections with contemporary views, reveal ways in which new techniques are employed in the realization of contemporary themes in art, indicate paths of interaction with national traditions. The 1960's in Poland's musical history was a period when certain developments could be

II. Music of the Second Postwar Decade (1956–1965)

clearly observed: a broadening of the musical lexicon, an emergence of mixed genres, and of new principles of form building.

As to the development of new compositional techniques in Poland at this time, two stages can be seen. The first one took place in the second half of the 1950's and the beginning of the 1960's, and went under the banner of dodecaphony; the second stage saw the formation of musical sonorism.

Let us begin our survey with dodecaphony, under whose sign the art of the second half of the 1950's evolved.

Serial dodecaphony (a term given by the Polish musicologist Józef M. Chomiński[1]), had practically no tradition in Poland's past. In the era between the two great wars, only one composer really studied this system: Józef Koffler, a pupil and disciple of Arnold Schoenberg. Koffler died during the Nazi occupation. He composed several works using dodecaphonic techniques. Yet in style and character, these compositions were closer to neo-Classicism (*String Trio*, *Variations for String Orchestra*, cantata *Love*, et al.). During the war years, the composer C. Regamey also worked in dodecaphonic technique, but generally dodecaphony in Poland was almost unknown in the post-war decade. The first compositions written in this tech-

Andrzej Dobrowolski with members of the Warsaw Accordion Trio (Jerzy Lukaszewicz, Jerzy Kaszuba, Krzysztof Olczak). "W.A." 1979.

nique were a *Suite of Preludes* for piano by K. Serocki, and *Nocturne* for strings by B. Schäffer (at the end of the first decade). From the start, composers showed a great interest in dodecaphony; however, in the majority of cases, composers used elements of dodecaphonic technique while retaining a modal-tonal basis in their way of thinking. In general, serial dodecaphony in its pure form did not "take" in Poland, and in the 1960's, other techniques came into use.

Let us examine some examples of dodecaphonic compositions from the standpoint of their relationship to national traditions in music.

Tadeusz Baird's compositions, during the second decade, show a crystallization of certain particular traits of his individuality. Lyric and romantic, by nature of his talent, he had a special affinity to Alban Berg's type of dramatic expressivity. His strength had always been for expressive melodic material as the main bearer of musical content. In the compositions of his dodecaphonic period, the significance of melody as a basic component of the composer's style is retained. This period encompasses the years 1956–1963 and includes chamber and symphonic music: *Cassazione* for orchestra (1956), *Divertimento* for flute, oboe, clarinet and bassoon (1956), *String Quartet* (1957), *Four Essays* for orchestra (1958), *Espressioni* for violin and orchestra (1959), *Variations Without a Theme* (1962), *Epiphany Music* (*Muzyka epifaniczna*) for orchestra (1963), *Egzorta* for narrator, mixed chorus and orchestra (1960), *Erotics*, six songs for soprano and orchestra (1961). In many compositions (especially later ones) dodecaphony is freely interpreted. Rows of thematic series are correlated, incomplete in their constructions, expressive from the standpoint of rhythm, timbres, and dynamics. Baird attempts to find the potential of vertical connections in the series, while preserving ties to traditional harmonic techniques. Separate segments of the series are combined in order to make a symmetrical structure (a device that also recalls methods of traditional composition). According to J. M. Chomiński's conclusion, the tendency to give prominence to monophonic (homogeneous, monochromatic) means, and to autonomy of horizontal structure emphasizes the melodic, non-pointillistic nature of Baird's dodecaphony.[2]

Baird consciously repeats a chosen intervallic system for the purpose of centering attention on the expressivity of the melodic cell. Both in melodic and rhythmic systems, elements of a motivic way of thinking are retained. For expressive declamatory types of themes, unison statements are characteristic, as are ascents and zigzag designs that stand out in relief. In a movement that ascends by way of rising ledges, upward jumps are filled with descending figures (solo parts in *Espressioni* and *Erotics*). Such themes contain great inner emotional power. Certain particular features in the chamber type of compositions, especially in the Quartet and song cycles, are in character close to the new-Viennese, "Webernesque" style: refinement of sound, economy in texture, a predilection for the 7th and 9th intervals, and individualization of voices. Yet, in spite of the similarities, Baird definitely remains himself, keeping his own original personal style.

In the *Four Essays* for orchestra, each part of the cycle is colored by its own definite emotional tone. Expressive means are chosen with strict care and are deliberately limited. The first *Essay (Molto adagio)* has a theme which is original in its rhythmic and melodic plans. It is distinguished by the breadth of its unfolding and the tremulous, personal tone of its statement. The development undulates. Attention is drawn to the principle of unification in the "wave"—variations by a central tone (pedal on *E* in the second phrase, and on *C* at the end). Intricacy in the motion of intervals, contrasting registers, transparent textures, changeable dynamic color nuances, all create a very special chamber style with a refined mobile inner fabric. A well-defined developmental line is drawn: the recitatival declamatory melody changes in the process of unfolding into a march formula (). Thus, a line is indicated—an evolution from an individual personal statement to a general one.

Its concrete form distinguishes the second movement, a rondo, which, at times, is an elegant, dance-like scherzo with a mischievously grotesque theme that first appears in the woodwinds; and at other times, a graceful waltz in the solo oboe against a light pizzicato background in the strings. A distinct transformation takes place in the middle episode as if two very different types of material were being joined together: the lyrically intimate statement by a solo violin and the firm marching step in ostinato repeats on the bass *D*. Baird's variational technique reaches a virtuoso level at this point: the genre picture is full of lively contrast—thematic transformations. In style and imagery this piece comes very close to neo-Classicism; in means, however, it is closer to the expressionism inherent in the new-Viennese school.

Example 14

The third *Essay (Allegro)* is more expressive, full of musical events, and dynamic changes. The chorale-like theme is replaced by a dialogue for two pianos, thereby giving an original concerto flavor to the third *Essay*. Percussively rhythmic elements appear in the dramatic culmination, recalling Bartók. Unusually prolonged in the continuation, it becomes a self-contained, separate episode, brutal in the strength of its expression. The imagery of this "angry scherzo" in the midst of a slow part, echoes episodes from "marches of invasion" in the anti-war type music.

In the finale (*Molto adagio*) rhythmically free, declamatory themes come back anew: typically expressive unison ascending flights in the violins (No. 10), fanfares (No. 40), intense culminations, tutti. A philosophic, contemplative coda constitutes the resolution of the whole cycle. The timbre of a clavecin, and Baroque ornamentations create an archaic flavor. Thus, again, in this composition, the neo-Classic style prevails. Dodecaphony does not limit the work's thematic system. Romanticism and Classicism, personal statement, the intrusion of general images from the outside, the juxtaposition of contrasting scenes, and a retention of unity of the whole form—such are the features of this multi-faced cycle. The music in *Four Essays*, with its expressive plasticity, attracted choreographers in Poland and also in other countries. It was produced as a ballet-pantomine in Gdańsk, Hanover, and other cities. Much later, the composer revealed the programmatic concepts in the *Essays*. Its first piece was originally written as incidental music to Shakespeare's *Henry IV*. Later, it served as the starting point for an independent composition.[3]

We see a continuation of the same creative line in *Espressioni Varianti per Violino e Orchestra* and in *Variations Without Theme* for orchestra. In *Espressioni*, intense emotion penetrates each motif. It is found side by side with the virtuoso character of separate episodes. In the symphonic *Variations*, there is, despite the large size of the orchestra, an astonishing transparency of texture, refinement of sonority, and richness in coloristic nuances.

The height of this line is reached in *Epiphany Music (Muzyka epifaniczna)* for cello and orchestra. Its characteristics encompass a chamber style in the presence of a large orchestral complement, a concerto virtuosity, the individualization of different parts, a rich imagination in the use of timbres, and unique harmony—all directed toward revealing musical thematic content.

The cantata *Egzorta* ("a warning," "an exhortation") is a typical example of Baird's dramatic expressionism. Using an ancient Hebrew text, the composition is written for narrator, mixed chorus and orchestra. It is permeated by the tragedy of the Second World War. The character of *Egzorta's* thematic structure and certain of its formal features, bring it close to Schoenberg's *A Survivor from Warsaw* and Milhaud's *Le Château de feu*. The same stylistics and reliance on literary sources, and "Sprechstimme" are present. Baird underlines the universal human, non-personal character of his composition, although there are moments when illustrational sounds direct the listeners' attention to the events of the war years, and evoke analogies to contemporary theater and cinema works. In style, Baird's cantata touches on French traditions (Honegger's *Danse des morts*, Milhaud's *Le Château de feu*). Imitation of actual sounds, graphic descriptions, the introduction of a narrator reading in a strict rhythmic style, all stem from the desire to make the cantata form theatrical; cinema art also makes its contribution by providing a structure of single still "frames" analogous to moments when a film stops. The complex of sharply expressive means, the character of the imagery, the technical system (dodecaphony)—all are close to Schoenberg (*A Survivor from Warsaw*).

The thematic material of the composition is presented in three series, which appear both simultaneously and separately. The character of the first two is related to the imagery of "the scene of action," and therefore includes rustling, percussive effects, tremolos, drumrolls, dry scattering sound effects produced by xylophone, tam-tams, temple blocks and piano. These series constitute single sounds, and whole-tone/tritone segments. Visions arise of the dreadful daily life in a concentration camp; of the face of death, of fascism's soul-numbing spectres. The concreteness of the imagery is further strengthened because the means are so economical. Baird found a vivid and effective device. Mimetic percussive and noise-eliciting sounds alternate with a realistic type of march; while rhythmic-declamatory speech segments change into an expressive cantilena. Such is the way in which theatrical elements, the arsenal of non-musical means, are interpreted in a seemingly inevitable way, through purely musical means of expression. "Scenes of action," alternate with "scenes of emotional states." Rampaging percussion and noise-producing elements in the central episode recall a

Example 15

terrible Danse Macabre, but a mournful requiem immediately follows. Segments of the third series are unified by means of stretti and the harmony of beautiful choral singing. Ex. 15.

Egzorta is not a large cantata, only eight minutes and thirty seconds long, yet because the expressive means are so strong and austere and because it is so intensely dramatic, it may be compared to a fresco. It takes its place next to the other big anti-war compositions of Polish art.

It is necessary to stress that in *Egzorta*, as in his other works, Baird goes beyond the rigid constructs determined by the rules of the dodecaphonic system. *Egzorta*'s structure approaches that of a ternary form within a frame. Periodically repeated structures, an undulatory development building up to intense climaxes, those are the marks of the traditional form of a cantata.

According to J.M. Chomiński, the belated acquaintance of Polish composers with dodecaphony had its positive side. They learned much from the actual experience of its use in other countries. They saw the limitations of its systems, the boundaries within which it had to be applied. This caused them to attempt to surmount the limits of the system, to search for a synthesized system, and to enlarge the boundaries of genres. These aims can be seen not only in Baird's music, but in that of others as well.

Kazimierz Serocki introduced a broad spectrum of colorful effects into his dodecaphonic works. It must be noted that a heightened attention to color had been present in Polish music since the time of "Young Poland." The desire to refine sonority, the accentuation of micro-motif as the carrier of fine nuances of mood characterizes the work of Serocki during his dodecaphonic period. In the *Heart of Night (Serce nocy)* cycles, poems by K. I. Galczyński (1956), and *The Eyes of the Air (Oczy powietrza)*, poems by J. Przyboś (1957), the composer continued in the Webern tradition. In *Musica concertante* (1958), Serocki becomes more interested in the technique of vertical structures, the pointillism of the Boulez school (*Structures* by P. Boulez). In Serocki's music, the technical system of dodecaphony is subservient to the solution of problems of sonority, especially in the vocal cycles. Already, in the first *Heart of Night* cycle for orchestra and baritone, a broadening of the coloristic spectrum in the orchestra can be seen. Here the percussion section plays a large role. The choice of instruments clearly indicates the intent to strengthen ringing, "fluid," "jingling" timbres: three piatti sospesi, gong, tam-tam, campanelli, xylophone, marimbaphone, vibraphone, celesta, two harps, piano. To them are added such non-traditional instruments as a mandolin and guitars—preferably electric. Poetically lyric verse is conveyed by refined means: delicate dynamics, fine nuances in sound. Sonority becomes one of the chief means for revealing musical substance.

In another cycle for soprano and orchestra, *Oczy powietrza (Eyes of the Air)* not only ringing timbres, but noise-producing effects are also emphasized (two tamburi, senza and con corda, two maracas, triangle, timpani), and provide ringing and rustling sounds. The vocal parts in both of the cycles are exceptional in their expressivity, in the smooth flow of intervallic motion, contrasting with the pointillistic design of the instrumental parts. Expressivity, tunefulness, deep feeling in intonation, all subtly convey the mood of the verse. In some songs, the theme is presented in a generalized way (*A Moment* in *Oczy powietrza*); in other songs, the import lies in their changeability and elusiveness. *Lilacs* from *Oczy powietrza* is an example. Filled with inner contrasts, it is made up of different segments. Lively motion, declamation, agitated and undulant (images of quickening earth and roots growing), motor ostinato figurations in the harps, clarinets and strings comprise the opening segment, which is contrasted to the calm, contemplative segments which follow. The themes alternate as in a two-theme rondo with frequent variational changes (inversions, transpositions, rhythmic alterations). In these songs a major role is assigned to the instrumental part in its character of figurational formation. Serocki is already developing the sonoric fabric of the composition, as if anticipating the tendency of the coming sonoristic period.

Serocki's songs often have a generic base. Elements of the musical genre seem to reinforce the text: features of the waltz in *Paths* (from the *Oczy powietrza* cycle); dance-like scherzo in *Message to Lovers*, a song of mourning in *In Memory of a Mother*, mimetic sound effects and lively rhythmic motion in *Sleighs*, landscape sketches, contemplation in *Moon, Night* (from the *Serce nocy* cycle).

Keeping to the text in all its particulars results in an original "moment-by-moment" structure of development, in which every passing instant is marked by its own special nuance in the construction of musical form. It is a method that was clearly revealed in *Musica concertante*, a seven movement cycle written in a serial technique. In it, however, a dependence on Boulez's style is felt in the way sounds are combined into vertical complexes—in a somewhat intellectual approach to the building of structures and the sonoric treatment of the orchestra. The pieces are differentiated from each other by the instrumentation, by the choice of articulation, and the distribution and type of timbres: at times, the themes consist of single sounds, played consecutively by each instrument; at other times, a noise color effect assumes prime importance. The pieces are written in different tempos, and further differentiated by their static or mobile character. However, vivid thematic contrasts are absent here. On the whole, *Musica concertante* is clearly not on the same level as the vocal cycles.

Serocki's next composition, *Epizody (Episodes)* for strings and three groups of percussion (1959) is another instance of the solution of the problem of sonority in a serial type of composition. The composer divided the ensemble into three groups, placed at different ends of the stage. The idea of antiphony, of stereophonic polyphony, and its opposite, the unification of all sound strata, leads to the formation of new types of textures—to textural thematicism, material of sonoristic composition. Thus, a succession of new technical systems gains acceptance while composers still keep their own concept of a total compositional form.

Changes in type of thematic construction can also be observed in the work of other composers; for instance, in the compositions of Grażyna Bacewicz. In *Music for Strings, Trumpets and Percussion* written in 1958, she already evinced a serial tendency in her approach to material, enlarging that technique to include rhythm, dynamics and harmony. However, in her *Sixth Quartet* (1960), Bacewicz showed that she was not a follower of the new-Viennese school, but of Bartók. Her interpretation of dodecaphony is very free, as an organizing principle of a thematic series, but, again in Bartók's sense, as a method of complementary tones. This cannot be called atonality, for individual sounds, methodically repeated, function as centralizing pivotal tones. At the same time, the functional tension is somewhat weakened due to a retreat from interval structures in thirds, and a move toward tritones. That is to say, modal-harmonic relationships become more complex; a changeover to a twelve-tone diatonic scale goes into effect.[4] Moreover, attention is increasingly centered on coloristic aspects; various techniques of color articulations are employed (saltando, col legno, sul tasto, sul ponticello, glissando, etc.). Although the traditional contours of the cycle and the generic function of its movements are retained (evenly paced motor motion in the second movement and in the Finale; intermezzo features in the third movement, Grave), an unconventional concept of the first movement is presented. Fragmentary and disjointed, with inner contrasts, this compound composition flows out of the new construction of the material itself. The further evolution of Bacewicz's musical language was to take it in the direction of stronger color means, penetrating not only into the area of timbre, but also of harmony, mode, and form.

A turn toward dodecaphony by a composer of the older generation, Boleslaw Szabelski, caused a sensation in Polish musical circles, similar to the one provoked by the venerable Stravinsky's ''change of faith'' to the new serialism. Several orchestral pieces by Szabelski belong to the dodecaphonic period: *Sonety (Sonnets)* for orchestra (1958), *Wiersze (Verses)* for piano and chamber orchestra (1961), *Aforyzmy "9" (Aphorisms on 9)* (1962), *Preludes* for chamber orchestra (1964), and also *Improvisations* for chorus and chamber orchestra (1959). It was characteristic for the composer to turn to chamber orchestral groups, which allowed him to bring out a transparent linear quality in musical texture.

Three Sonnets for orchestra is an interim type of piece—transitional from the standpoint of form. In it, Szabelski moves away much farther than Bacewicz from the traditional treatment of a form of a sonata symphonic cycle. Serial themes, at times pointillistic, whose characteristics are: transference of sounds from one instrument to another, composition fractured into small fragments, phrases, motifs; absence of broad melodic lines and large waves of development—all these are traits of dodecaphonic writing in *Sonnets*. But unlike Webern, in whose works similar techniques are used in small forms, Szabelski's compositions are framed in large forms, which then creates a certain contradiction between the means and the form. "This music is dynamic and expressive, but it is short of breath," justly noted the critic T. Zieliński.[5] What remained from Szabelski's former type of romantic expression were vivid dramatic climaxes, strong symphonic tutti, contrasting images evoking analogies with a variety of genres. From time to time, along with the atonal material appear progressions of a major-minor derivation. The composition ends on C, which is perceived as a cadential tonic. But stylistic lack of homogeneity does not eliminate the artistic worth of the piece, in which one feels the big talent and individuality of its composer.

Correlation of form and means is achieved by Szabelski in a not very large orchestral piece, *Aphorisms "9"*—the most "Webernesque" of his compositions. The small size of the piece (five minutes), the chamber style (the ensemble consists of nine performers: five winds, three strings and a percussionist), the disjointed phrasing—all these factors are in accord with serial composition. Here, the composer employs intervallic tension (chords of minor 2nds and 9ths, major 7ths, tritones) for the purpose of strengthening the sharpness and expressivity of emotional tone. In this piece, the role of sound coloristics is clearly intensified. Unusual methods of articulation are employed. The highest sounds in the strings (unnotated), diverse figurative complexes, rhythmic-percussive noise effects abound. A unique undulating development is promoted by the ternary structure of the composition with an intense culmination and then an abatement in the recapitulation. Such is the relationship between the new and the traditional in this miniature piece, demonstrating Szabelski's desire to introduce an individual, original note into serial composition. In the future, Szabelski would revise his position of this period. A return to national traditions, a turn towards large symphonic forms was to be the next step in the evolution of his music.

At a time when the acceptance of strict limitations in the West gave birth to numerous monotonous compositions with little to distinguish them from each other (epigones of Webern and early Boulez), Polish musical art kept a vivid emotional content. The development of Polish music lay along two lines. In the first, dodecaphony intersected with other systems, with traditional forms; in the second, dodecaphony led to other principles of composition, and lost its primary significance. In the first instance, new perspectives were opened up by Lutoslawski's *Musique Funèbre (Funeral Music)*; in the second, by Górecki's work of that period.

Musique Funèbre in Memoriam to Béla Bartók (1958) is the only composition of Lutoslawski's in which he partially accepted thematic dodecaphony. Opposing the technique on principle, he nevertheless made use of it in the exterior sections of a ternary composition for the purpose of creating a definite type of expression. These two sections stand in contrast to the middle one, written in a complex system in which twelve-tone chromaticism is combined with diatonicism. In the *Prologue* and *Epilogue*, an acutely expressive, somewhat archaic character of sound is created by a canonic statement of a twelve-tone dodecaphonic row and its inversion at the tritone. The theme itself, austere in expression, is built on only two alternating intervals, a tritone and a minor second—both belong to the contemporary musical lexicon, but appear frequently, especially in Bartók. Ex. 16.

The means were meticulously selected and so economic that the composer was able to foresee all the possible variants which might arise from the combinations of unfolding lines in the vertical. Tritones and fourth-fifth harmonies, unisons, and seconds contribute towards strengthening the somber and austere character of this music. Tritones, bared and emphasized at the climax, pulsate in percusive fanfare, clanging sonorities which resemble the nerve-wracking ringing of alarms.

In contrast to the ascetic color of the framing movements, the middle part of *Metamorphoses* is a row of freely unfolding episodes. Out of the core of a cyclically repeated variationally changeable, gradually lengthened melody, an undeviating dynamic augmentation emerges. The twelve phases of *Meta-*

Example 16

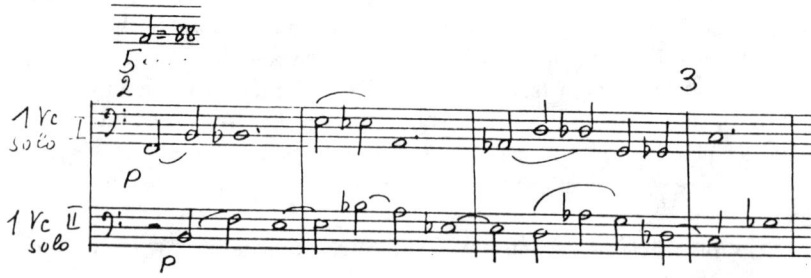

morphoses are built on a technique of rhythmic contractions and a constant filling in of the diapasons of registers. A growing dynamic surge leads to the *Apogeum*, the colossal height of the whole work. Here, twelve tones distributed over three diminished seventh chords are gathered vertically in all the registers at the same time, in "alarm-bell" rhythmic, percussive sonorities. The powerful artistic impact of *Funeral Music* gives proof that the path proposed by Lutoslawski opened up new perspectives and broad possibilities. It is a path of mixing various technical systems within the framework of a traditional understanding of form. The limitations of the influences of each of these systems are surmounted by their interpenetration, and by the use of each in its own definite, designated section of the form. This functional approach to technical systems determined by their semantic meaning, and it could be said, "affixed" to different sections of the form, stems from a traditional understanding of the form. It is an understanding to which Lutoslawski would remain faithful in his later compositions.

Similar aims are pursued by Henryk Mikolaj Górecki, although via a different path. He overcomes the limitations of the influence of dodecaphonic devices, by exploding the system from within, subjecting the material itself to a re-evaluation as a possible source of a different type of sonoristic system. At the same time, he ignores the obligatory rules of serial composition. The composer is interested in the techniques of organizing dodecaphonic serialism only as an impulse toward forming the theme of a new, purely sonoric quality. True, Górecki did not arrive at this point all at once. In an early *Concerto* for five instruments and string quartet (1957), dodecaphony was used quite traditionally; although there, already, a search was under way for methods to diversify color characteristics. In that instance, he was helped by his choice of instruments: flute, clarinet, trumpet, xylophone, mandolin, and quartet.

In the small cantata *Epitaphium* (1958) the force of tragic expression is achieved by the gradual transition from spare one-voiced monodies and pointillistically diffused sounds in various instruments to a tense harmonic vertical of the chorale in the climax. These condensed orchestral verticals are further interpreted as the tools of sonoristic expression. Here, already, Górecki showed his strong dramatic talent. Ex. 17.

In the *First Symphony, 1959* for strings and percussion, Górecki's search for his own system of imagery becomes more active. Two themes are counterposed here. The first, unpolished and powerful, produces its effect through an ostinato of repeated clustered verticals, tutti. Again we see a striving for harmonic synthesis: these powerful chords bear little resemblance to serial organization of material. And only the second theme—finely articulated, differentiated in color—is within the sphere of dodeca-

Example 17

phony; solo melodies follow one another along the horizontal. This work, with its carefully selected material, anticipates Górecki's new method of composition, which later will be labeled "limited sonorism."[6]

A crucial point in Górecki's turn from serial to purely sonoric composition was *Scontri (Collisions)* for orchestra (1960). Employing serial "sets" of sounds produced simultaneously by twelve instruments, each playing a figuration of twelve tones, Górecki treats the material as purely color-oriented; the overall effect is one of an audibly indistinguishable mix, in which the chief factors are coloristic effects produced by the highest tones of the wind instruments, percussive soundings, and clustered mixtures of chords.[7] Ex. 18.

Thus, the composer, having used the techniques of integral serialism, turned it into an element of sonoristic composition. But in the future, Górecki was to reject serial dodecaphony completely.

"Total" serialism, also in its color-oriented sonoric sense, drew the attention of another composer, Boguslaw Schäffer. In *Concerto per sei e tre*, in *Monosonata* for 24 string instruments, and in *Four Movements* for piano and orchestra, he demonstrated the diverse possibilities present in the application of serial techniques to concerto and symphonic forms, focusing attention on the technical side. However, even in this music, the analogies to traditional forms are obvious.

An original page in Polish dodecaphony is to be found in the early works of Krzysztof Penderecki, a unique manifesto rejecting the influence of the Darmstadt school. Even though Penderecki utilized some of the specific techniques of dodecaphony in his early compositions, he relegated it to a purely subservient role: a method of constructing intervallic structures and their relationships in the development of form (*Emanacje*, 1958, and *Strophes*, 1959). The composer tried to resolve technical and expressive problems at the same time. Expressivity permeates his works at all levels, from thematics and types of texture to the dynamic unfolding of form as a whole. In his early compositions, the composer posed for himself complex

Example 18

technical problems. In *Emanacje (Emanations)* for two string orchestras, the whole second orchestra is tuned a half-tone higher than the first, not for the sake of a formal experiment, but to obtain a specific color in the performance of the composition. As J. Rychlik noted, the form of *Emanacje* is constructed from a row of textural models, especially chosen because of their expressive potential.[8]

A similar balance, weighted toward expressive content versus the constructive side, may also be observed in other works by the composer, although due attention is always given to solving new technical problems. *Strofy*, for soprano, narrator, and ten instruments, set to the original texts of Menander, Sophocles, and other ancient Greek and Eastern poets, gives evidence of a careful study of L. Nono's and P. Boulez's scores, especially of *Improvisations sur Mallarmé*. Penderecki combines a fine pointillistic texture with vocal and spoken declamations. At the same time, rhythmnic organization of the text, time relationships, accentuation of separate syllables and words remain important factors in conveying intonations, meanings, and so to speak, the "melodic" line. The composer concentrates on creating a complex system of verbal accents, underlining the meaning at those moments when interaction between word and music is specially close.[9] The general theme which unifies the text is the humanity of man: "What a wonderful being is man, when he is indeed human." A comparison with analogous cycles, those of Boulez, for instance, shows that Penderecki's concept is focused to a far greater extent on sonoric problems. Young Penderecki uses texts in their original languages, setting their semantic content aside, as did Stravinsky in his time when he wrote *Oedipus Rex*. But again, here the aim is different. The subject matter of *Oedipus* is familiar to the listener, and moreover there is a Speaker who comments. Stravinsky wished to focus attention sharply on purely musical laws of development, while maintaining a traditional approach to the genre. Penderecki looks on the text more as phonic material. And although, as in the Stravinsky work, a narrator's part is added to the soprano's, his rhythmic declamation serves to strengthen the sonoric color of the total image, for the language he speaks is unknown to the audience. Penderecki's aim is to create the universal image contained in the verses, but through musical means alone.

Thus, in *Strophes,* the composer for the first time took the path of transforming the semantics of a text, converting it into a phonic apparatus, one of the components of Penderecki's sonorism. In a composition which followed shortly, *Dimensions of Time and Silence* (*Wymiary czasu i ciszy*, 1960), for 40-voice chorus, strings and percussion, the composer took the next step on the same path, changing the word into a formal element of the score, singling out from the Latin verse a group of consonants in circular

K. Penderecki, 1978

motion, a device somewhat like the "magic square" in rebus.[10] The chorus, treated as a percussion apparatus, joins an enormous and carefully selected group of percussive instruments. The chorus is used for the timbre they contribute as producers of a noise element, a timbre attained by emphasizing only consonants and sibilants, by whistling and so forth. These compositions, extraordinarily subtle in color, belong to a particular neo-impressionistic line that runs through Penderecki's artistic path, and is distinct from the other, parallel development, that of expressionism.[10]

In summary, we come to the conclusion that serial dodecaphony in Poland assumed a completely different character than it did among the new-Viennese composers or their contemporary followers in other countries. Appearing much later in Poland than elsewhere, the given system was almost always subservient to the idea of "coloristics." More often than not, composers regarded it as a sonoristic means, and that became the foremost special quality of dodecaphony on Polish soil: a fact that accounts for the short-lived, episodic nature of the fascination with serialism. Having transformed the system composers soon took other aesthetic-stylistic positions.

At the beginning of the 1960's, Polish musical art was already developing under the banner of sonorism. Dodecaphony was, to some degree, an alien phenomenon. Sonorism, on the other hand, was much more compatible with certain deeply rooted features of Polish musical culture. The stability of sonorism, its all-inclusive character, its omnipresence and various manifestations can all be attributed to that fact. Therefore, it is essential to examine this trend fully.

The term "sonorystyka" ("sonorism") came to us via Polish musicology, stemming from the French word "son"—sound;—hence, 'sonorité'—sonority with all its derivatives: "sonorous," "resonant," etc. Other musical definitions of "sonorism" also exist: "the music of timbres,"[12] for one. Sonorism is a special system of musical expression, in which the color of sound acquires an all encompassing meaning: it becomes the sum-total of timbre, coloristic, textural and rhythmic-harmonic sides of musical language.

The term "sonorism" was coined in the 1950's by the prominent Polish scholar Dr. Józef M. Chomiński,[13] and served to define more specifically several aspects of "sound colorism," a concept evolved earlier in Polish musicology that reflects certain particular qualities of the national music.

Sonorism is one of the wide-spread stable phenomenon that influenced the national school of Polish composers of the post-war period. Sonorism absorbed a large variety of stylistic tendencies of the 20th century. Its preconditions are rooted in the style of national music of the 1920's ("Polish colorism").[14] The coloristic discoveries of Karol Szymanowski were enhanced and developed in an original manner by composers of the post-war generation. In his article "Musical Work of the Last Decade," Malinowski writes, "Szymanowski steered Polish music even before 1920 on a path of sound refinement and of reflection of the instrumental texture as a means of artistic expression."[15]

Starting in the 1960's, this trend in music was developed in the works of Penderecki and in a whole group of compositions by G. Bacewicz, H. M.

Górecki, K. Serocki, W. Kilar, W. Szalonek, Z. Rudziński, Z. Bujarski, Z. Penherski, Z. Krauze, and many others. The mere enumeration of these names speaks of the fact that composers with utterly diverse creative and aesthetic leanings, writing in different styles, and using different compositional techniques, all showed an interest in sonorism in its broad sense.

Sonorism, at first, was perceived by composers as a way to gain freedom from the strict canons of serial techniques. The technique of mobile structures, aleatory music (aleatoryzm), and sonoric compositional technique with their independence from metro-rhythmical rules, and, at times, even from the organization of pitch, were a specific form of protest against all manner of limitations, but artistic results were sometimes at variance with the aesthetic goals of the movement. As so often happens, the new wave led to extremes. Having repealed the strict laws and rules governing composition, composers found themselves imprisoned in other excesses, while their compositions, built totally on narrow sonoric devices, often turned out to be just as monotonous and colorless as those of dodecaphony. Sonoristic means acquired an all-encompassing character, functioning as theme, texture, form, etc. Pitch relationships, metro-rhythm, the process of development of form—all were incorporated into sonoristic forms; hence, the great attention to unusual coloristic effects, the overgrown percussion section, the introduction of rare, exotic timbres, the eliciting of imitative, illustrational effects, the use of the chorus for its capacity to produce noise as a color, and so on.

It was becoming obvious that narrow sonoristic devices could not be a substitute for all other components of musical speech. Sonorism began to be approached as a means, commanding a specific imagery, but sharing its place equally with other means of musical expression. Composers who understood sonorism in this way were still able to interpret it in an individual manner. Sonorism does not have the same character in the works of Penderecki, Górecki, Varèse, Messiaen, E. Denisov, and G. Kancheli; for instance, in compositions in expressionistic or classic styles, the introduction of sonoristic means is dictated by a compositional concept.

In the works of some composers, sonorism acquires neo-constructionist traits, when the phonic-acoustical system is invented and arrived at through calculation. Examples of such trends can be seen in some compositions by Z. Penherski, T. Sikorski, and other composers. These composers incorporate in their music, impressive static concepts.

The *Instrumental Quartet* for piano, clarinet, trombone and cello by Zbigniew Penherski (1971), demonstrates this point.** Throughout the length of the composition, a timbre-rhythmical combination is repeated.

**Some of the compositions cited were composed after 1965.

According to Penherski, at the center of his concept lies a search for new constructions. Within them, because of a unique interpretation of development, appear special intervallic relationships in different registers, and changes of dynamics in sonority. The composition is made up of several segments separated by rests. However, the juxtaposition of a few variants, of what are, in fact, monochromatic models, is by no means sufficient for the creation of an integrated form. The result is the reverse of what the composer was attempting to achieve. Instead of a dynamic development and a juxtaposition of contrasting sonoric blocks, there is an incredibly static quality to this music. That phenomenon of process, as the very essence of form, which is impossible to attain outside of dynamic development, is here negated.

It is characteristic that during the performance of the *Quartet* in a *Warsaw Autumn* concert in 1971, the audience interrupted the performance by laughter and by applause—all of which is documented on the recording of that concert. The *Quartet* is a composition that lacks individuality. One of a fraternity, it resembles its brothers of American, Swedish, and other origins, all as alike as drops of water.

Compositional problems of a different type occupy Tomasz Sikorski, one of the Polish representatives of minimal music. The structural element, the "building material" which gives the whole composition its particular quality, is made up of only three or four intervallic structures. With no change in pitch, they reappear throughout the length of the piece. But they do undergo color-timbre alterations. Here is an original variational approach; an attainment of maximum possible color effects by a limited instrumental group. Does the process of development exist here? Is it possible to find the dialectic of the transformation of an image in this type of composition, the dynamic of the advancement of form? The answer seems to be "yes," but with many reservations, since this kind of understanding of theme, development and form as a whole, is one-sided. It is doubtful that such a novel approach can lead to new perspectives.

The compositional concept is clearly demonstrated in Sikorski's work *Holzwege* (*Roads to Nowhere*, 1972). The title is steeped in Heidegger's poetic metaphor. The composition is based on the sound of one figuration only in the whole form. From beginning to end, violins provide a background of a monotonous ostinato in a melodic figuration on the tritone e''—$b^{b'}$. Against this rocking, at evenly spaced periods of time, separated by rests, the brasses play chords which are layered on the figuration. The effect is unusual; an "ostinato of mood," congealed in one color. This static state is permeated by the programmatic symbolism contained in the title of the piece. Only at the very end does some unexpected harmonic movement occur. However, no resolution of the questioning intonation ever follows.

II. Music of the Second Postwar Decade (1956–1965)   71

Tomasz Sikorski and Jerzy Maksymiuk, the conductor of the Warzaw Philharmonic Orchestra. "W.A." 1983.

The examples given show that the problem of incorporating sonorism is extremely complex and many sided. Composers may be pursuing diverse aesthetic aims, while employing similar techniques. Moreover, the selfsame technique cannot always serve the same basic function. Thus, within the rather small dimensions of Penderecki's *Threnody*, two sonoric devices are sufficient to create an expressive image; but they would not be enough in the construction of a large form. In the coming period, oratorial and symphonic works by this same composer were to bear witness to this fact.

Krzysztof Penderecki came to the fore at the beginning of the 1960's as one of the most successful representatives of sonorism. In his early compositions he proved himself a subtle colorist, a master of the impressionistic sound palette. Another direction in his work is its expressionistic side, revealed in *Emanations* for two string orchestras, in which new articulative and percussive effects are already encountered. The first orchestra is tuned a semitone higher than the second one, creating a special sonorous effect. However, it would be a mistake to accentuate only purely technical innovations in Penderecki's compositions. They are there to serve the composer's main goal of creating a sharp dramatic expression. By making use of the percussive effects of non-traditional sound-eliciting properties of the strings, by introducing whistling sounds at pitches beyond the strings' ordinary range, and by powerfully intensifying dynamics through gradual ascents or descents of wide cluster-streams, Penderecki frequently achieves great emotional tension. *Anaklasis* for percussion ensemble and string orchestra (1960); the famous *To the Victims of Hiroshima—Threnody* for 52 strings (1960); *Polymorphia* for 48 strings (1969); *Fluorescences* for large orchestra (1962); *Canon* for 2 String orchestras and 2 tapes (1962)—all these works vividly represent Penderecki's sonoristic expressionism. However, his aesthetic and technique are far from the new-Viennese school. Penderecki's style and imagery system is much broader than a system of expressionism. He consciously produces analogies with the arsenal of traditional genres and forms, although frequently in a cryptic fashion. For example, the origin of the genre becomes apparent in the meaning attached to rhythm. Here, much stems not only from Edgard Varèse's aesthetics, but also from the "classics" of the twentieth century: the ostinati of Stravinsky's *Rite of Spring* (*Printemps*) and *Les Noces*, (their pagan rite themes and rhythms); the "scythiannes" of Prokofiev, and Bartók's barbarisms in their primeval, spontaneous force. Besides this, we can trace, in the choral work which followed the early *Psalms of David* (1958), Penderecki's neo-Classic tendency; it foreshadowed his turn, in the 60–70's towards traditional monumental form: passion, opera, Catholic and Orthodox liturgy and so forth. The titles of Penderecki's works of the 1960's refer sometimes to the genre prototype (*Strophes, Threnody, Psalms, Canon*) or sometimes in symphonic "pure" music, to a compositional—"technological" task, a reflection of the interpenetration of science and art common to most Western countries in the 1960's. Thus, "Anaklasis" is a Greek word referring to the breaking up of light, "Polymorphia" deals with the transmutation of diverse types of sound, "Fluorescences" has to do with the luminescence of phosphoric bodies that absorb light. Finally, *De Natura Sonoris (On the Nature of Sound)* quite directly reflects the essence of the composer's intentions in the field of sonorism.

For all the diversity of the dramatic-compositional solutions, these compositions are united by one constructive idea: the primary importance given to sonoristic problems. Furthermore, although the external contours of the forms resemble traditional ones, the composer had elaborated on his own concept of the form, a sort of "through-compositional" technique.[16]

The combination of new sonoristic means with transformed traditional forms is unusual and surprising. Therefore, listening to these works, one does not immediately grasp what their generic roots might be. In order to comprehend their nature one must first become accustomed to the unusual type of thematic material and its development.

For example, the genre of *Threnody* is an epitaph, a lament for the dead, rooted in the time honored traditions of Polish culture. Especially popular were the "Threnodies" of Jan Kochanowski, the Renaissance poet of the sixteenth century, much esteemed in Poland. But there are no direct ties between the traditional genre of elegiac lyric poetry and Penderecki's composition; yet it remains truly a "Threnody," a title Penderecki gave it post factum, having found a correspondence with the thematic image content of the already finished work. Its style, already worked out in earlier compositions, is a clear example of Penderecki's sonoristic expressionism. The means of expression, intentionally exaggerated in the development, as well as in the exposition, border on the non-musical. Such are the high-pitch sounds in the strings that begin the composition. They are not notated, for they are beyond the strings' ordinary range.[17] Whistling sounds seem to emit an unbearably bright light. These sounds conjure up a terrible vision. An ominous effect is produced also by the rhythmic weavings of several strata of dry percussive knockings. Here the strings are turned into percussive instruments. The composer makes use of the expressive potential of dynamics, at times frighteningly strong, at times enfeebled to a ppppp. The diapason of soundings of the string orchestra is broadened beyond recognition.

Out of sonoristic expression the composer elicited the hidden generic features of a threnody, a funeral chant. First, long, extended melodic lines lie at the base of the exposition. Complexes of prolonged linear pedals laid one upon the other form the "theme" of the introduction. Protracted in time, this theme generates an "epic" mood and, in keeping with the character of the genre, plunges the listener into lugubrious reflection.

Second, there is a gradual glissando: a narrow cluster widens, narrows again (Nos. 10-17), then drops in pitch. In its slow downward slide, it resembles a moan. The widening of the field of sound outwards from the center in a pointillistic, zigzagging design (No. 18) recalls a sharp cry full of pathos. One more articulative device helps to attain this moaning, a vibrato in cello unison (No. 23). This vibrant swaying somehow evokes the even back and forth rocking of mourners.

Apart from specific sonoristic devices, we should note a special feature of development that is related to the threnody genre. The dynamics of the piece are wave-like and the direction of the waves is regular: from ascent to descent, from gathering to breakup, from the tonic complex to its shattering.

The structure of this work is quite easily grasped. A certain simplification of the contour of forms can be seen as defiance of the spirit of the Darmstadt school, with its dominance of complex technical rules.

Compositionally, the piece is built as a sequence of contrasting episodes which are related in two different ways, by development and by opposition; its general contours are of the ternary form. A series of contrasting episodes function as an exposition. The main conflict of the piece is presented here (Nos. 1, 6) in the contrast of extended pedal sounds like "whistles" and "sparks"—with knocking percussive complexes. In the center of the piece there is an isolated large descriptive episode—the brilliant elaboration of percussive material, which calls forth visually associated analogies (Nos. 26-61).

In place of a recapitulation is a short section (Nos. 62-70) with a return to the prolonged, steady glissandi of the exposition. Percussive sounds, stemming from the central episode, are elicited by playing on the bridges and tailpieces of cellos and double basses. These sounds are superimposed on perpetual progressions of glissandi, as if in a variant of a "synthesizing" recapitulation.

Polyphonic devices borrowed from serial music (such as imitations, inversions and retrograde), may also be classed as a traditional aspect of the score, although they are formed in a sonoristic way. In the central episode, one passage, pointillistic in texture uses a 36-voice canon with inversion (Nos. 50-55).

In many segments of *Threnody* the composer again retained pitch and intervallic relationships. In the scores that followed, sonoristic exploration was even more intense.

The tendencies noted in *Threnody* continue, with variations, in Penderecki's subsequent works. The genre prototype for *Anaklasis* is the concerto for strings and percussion. The contrast of solo and tutti, the numerous solo passages, the alteration of various contrasts in the tone color of passages point to the concerto origins of this piece. The form approaches the ternary. The composer focuses attention on the central episode, in which a greatly expanded percussion group plays unaccompanied. An unexpected refinement of soundings, transfers from idiophones to percussive effects and back, and the combination of the two, and an exceedingly complex rhythmic system dependent on numerical combinations—all increase the vast scale of the nuances of tone color and, in the final analysis, intensify the expressive effect of the composition.

The composer unifies all previous achievements in the field of sonorism in *Fluorescences*, which is scored for full orchestra in four groups and six sections of percussion. A series of contrasting episodes demonstrate different sonoristic kinds of sounding: knocking, wailing, whistling. Certain combinations of timbres carry the function of themes. Rhythmically fixed figures of percussive soundings and quasi-fanfare chime complexes are counterposed to extended lines of clusters, streams of complex figurations composed of unusually articulated fanciful timbre soundings, glissando lines, and pointillistic structure intervals. In the climax of the form (central episode) percussive-rhythmic means replace the traditional orchestral tutti. The orchestral crescendo and diminuendo also are rendered by unusual means of dynamics and articulation.

The formative principle of the composition is the combining of episodes based on different approaches to tone color.

Distinctly delineated in the composition are an introduction and six unequal sections in a through-compositional technique. They comprise a variant on a form with contrasting sections. In it two form-shaping principles employed previously by Penderecki intersect. The first consists of the advancement and continous development of form by the gradual transformation of sounds and sonoristic complexes (in Erhardt's expression *forma ewolucyjna—evolutionary*).[18] The other form-creating principle stems from a montage of timbre-contrasting instrumental models. Properly speaking, the first principle involves details and development within the episodes, while the second concerns general composition. In the sphere of general dynamics there are numerous analogies with the full symphonic form in the construction of the whole—the broad strokes, the rough-hewn quality, the grandiose intensification, the striving for a continuous line. Zieliński, and later Erhardt, defined *Fluorescences* as a symphonic poem.[19]

Fluorescences is a peculiar anthology of Penderecki's sonoristic devices. Besides eliciting new sounds from standard instruments, converting strings and winds into percussion, Penderecki uses lastra (sheets of steel), sirens, an electric bell, and a typewriter. However, the inclusion of such extraordinary "instrumentation" does not indicate any desire on the part of the composer to shock the audience. Its function is to strengthen the dramatic intensity of the music.

The imagery of *Threnody* is definitely continued in *Fluorescences* through mimetic sound effects, the introduction of the awful howl of a siren, and finally, the hypertrophy of dynamic means in the unwinding process of the piece. Here, even more than in *Threnody*, analogies with Apocalyptic themes are evoked. But, we also can discern a foreshadowing of another theme that enticed the composer, the idea of the cosmos. In 1970, it was to be presented in *Kosmogonia—Cosmogony*.

Concluding this overview of the early, so-called "sonoristic" period of Penderecki's work, we should note how the composer resolves the problem of the tonal center. It would appear that the sonoristic type of style quite excludes traditional tonality, especially as, in it, normal pitch relationships are replaced by interactions of coloristic blocks, cluster-streams, and by noise-making and rhythmic-percussive complexes. All the more characteristic is Penderecki's striving to affirm, at the end of the whole composition and of major sections, the form of a chord acting as a tonic, which could function as a tonic complex.

In some pieces, *Polymorphia* for example, the final "tonic" comes in the shape of a major triad—somewhat unexpected after the percussive soundings of indeterminate pitch. In other works, various sounds and thematic or figurational complexes may function as a tonic, and in any given concrete instance behave as a tonic complex (*Anaklasis*, *Threnody*, *Fluorescences*). Ex. 19.

These heralds of a return to harmonic language along with traditional understanding of form prove to be the preconditions that paved the way for Penderecki to turn in the 1960's to genres of classical music.

Sonorism in Henryk Mikolaj Górecki's music is different in kind. This composer, who today occupies an increasingly prominent place in Poland's musical culture, went through an important evolution in his musical thinking. His sonoristic aesthetic grew out of resistance to post-Webernism, an influence he had not escaped in his early works. At the beginning of the 1960's, his attention focuses on the coloristic side of music; but by the middle 1960's, Górecki rejects the search for all-inclusive sonorism, and arrives at the idea of a maximal limitation of expressive means. Thus, in *Refrain*, musical material is reduced to two counterposed types of clusters: wholetone and semitone. In the *Genesis* cycle (1963) (I—*Elementi*, II—*Canti strumentali*, III—*Monodram*) the musical material consists of several elementary sound formulas. Górecki selects, for his music, a particular type of texture, made up of nothing but vertical sonoric complexes which then appear either over the length of a composition or over a large section of a form, and fulfill a thematic function.

Example 19

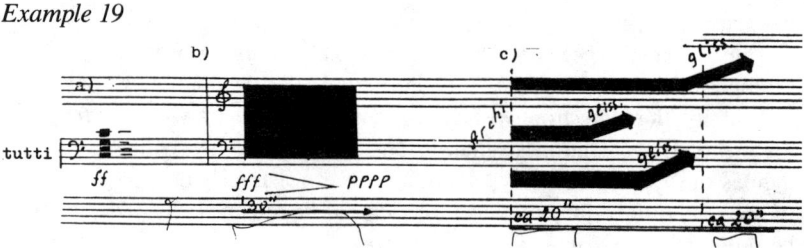

However Górecki's method differs from that of minimal music, for it is connected to the large scope of the symphonic form, and is usually comprised of a row of sections. The thematic material is in a constant process of development. This type of sonorism was aptly defined by the critic Krzysztof Droba, as "limited" or "reduced" ("redukcyjny") sonorism.[20]

A great symphonic sweep can be sensed in the writing of the single-movement *Muzyka Staropolska (Old Polish Music)*. In it, serving the function of thematic images, are two contrasting sonoric complexes: (1) a fanfare formula in the brasses, the theme of a call to battle; and (2) a complex of quiet multi-level verticals in the strings moving in a broad band at a measured pace,—a lyrically serene theme. The first is full of dynamic potentials, the second is sustained at a still point. The generic prototype of the first theme is an ancient call to battle, a reveille; of the second, a hymn. The themes' sources were the organum *Benedicamus Domino*, taken from the Klaryski Antiphonarium of 1300 A.D., and a cantus firmus from the Song of Waclaw of Szamotuly*** of 1556 A.D. An image arises of Poland's heroic historical past, a knightly epic is evoked. At the end of the composition, the interaction of influences leads to a thematic synthesis. A long crescendo emerges from the matrix of quiet, sonoristic themes and leads into a fanfare type of chorale. The fact that such a transformation is possible speaks of the latent ties, the common generic roots of the two musical themes.

In the future, Górecki would retain his individual conception of form-building, no matter how old the traditions in which he delved. Among traditional genres, he was drawn to various psalms of praise. In Górecki's work, we will come across strongly transformed chorales set to words from liturgical texts, or from the hymnology of the Polish Renaissance. But again, it must be underlined: Górecki does not use direct quotations, but recreates an epoch's ambiance.

Among liturgical forms, Górecki was attracted chiefly to old chants. The title of his instrumental and vocal works speak of this: *Canti strumentali* (from the *Genesis* cycle), *Cantata* for organ, *Choros I* for string orchestra, *Canticum Graduum* for orchestra.

In discussing the thematic content of Górecki's compositions, we must note that his attention centers on the creation of a universal humanistic theme. The composer's typical method of incorporating content is to prolong a mood through the lengthy unfolding of each theme directed toward revealing a primary idea. In vocal compositions, Górecki takes the text of a Psalm, or a part of the Mass, and selects one or two verses, and sometimes

---

***The Polish composer polyphonist of 16th century.

a few words, which contain the main idea of a large section. It is an approach that corresponds to his compositional method and the stylistic basis of his music—a "super-economy" of means: to express the main thought, a short aphorism is sometimes sufficient. "Mater mea, Lacrimosa, Dolorosa"—there stands the complete text of the cantata, *Ad matrem*. The textual fragment on which the big finale of the *Second Symphony*, the *Copernican*, is based is just a little longer.

Affirmation of a positive idea, monumental forms (even in short pieces), a rare harmony of relationship between content and expressive means, such is the framework of Górecki's limited sonorism.

Not only sonorism, but aleatoric music, too, must be examined. Not infrequently, the two phenomena are closely connected, although they belong to different musical categories. As we know, "aleatory" stems from the Latin "alea" meaning dice; hence aleatorism is knowledge about the fall of dice, or in a broader sense, knowledge about chance itself. In music, the role of chance may touch upon the problem of form-building in composition (the choice of the sequential order of the different parts) or it may touch on more specific areas, such as the texture of a composition. In its creation, each member of an ensemble may improvise on given sounds. In that case, the composer allows the performers to participate in the realizaiton of a composition. Arising as a reaction against the strict rules of dodecaphony and post-Webernism, aleatory music like sonorism, at first took on some undoubtedly exaggerated aspects. There were composers who introduced "total" improvisation in each part by every member of the ensemble. On the whole, this led both to chaotic sonority, and an actual disintegration of form. Such systems, in which excessive freedom and chance hold sway, fundamentally lie beyond the frontiers of musical art. Examples may be seen in certain works by John Cage, Sylvano Bussotti, Vinko Globokar, Andrzej Krzanowski. As a specific example, we cite Krzanowski's audio-visual play, *Transpainting* with libretto by K. Urbański.[†]

Generally, such excesses are atypical in Polish art. Only a few, isolated compositions of this kind can be named. For the most part, they are found in the work of Zygmunt Krauze, well-known for his experiments with form. In his compositions, the performer may, according to his inclination, change the order of movements, arbitrarily lower, lengthen or shorten whole sections, begin or end a work at any point. One of the first composers in Poland to use aleatory techniques in the area of form was Kazimierz Serocki. In his piano piece, *A piacere* (1963), he left it to the performer to choose the order

---

[†]It was performed in an evening concert at the *Warsaw Autumn* festival in 1977.

II. Music of the Second Postwar Decade (1956–1965)

and length of the textural-sonoric segments. Among Polish composers, Serocki remained the most constant and consistent adherent to aleatory, continuing to explore its new potentials up to his death in the early 1980's.

For Krauze, aleatory methods proved to be suitable for creating a "contrastless" form. Krauze stated his aesthetic principles in an annotation to *Piece for Orchestra No. 1* (1969): "That which the listener meets in the first seconds of the performance of the composition will continue through to the end. The beginning of the composition is also the exposition of the total sonoric diapason of the composition, and in the process of development of the sonoric material nothing alien or new to it will appear. There will be no surprises. This music does not intrude into the world of the listener; it does not attack. He listens only to those fragments and musical parts which please him. . . . Such a 'contrastless' form has, in reality, neither beginning nor end. The composition may be stopped abruptly at any moment, and this would not alter any of its essential features. It may also last for as long as seems desirable."

"This is music which may be 'taken in' in different ways. An ideal situation would be for the music to be played continuously, while the listener arrived at a time convenient to himself, and left whenever he found it necessary. This could be possible in a new type of auditorium whose architecture was especially designed for this purpose."[21]

The composer's idea, however, was not new. Something similar, although under different conditions, had been tried by Eric Satie in his "Musique d'ameublement" in the 1920's in France. The experiment, as everyone knows, was not successful. In fact, it failed from the start. Stockhausen, too, at the beginning of the 1970's expressed ideas that were close to Krauze's. The character of Krauze's experiment is also contained both in the formal conception and the sonoric material of his compositions. The projected length of *Piece for Orchestra No. 2* (1970), allowing for differences in performance versions, ranges from 10 to 40 minutes (!)

A schism appears between the limited emotional range of the musical material and the massive form of "contrastless" composition in those works of Krauze which are based on folklore. His aim in working this material is to bring timbre to a common denominator. He consciously neglects the character and the expressive, stylistic qualities of folk music. A specific example is his *Folk Music* (1972).

In the pursuit of his goal, the composer used many melodies in this piece gathered from different areas of Europe by the Polish folklorist, Dr. Jan Stęszewski: songs and dance melodies of Bashkir, Vladimir, and Pskov districts in the USSR, Latvia, Czechoslovakia, Hungary, Yugoslavia, the Austrian Alps, and other historic Polish and East European regions—21 melodies in all are represented here. The orchestra is, correspondingly, divided into 21 groups (in reality some are solo instruments, while others form small ensembles resembling folk groups). Each of these "groups" plays its own melody whose complex carries its own particular features. For instance, at the opening the oboe plays, in a free moderate tempo, a melody in A-minor comprised of different lyric songs; these vary in length, time signature and tonality. The 1st violin plays a single voice dance melody in D-major in 3/4. The next group, an ensemble of two violins and a cello plays a Czech dance in 2/4, with the tonic alternating from D to A, etc. National folk tradition is consciously rejected here, for these melodies are put into an environment that is completely alien to them. They are connected mechanically for purely sonoristic purposes. Other melodies could have replaced them with equal success, and, in spite of the fact that from time to time, out of the hooting mass of sound, a newly introduced melody makes its ways to the fore, strengthened by dynamic devices (a collage method is at work here), it is soon drowned, beaten down by a flood of sound waves. Scattered on the stage, various ensembles completely unrelated to each other, play Austrian or Polish songs, and if at the start there were 21 melodies, that number soon multiplies, for each group, having played its own song two or three times, introduces a new one. A dense heterophonic mass of sound arises, in which the human ear can distinguish nothing. According to the composer's concept, the composition as a whole must be "contrastless" and as homogeneous as possible in form. In the performance of the piece, the conductor and players are allowed great freedom. Choice of tempi is left to the latter's discretion, while the order of the quotations, the number of repeats, and which group of instruments is to have a dominant role in the sonoric process is determined by the conductor.

In *Folk Music*, aleatorism, sonorism, collage, and other techniques are eccentrically interwoven. The sonoristic result also varies, depending on the combination of instruments at any given moment. The composer used unusual timbres for an orchestra, introducing such instruments as a hand lyre, a Góralski duda,[††] an old shawm, squeaky pipes and harmoniums. But how is all this reflected in the character of the color, the sonoric essence of the composition? The timbres are drowned in a general, homogeneous melange of sound.

A peculiar situation arises—"a sonorism in reverse." The phonic sounding, which the composer aims to achieve must be deliberately flattened out, and lose its character.

[††]Góralski duda is a type of bagpipe.

II. Music of the Second Postwar Decade (1956–1965)

Example 20

Let us cite as an example part of the score. Vertically, there are in all 40 parts written. A recording with Kazimierz Kord as conductor gives but a rough impression of the composition. Ex. 20.

An eclectic mix of national styles, a reworking of folkloric melodies into an alien type of material in a search for new coloristics, this was the method that Krauze was to "replay" at a later date in other compositions, such as *Aus aller Welt stammende* (1973) in which ten soloists play simultaneously several Polish melodies from the Sandomir region in different combinations. Here, because of the small ensemble, a fairly integrated performance becomes possible. Yet, even in this instance, the intentional lack of contrasts, and the heterophonic mixture of melodies results in a dull, monotonous color and a blurring of genres.

We must note, however, as we glance into the future, that in the 1970's, Krauze would, in many respects, move away from such extreme positions in his aesthetics. His piano *Concerto* (1976), which received contradictory evaluations from the press, indicated ways to surmount "total" static form, and contains a set of contrasting, expressive fragments. Echoes of romanticism may be heard—a live national tradition is continued, but of a new quality. A turn in direction in Krauze's work shows that he did not remain untouched by the wide trend toward synthesis that encompassed music in the 1970's.

"Pure" and absolute aleatorism (C. Kohoutek)[22] where chance dominates, may be contrasted to partial and controlled aleatory music, whose theory and technique Witold Lutoslawski worked out in the 1960's. He named his system, "composition of the limited action of chance," or "controlled aleatorism," or "technique of aleatory counterpoint." Thus, he underlined its essential difference from those systems in which chance is the arbiter. In Lutoslawski's system, the element of improvisation touches on only one component of musical expression: rhythm. All that concerns pitch, however, is determined strictly by the composer. Therefore, he is able to foretell what the overall character of each musical segment of the form will be. The introduction of the element of rhythmic improvisation serves to create a special effect of a vibrant, mobile sound fabric, an effect hard to attain if a common measure is present. "Aleatory counterpoint," or "aleatory texture," a specific coloristic means, creates an imagery of a particular type. It is irreplaceable for the realization of some of Lutoslawski's complex conceptions.[23]

The technique of controlled aleatorism was first used by Lutoslawski in an orchestral piece, *Les Jeux Venitiens (Venetian Games*, 1961). Later, came compositions of different genres, in which the potentials of aleatory methods were revealed in many different ways. *String Quartet* (1964), *Trois*

II. Music of the Second Postwar Decade (1956–1965)

Poèmes d'Henri Michaux for 20-voice chorus and orchestra (1963), *Paroles Tissées* for tenor and chamber orchestra (1965), *Second Symphony* (1967), and *Livre pour orchestre* (1968) marked the transition to a period of increasing maturity in the composer's music. Each of the above-named compositions is a significant work, and absolutely unique. Their great value lies in the complete correspondence between concept and realization. In spite of the complexity of the technical system, construction always remains subordinate to expressive and artistic values. This becomes especially clear in Lutoslawski's vocal and instrumental compositions.

A new sonoristic quality appears as the result of rhythmic relationships of voice in the texture. The effect of inner mobility is incomparable. Resemblances may be found in the irregularly accented rhythmics described by V. Cholopova.[24] In general, Lutoslawski's compositions are made up of sectional segments of differing lengths which substitute for the measures and

W. Lutoslawski during a rehearsal at the 10th Festival Polish Contemporary Music in Wroclaw, 1974.

periods of traditional music. Each of these sections is performed by a group of instruments. The beginning of each section is marked by a signal to be given by the conductor. However, here his function ends; the instrumentalists play their parts independently of each other, each in his own individual rhythm, until the conductor gives the next signal. The orchestra becomes an ensemble of soloists playing with considerable rhythmic freedom. But, in Lutoslawski's scores one never meets a chaotic lack of accord of voices on the veritcal. The total resultant sound has been foreseen in all its details by the composer, who notates precisely all pitch relationships in all parts. Thus, metro-rhythmical freedom cannot influence the total sonoric result in any segment of the score.

All innovations connected with new methods of playing serve expressive ends. "The aim of my experiments is to achieve a definite sonoric, rhythmic, and expressive result which cannot be attained by any other means," writes Lutoslawski on the occasion of the premiere of his *String Quartet*.[25]

A quartet, however, has only four voices which create the sonority, and the problems encountered in a large composition for a big orchestra, or orchestra and chorus, are far more complex. Again, Lutoslawski builds the vertical in such a way as to allow him to foresee the structure of any timbre complex in all instances.

In the ranks of innovative compositions employing limited aleatorism, *Trois poèmes d'Henri Michaux* for chorus and orchestra occupies a special place. The composer turned to symbolist poetry and combined into a whole, verses from Michaux's different poetic cycles. Lutoslawski's musical interpretation endows the verses with a universal, philosophic meaning. At the heart of the conflict lies an almost romantic concept of collision: skepsis and doubt (First movement: *Pensées—Thoughts*); combat and death, grotesquely refracted (Second movement: *Le grand combat—The Great Battle*); catharsis, moral purification, the search for an ethical ideal (Third movement: *Repos dans le malheur—Peace in Sorrow*). In the realization of the total concept, we see the sensibility of a 20th century artist who speaks about the condition of the world in the language of our time.

The theme of *Trois poèmes d'Henri Michaux* echoes, to some extent, one of the leading themes of post-war cantatas and oratorios, that of disturbing reflections on the fate of a generation which experienced the horrors of war. Yet, there are no direct analogies to war themes here. The new interpretation of the theme is connected to the tendency, common in contemporary art, of psychological analysis, and to a search for deeper meaning, the intensification of interest in the moral-ethical side of problems.

The originality of Lutoslawski's substantive ideas in this composition lies in the two-fold plan of its semantic lines. For the theme unfolds in two aspects; the first, appearing in the exterior movements, is philosophic: reflections on life and death and existential meaning; the second, the subject of the poem in the middle movement is dramatic: cruel combat and defeat. Such a distribution of emphasis determines the dramatic solutions in the cycle. The philosophic line is incarnated in imagery of an intensely meditational character (the first and third poems); while the tense, aggressive action in the second poem is presented through illustrational, theatrical, mimetic techniques. The composer underlines the idea that "the second movement must fulfill the same role that conflict (its development and resolution) plays in a classical tragedy."[26] Associations with timeless, old dramatic forms arise and reverberate in the themes of those works which belong to Lutoslawski's classical period.

It is interesting that, despite the newness of the expressive means, it is still possible to find analogies with traditional forms in the structure of the movements. The first poem is an unusual meditative variant of a sonata form. Evidence of its relationship to a sonata scheme can be seen in the two contrasting sonoric themes: one vacillating and elusive, as if lightly sketched in by a dotted line; the other, full of vivid, lyric expression. The action evolves slowly, in an unhurried unfolding of musical images. This is a natural development of the inner act of intense contemplation of symbolic imagery. For this section, an expository type of statement, the alteration of contrasting elements, is characteristic. In the middle, developmental section, the dynamic is wave-like. A symmetry becomes apparent as, in each segment, sound accumulates and dies out. One becomes aware that segments are ending in complexes that fulfill the function of tonality. All this gives grounds for drawing an analogy between the innovative, mobile forms of the *Trois Poèmes* and the contemporary, but more traditional contrasting compound form.

A ternary form also lies at the base of the second poem, whose dynamic outline is expressed by a great surge of movement towards the climax and then a sudden drop into a quiet recapitulation. Lutoslawski goes beyond the framework of purely musical laws of form in *Le grand combat*. This composition is literary and theatrical with elements of musical form-building. Its theatrical quality becomes apparent through the depictive use of the orchestra's noise-producing and sound effect apparatus; while its literary side has for its instrument the speaking chorus—muttering, reciting fast tongue-twisters, "glissandoing" and exclaiming. These techniques endowed with corresponding color nuances, naturally evoke vivid generic associations. Thus, neologisms introduced into the text acquire semantic meaning.

The tranquil, lyric finale, focused around a single image, is a variant of the free one-movement form. It can be seen that, although Lutoslawski treats the poem genre in a highly individual fashion, he never allows chance to penetrate into the form of the composition. The main areas for new means are in thematic structure and texture. The unusual imagery of H. Michaux's poetry is embodied in mobile structures, in an aleatoric counterpoint. And here, the imagery is indeed apposite.

Poèmes is an example of Lutoslawski's astonishing ability to balance the new with the traditional. As the Leningrad musicologist, E. Ruch'yevskaya noted: mobility, the principle of improvisational structures, "appears only at the level of segments. However, the arrangement of the mobile segments is subject to a strict system, and therefore, form, as a whole, remains stable, organized by the composer."[27]

Ruch'yevskaya also draws analogies between the design of the separate motifs and traditional "fanfare" melody. However, such analogies are highly strained: the impulse signals are spaced irregularly, the timing for their entrances arbitrary, as they push their way through a thick, amorphous mass.

All the means promote the creation of a special inner mobility, a vibrant texture. To be specific, the composer intentionally counterposes the timbres of the orchestra and those of the chorus, treating them as two interacting but relatively independent component entities, each with its own conductor, and its own function in the creation of the total sonority. The idea of antiphony stemming from tradition of the Passions is thus uniquely incorporated. However, Lutoslawski creates completely new models of heterophonic texture, whose interior mobility is essentially different from the texture of the old polyphony.

Everything that Lutoslawski presents here is unusual: the thematic material itself, its sonoric-textural complexes, its formation, the development, and the composition as a whole. An analysis follows of the new models of musical texture, or (to use Lutoslawski's own term) "the sound image."

At the beginning of the first poem, after the orchestra has made its entrance, comes a choral exposition. The chorus enters as a dense mass, subject to inner oscillations; for the rhythmics of the vocal parts are as free as those of the orchestra. This texture with its special inner mobility, Lutoslawski defined as "a 'sound magma' which is in constant irregular motion."[28] The whole mass, encompassing twelve tones is divided into four groups, which, in their turn, are subdivided into five parts. The material is economically constructed on a segmented scale comprised of two to six tones. Within each group, the time coordinates are deliberately displaced. The same tones are repeated at irregularly spaced durations of time.

Thus, Lutoslawski creates a distinctive type of heterophonic texture, formed by simultaneously combining different unconnected lines; its special quality: a unique correlation between verticals and horizontals, the sequential unfolding of a given complex. In other words, a gradual gathering—the formation of a vertical group of tones within a time sequence. The reverse also takes place: a chord is prolonged on the horizontal. After an initial simultaneous attack, each component of the chord is taken melodically in a different figuration in each line, in the time freely chosen by any one of the performers. Ex. 21.

The effect arises of an undulant, oscillating, quivering mass. Desiring to create a new type of imagery, Lutoslawski manages to avoid the danger inherent in unification, that is, the erasure of the sonoric character, a possible consequence of the heterophonic technique. But here, no blurring of color

Example 21

occurs, nor does the sonority lack individuality. Each interval, as well as the whole irregularly shifting mass, becomes the carrier of meaningful expressivity.

Two kinds of intonational phrases are typical of Lutoslawski's melody: a broad intervallic pattern, whose unique zigzag design rivets attention on itself; and its opposite: narrow, close spacing, a creeping chromatic line, almost a glissando, with its idiomatic character deliberately erased. In this way, two complementary methods are combined: one that levels and conceals the interval in the general sound "magma" and the other that highlights vivid inflections and attracts attention to them by virtue of their contrast to the mixture of similar, barely distinguishable motifs. Ex. 22.

A different type of sonoric material was used by the composer in the second poem, *Le grand combat*. It is written for a speaking chorus, whose part in the choral score is not notated. Only the direction of the intonation is indicated; the heightening or lowering of the vocal register. "*Le grand combat*," says Lutoslawski, "is not a mass declamation. It is a composition which operates via groups of sounds; although these sounds originate in words spoken in various ways. . . . In many places, they appear as a pure sound element, perceived by the listener only as different kinds of noise, hubbub, cries—sound complexes not lacking expressivity, but having no concrete meaning. Out of these sound complexes, the form of this movement is built on a purely musical base."[29]

At the same time, certain vocal techniques, such as glissandi, have been retained, and also a free, irregular rhythmic network. Principles of limited aleatorism introduced into the area of choral declamation are subject to problems inherent in sound imitation and expressivity. Techniques, worked

Example 22

out in compositions of the preceding period, here acquire a new aspect. In particular, the polyphony of strata is now presented in a new way, possessing an independent, rhythmic-motivic design. The climax of *Le grant combat* is a rare instance of writing for 20 voices, each of which is different from all the others. Furthermore, each voice is assigned a separate verse, everyone of which has its own rhythmic and intonational pattern. The effect is of a mass dispute, such as may arise in an excited crowd, when all express their reaction to some event at the same time. The use of heterophonic structure in a musical-poetic composition is an innovative technique. Lutoslawski's understanding of music as an art which can absorb certain features of other arts is carried through with extraordinary strength in this composition.

In spite of all the innovative techniques, the generic basis of themes, the contours of familiar forms, and the logic of dramatic development have been preserved. Lutoslawski never severed his connection with principles governing extended forms. His high artistic achievements give proof that his chosen path is productive and opens up on new perspectives: hence, the great musical authority commanded by Lutoslawski. In the coming years, controlled aleatory technique was to spread to many other countries.

Musical art in the second post-war decade in Poland was truly rich. The creation of many significant compositions in which new technical systems were assimilated and developed put Polish music on an equal plane with the best compositional work produced in the western world at that time. The ground was now prepared. The time was ripe for the Polish school of music to come to full flower.

Notes

Chapter II

1 The term "serial dodecaphony" was coined by Józef Maria Chomiński in his book: *Muzyka Polski Ludowej* (Warszawa: PWN, 1968), chap. VI ("Dodecafonia seryjna w Polsce"), pp. 111–126.
2 Józef Maria Chomiński, "Muzyka polska po 1956 roku," *Polska współczesna kultura muzyczna 1944–1964* (Kraków: PWM, 1968), p. 87.
3 Tadeusz A. Zieliński, *Tadeusz Baird* (Kraków: PWM, 1966), p. 44.
4 The term "twelve-tone diatonic 'scale'" was coined by the Soviet musicologist Michail Skorik in the article, "The specifics of Prokofiev's modes." in a volume: *Problems of Modes*, compiled by Kiroline Yujak (Moscow: Muzyka, 1972). The author writes about the emancipation of all twelve tones in Prokofiev's complex diatonic natural modal system.
5 Tadeusz A. Zieliński, "'Sonety' Bolesława Szabelskiego," *Spotkania z muzyką współczesną* (Kraków: PWM, 1975), p. 144.
6 See: Krzysztof Droba, "Droga do sensu tragicznego," *Ruch Muzyczny*, No. 15, 1978, p. 3.
7 See: Józef Maria Chomiński, *Muzyka Polski Ludowej*, opus cit., p. 93. Chomiński cites this work as an example of a successful solution of harmonic problems in serialism.
8 Józef Rychlik, "Punktualizm we wczesnej twórczości Krzysztofa Pendereckiego," *Muzyka*, No. 2, 1976, p. 10.
9 Ibid., pp. 12–20, a detailed analysis of semantic and musical texture and their interaction.
10 Ludwik Erhardt, *Spotkania z Krzysztofem Pendereckim* (Kraków: PWM, 1975), p. 25. The idea of the "magic square" based on a 12-syllable five-line Latin verse probably was borrowed by Penderecki from Webern. Webern used to bring us this example in his lectures on music. See:

Anton Webern, *Der Weg zur Neuen Musik*, (Wien: Herausgegeben von Willi Reich, 1960). Cited: Anton Webern, *Lektcii o muzyke. Pis'ma* (Moscow: Muzyka, 1975), p. 83. Penderecki reworked the finale of *Dimensions of Time and Silence* for the 2nd edition, and withdrew the "magic square" in order to give greater clarity to the form.
In the program notes to the premiere of *Dimension of Time and Silence*, given at the Warsaw Autumn Festival 1960, Penderecki points out that he tried to apply to music certain principles from the art of Paul Klee and Yves Klein.

11 Tadeusz Zieliński's definition. *Spotkania z muzyką wspólczesną*, opus cit., p. 18.
12 Ctirad Kohoutek introduces the term "music of timbres," and ties it to aleatoric technique. See: Ctirad Kohoutek, *Technika kompozicii v muzyke XX veka* (Moscow: Muzyka, 1976), p. 236. In original: Ctirad Kohoutek, *Novodobé skladebné teorie západoevropské hudby* (Praha: Státni hudebni vydavatelstvi, 1962). 2nd edition: Ctirad Kohoutek, *Novodobé skladebné směry v hudbě* (Praha: SHV, 1965).
13 Józef Maria Chomiński, "Z zagadnień teckniki kompozytorskiej XX wieku," *Muzyka*, No. 3, 1956, pp. 23–48. See also: same author, "Istota sonorystyki muzycznej," in *Muzyka Polski Ludowej*, opus cit., p. 127. After Chomiński, younger scholars elaborated on the theory of sonorism using examples from Polish classics. See: Wladyslaw Malinowski, "Problem sonorystyki w 'Mitach' K. Szymanowskiego," *Muzyka*, No. 4, 1957. Anton Prosnak, "Zagadnienia sonorystyki na przykladzie etiud Chopina,"*Muzyka*, No. 1/2, 1958.
14 The term "polish colorism" relates specifically to the art of painting, and was later adopted by musicologists. See above-mentioned book by Ludmila Tananaeva (note 12 to Chapter 1), pp. 33–34.
15 Article in the collection: *Muzyka v Pol'she*, an Informational Bulletin of the First Polish Musical Council (Warsaw, 1969), pp. 19–27.
16 The concept of through-compositional technique is examined in the book by Sergei Slonimski, *Simfonii S. Prokofieva* (*The Symphonies of S. Prokofiev*, Leningrad: Muzgiz, 1964).
17 Penderecki uses in his notation a system of symbols, signs and graphic designs supplied with detailed explanations. This is necessitated by his system of sounds, which includes sounds of unchartable pitch, striking of the sounding board of instruments, and various noise-producing effects.
18 Ludwik Erhardt, *Spotkania z Krzysztofem Pendereckim*, opus cit., p. 50.
19 Tadeusz Zieliński, *Spotkania z muzyką wspólczesną*, opus cit., p. 155. Also see: Ludwik Erhardt, opus cit., pp. 49–50.

20 Krzysztof Droba, "Droga do sensu tragicznego," opus cit., p. 3.
21 See the Program notes to the Warsaw Autumn Festival 1970: XIV *Warszawska Jesień*, pp. 12-13.
22 Ctirad Kohoutek, opus cit. (Soviet edition), p. 241.
23 For further information see Lidia Rappoport's book *Witold Lutoslawski*, (Moscow: Muzyka, 1976), pp. 56-57, 87. See also: Witold Lutoslawski,"About the element of chance in music" in *Three Aspects of New Music* (Stockholm: Nordiska Musikförlaget, 1968). See also listing of other Lutoslawski's works in bibliography.
24 Valentina Cholopova, opus cit.
25 Witold Lutoslawski, "Uwagi o sposobie wykonywania mego Kwartetu smyczkowego," *Ruch myzyczny*, No. 17, 1965, p. 3.
26 Stefan Jarociński, *Witold Lutoslawski, Materialy do monografii* (Kraków: PWM, 1967), p. 51.
27 Ekaterina Ruch'yevskaia, "Tematism i forma v metodologii analiza muzyki 20 veka," in: *Sovremennyie voprosy muzykoznaniya* (Moscow: Muzyka, 1976), p. 167.
28 Tadeusz Kaczyński, *Rozmowy z Witoldem Lutoslawskim* (Kraków: PWM, 1972), p. 13.
29 Ibid., p. 12.

III
Music of the Third Postwar Decade (1966–1977)

In the history of post-war Polish music, the third decade "appears as a period of relative stabilization,—a stabilization that is in no way related to a stop in development, for in this period a renascence of large instrumental and vocal-instrumental forms occurs. Stabilization comes about as the result of processes which join and integrate contemporary and traditional trends."[1]

As in the second post-war decade so in the third, a progressive movement encompassing all genres continues to evolve in Polish music. A continuous line of development in post-war music is delineated. While music in the second decade moved forward under the banner of an active search for new musical language, in the next period, various systems are combined to create a new quality. These systems generate large forms; in many ways, they intersect with traditions. Not only the forms and genres which comprise the primary source of neo-classicism are now employed (Baroque, Bach and pre-Bach, Passion, Magnificat, Mystery), but also the large symphony of the Viennese classical period, the romantic symphonic poem, the vocal cycle and other forms.

New operas and ballets are written in the third decade. As in the preceding period, composers are drawn to both historical and contemporary themes.

Let us begin with opera. In *The Devils of Loudun*, Krzysztof Penderecki took for his subject an actual trial of a parish priest, Urban Grandier. The action takes place in Loudun, France, in the first half of the 17th century.

Grandier was accused of being in league with the devil, and of enticing some nuns of the Ursuline order and their abbess, Mother Joan, into "His" power. The underlying cause of Grandier's fall from grace was his secret alliance with civic rulers against the powerful Cardinal Richelieu, who was determined to deprive Loudun of its independence. The trial ended with Grandier condemned to be burnt at the stake. This affair drew the attention of numerous prominent people of the era. Subsequently, artists of many periods immortalized this extraordinary man. The British playwright, George Whiting, adapted Aldous Huxley's novel, *The Devils of Loudun*, for the stage. Basing the opera on the play, Penderecki, himself, wrote the libretto; its primary theme: the fight against evil and coercion, a theme of martyrdom to which Penderecki repeatedly returns.

"Loudun is separated from Calvary, Guernica, Auschwitz, and Vietnam by but one step; only the scenario and production are different." These words of A.D. Hogarth correctly reflect the ideological problems posed by the opera.[2]

Let us note that the subject of *The Devils of Loudun*, containing possibilities for broad interpretations and examinations of different aspects of religious themes, attracted Polish artists again and again. Jaroslaw Iwaszkiewicz used it in his novel, *Mother Joan of the Angels*. Jerzy Kawalerowicz made a film of the same title. Romuald Twardowski used the same material in a radio play, *The Fall of Father Suryn*. And, in 1963, the Warsaw theater, "Ateneum," produced Whiting's play *The Devils* under Andrzej Wajda's direction.

Penderecki's opera is a large three-act work containing big choral mass scenes. Many of them, in accord with the subject of the composition, are sharply expressionistic, especially scenes depicting the nuns' hysteria and madness. The opera's style reflects Penderecki's compositional achievements in the second half of the 1960's and the 1970's, and echoes such large oratorial works as *St. Luke's Passion*, *Morning Prayer* (*Utrenya*), and others.

A different kind of highly expressive drama was created by Tadeusz Baird. His one-act chamber opera, *Tomorrow,* made use of narrative material taken from Joseph Conrad's short story. In preparation for this work, Baird conducted a long search for a subject which would answer his ideas on contemporary opera. Conrad's *Tomorrow* contained both a sharp conflict and psychological drama. Without such features, Baird could not envision the musical dramatic line of opera. Here the action is greatly compressed in time, and "develops on two levels: that of the plot and that of psychology. The former is expressed on the stage by the action and the dialogues, the latter, developing mostly in the characters' subconscious, is conveyed by the music."[3]

The action centers around the tragedy of the three main protagonists. Ozias, the old father, waits for the return of his son, Harry, who ran away to sea many years ago. Crazed by the long wait, Ozias builds an imaginary world of the perfect "tomorrow," and involves in it Jessica, the young girl who cares for him. The return of Harry, a commonplace, coarse character, shatters illusions. The father fails to recognize the son, and forbids him to enter the house. Out of the kindness of her heart, Jessica attempts to help the young man. Misinterpreting what is happening, Harry tries "to take advantage" of the girl. In answer to her cries, Ozias comes running and kills his son. The dramatic situation in Jerzy S. Sito's libretto is sharper than in Conrad's story; emphasis has been shifted—the center of attention moved from the figure of the hopelessly waiting father to the sufferings of the deceived and violated Jessica. The rape scene, accompanied by hysterical cries, is both the climax and the finale of the drama.

Both the extent to which expression is condensed and the character of its emotional tone place *Tomorrow* (a typical expressionist drama), in the same rank of compositions as A. Schoenberg's *Erwartung* and A. Berg's *Wozzeck*. However, here there are no neurotic distortions, none of the overheated, negative emotions typical of expressionist compositions. Baird's music is laconic and restrained to the utmost degree; focused around the central conflict. The composer's purpose was not so much to draw character portraits as to convey a general emotional atmosphere, the protagonists' psychological states.

The composer employs as a major device, the technique of dramaturgic "separation." Of the four roles in the opera, three are for singers; the fourth, a speaking part. This contrast polarizes characteristics: Harry's alien quality, the negative essence of his personality is underlined. An actor takes the role of Harry, the speaking part. Theatrical techniques of this type are not unknown and appear in both operas and oratorios (Schoenberg's *Moses and Aron*, Honegger's *Jeanne d'Arc au bûcher*, etc.).

Emotional states and characterizations are conveyed chiefly through the timbre-coloristic aspect of music. Since the language of the opera's protagonists is based on recitatives and declamations, orchestral means become a major factor in the delineation of characters. The primary purpose, here, is to reveal behaviour; to show the inner, subconscious motivations for actions. This is the reason why the system of the leit-motifs is so varied and branches out in so many directions. A group of specific leit-timbres accompanies each character. Thus, Jessica enters to the sounds of strings, harps, flutes, and alto saxophone; Ozias is accompanied by oboes, bassoons, horns; Jozue, Jessica's father, by clarinets and contrabasses; and Harry by brasses, trumpets and trombones. These timbre complexes vary, creating definite "atmospheres of mood."

Moreover, each particular emotion is connected to a specific leit-motif. Motifs for waiting, joy, anger, helplessness, horror and love, all have their own particular color. It is these leit-motifs that create the authentic unfolding of the musical action, the inner movement of the psychological drama. And as the climax is reached, the inner and outer action intertwines. Extreme, specific "realistic" devices intensify expressivity: cries and laughter (used discriminately and in moderation) are combined with colorful techniques: ascending figurations, vivid timbres, dynamic outbursts. In *Tomorrow*, Baird worked out special types of textural-sonoristic themes. Commanding strong emotional power, they serve the function of elucidating the content of this laconic psychological drama.

In the majority of operatic, as well as balletic compositions of the late 1960's and the 1970's, a tendency to mix features of different genres can be observed. Examples of "pure" opera or ballet are few. They can be found in the compositions of W. Rudziński: *The Dismissal of the Greek Envoys* (1962); *Sulamith* (1964); *Peasants* (1974).

Rudziński's one-act opera, *The Dismissal of the Greek Envoys*, is based on a tragedy of the same name by the well-known dramatist of the Polish Renaissance, Jan Kochanowski. Epic in tone, it has a clearly defined dramatic line that strengthens and thickens as it moves towards the conclusion. The main characters are: Helen, Antenor, Alexander, Priam, Cassandra, Narrator. The characterizations lack individuality; but to compensate for this, occasional short but vivid episodes are brought out; they recall marches of invasion, threnodies and war signals such as reveilles.

The opera's neo-Classic style is attained via original sonoric means. Futhermore, the palette of means that the composer uses is extremely limited. The soloists' language is recitatival; a system of leit-motifs is made up of laconic, harsh sounding serial segments; the instrumental ensemble (piano, clavecin, "knocking" percussion and occasional brass clusters), is stylized so that it sounds like various ancient cymbals. Certain devices (recitatival language, cymbal sounds, frequent ostinato rhythms) are reminiscent of the neo-Classic style of Stravinsky and Orff; but unlike them, Rudziński focuses attention on strictly selected sonoric means.

All the means (rhythm, harmony, instrumentation, timbres-hues) are employed in such a way as to sharpen their sonoric qualities which were enlisted to evoke the ambiance of an epoch, and also to stylize the dramatization of the described events. Here, one finds a masterly and apposite use of such special colors as moaning glissandi, a speaking chorus, ostinato rhythms in the "cymbals" and percussion, and artfully realized counterpoints, all of which create aleatoric effects.

In the book of Polish operatic art, this rather small neo-classic-sonoric opera presents an original page.

A group of operas and ballets were composed by Romuald Twardowski. In the 1960's, looking for source material, Twardowski, typically, turned to old music ranging from the Renaissance to ancient Russian Orthodox Liturgies. Twardowski's purpose, at all times, was to stylize a given national prototype in the tradition of its own particular epoch (*Florentine Triptych*, 1967, and *The Small Orthodox Liturgy*, 1968). Twardowski's characteristic interest in the coloristic side of composition is reflected in this style which grows out of his ethnographic studies: *Jaworowy Pieśni (Jaworow Song), Lullabies,* and *Bucolics* for mixed chorus (1960–1961); *Antifone* for three orchestral groups (1962); *Canti antiqui* for soprano, clavecin, piano and percussion (1962). The music of an early ballet, *The King is Naked*, contains a group of stylized dances of the Baroque period introduced to give the ballet a satirical, grotesque flavor. *Cyrano de Bergerac* (1963), a four-act opera, belongs to a different style. The composer takes advantage of experiments carried out by G. Puccini, S. Prokofiev, and M. Ravel in their operas, and consciously mixes different stylistic traditions. However, the special traits of the lyric genre dominate. This somewhat eclectic style is the cause of the unconvincing quality of the solutions in the Rostand drama.

In 1969, in Lodź, Twardowski's *The Tragedy of John and Herod*, based on an old Polish version of the Biblical text, was produced.

In 1974, Warsaw saw the production of the ballet *The Sculptures of Master Peter*, a musical paraphrase of Goethe's ballad, *The Sorcerer's Apprentice*. Twardowski (as author of the libretto) changed the ballad's content and built his plot on the "immobilized figures" coming to life, throwing off their enslavement to the apprentice and at long last overcoming their taskmaster. It is obvious that the romantic tradition in the music stems from R. Strauss. At the same time, the influence of Stravinsky's and Bartók's rhythms can be felt. Fiery in temperament, Twardowski's music is eminently danceable.

A fusion of those means which are characteristic of late romanticism and modernism can also be observed in other operatic compositions by Twardowski. We cite: the radio drama *Upadek Ojca Suryna (The Fall of Father Suryn)* based on J. Iwaszkiewicz's story, *Mother Joan of the Angels* (1969); and the opera *Lord Jim,* based on Conrad's story.

The plot of *Lord Jim* revolves around its main character, Jim, around his external conflict with his environment and the inner one with himself. Out of these clashes grow the multiple dramatic lines and levels on which the action develops. The genre here is lyrico-dramatic; its theatrical characteristic: a mixture of different types of operatic and stylistic devices; transitions from singing to speaking and visa versa. The opera's plot provides a favorable ground for stylization of oriental motifs. (Jim departs for Patusan, and lives among Malayans.) Twardowski, however, avoided direct stylization of the native music and instead created a generalized exotic variant of "oriental music" (in the broad meaning of that term), distinguished by atypical, unevenly grouped rhythms and a special manner of inflection. The connecting link between the two contrasting stylistic spheres in the opera, is the musical portrait of Jim, his accompanying leit-motifs. Some specific devices in the opera are taken directly from the play version of the novel; as, for instance: the figure of a narrator in the Prologue, who represents Conrad himself. Such are some of the features of Twardowski's opera.

Augustyn Bloch envisions the musical stage in a different light. Lyric by nature, he leans toward gentle humor, jests and the expression of heart-felt warmth. In his musical thinking, he attaches great significance to the role of generic associations. The range of his creative endeavors is indeed broad; at one end of the spectrum are compositions in which the artist presents his interpretations of "timeless" themes: the ballet *Gilgamesh* and an operatic Mystery play, *Ajelet, Daughter of Jeft*; at the other end of the spectrum are the humorous fables: the musical fairy-tale *Very Sleeping Beauty*. Somewhere between these two works stands his first ballet, *Awaiting* (1963). Here his music is lyric and restrained, elegantly danceable, full of things left half-said, languid in mood. The primary motif (an original refrain that runs throughout the ballet) is a clearly stated jazz rhythm. Small wonder that the composer assigned it to the saxophone. An electric guitar, also, was introduced into the orchestra. Languorous jazz passages, a fanciful coloring of certain images, muted tones, a tender lyricism—all this, wrapped in a wry, sad mood bears Bloch's own particular signature.

A synthesis of different forms may be observed in all his compositions of the third decade: *Gilgamesh; Ajelet; Very Sleeping Beauty. Gilgamesh*, a one-act ballet with chorus, takes for its subject material from a Babylonian epic. The music is supple and expressive; its vocal part, a men's chorus (baritones), sternly ascetic. In sound color it comes closer to Gregorian chant than to eastern melody. (There are melismas, jubilus, melodies sung on single vowels, and free rhythms.) Eastern elements are reflected in some orchestral tutti episodes, in the orgiastic clanging of exotic percussion instruments, which evoke scenes of ritual processions. A mixture of heterogeneous stylistic means (elements of serial techniques, colorful "exotic" instrumentation, traditional harmony, etc.) makes up the individual personality of *Gilgamesh*.

The one-act Mystery-opera, *Ajelet, Daughter of Jeft (Ajelet, córka Jeftego*, libretto by Jaroslaw Iwaszkiewicz), reenacts the Biblical tale of a daughter of the Israelites, Ajelet, who, in the name of peace, was sacrificed to the Gods. The composer stresses the contemporary sound of this tale. It is contiguous to the theme in praise of patriotism and the heroic sacrifices made by nations in the second world war. As in *Gilgamesh*, what is timeless and immortal is vested in significant universal forms of stylizations: "The ancient in a modern guise." Archaic melodies are combined with contemporary, fractured melodic designs. A mood of ardent emotion suffuses the music. The beauty of fragile melodic lines, of sinuous timbres in heterophonic choruses and orchestral ensembles is underlined. Refined colors and a poetic narrative tone captivate the listener in this extraordinarily integrated score—integrated in spite of the many component elements in the Mystery-opera, in which traits of operatic, balletic and theatrical genres all merge.

"The charm of the natural," that, perhaps, is the best definition for the prevailing tone in all of the diverse genres of Bloch's music. His spontaneity is specially felicitous in a show for children, *Very Sleeping Beauty (Bardzo spiąca królewna)*. Here, too, genres are mixed, with opera, ballet and pantomine all combined. "A story for children from 8 to 80" (as the subtitle declares) is a composition in which jest and gentle humor, lyric feeling and the grotesque are expressed through a compositional technique that is both modern and highly accomplished. Witty instrumental invention, musical jokes, brilliance in the orchestral and vocal parts (polished in every detail)— are all purely "Blochian" features in this merry show.[4]

Other composers, too, were working in the area of musical theater, and here a general tendency may be observed: composers who had shown themselves to be quite radical when working in other genres, usually took into account the specific nature of the musical theater and its audience, and modified in their choice of means, subordinating the newest systems to traditional forms. Innovations are mostly seen in the area of dramatic composition, in a reinterpretation of the operatic and ballet genres. In the field of ballet theater, we find Juliusz Luciuk. His compositions include: the pantomine-ballet *Niobe* (1962); the pantomine *Marathon* (1963); the choreographic drama, *November Night's Dream* (1971); the ballets *Death of Eurydice* (1972), *Orpheus' Love* (1973), *Medea* (1975). The choice of themes here is characteristic, taken in most cases from ancient or modern literature.

An interesting treatment of the operatic genre was presented by Zbigniew Penherski in *Peryn's Twilight (Zmierzch Peryna*, 1975). Its libretto was based on a legend about the establishment of a Polish community. The material came from J. Kraszewski's narrative, *An Old Legend*. In this opera, also, musical dramaturgy enters into complex interaction with elements from other arts.

Zbigniew Bargielski presents different types of opera: the big opera, *Danton*, after Büchner's drama (1969); a children's opera, Lewis Carroll's *Alice in Wonderland* (1972); a tragi-comedy, after S. Witkiewicz, *On a Small Estate* (1972).

Maniola Kowalczyk (alto) and Bernadetta Matuszczak after a performance *Canticum per Voci ed Orchestra.* "W.A." 1981.

III. Music of the Third Postwar Decade (1966–1977)

Bernadette Matuszczak's works give evidence of a desire to enrich the dramatic scope of chamber opera. They include: *Chamber Drama* (T.S. Eliot's poetry), for baritone, reader and ensemble (1965); the chamber opera *Romeo and Juliet* (1967); *Invocazione* for children's chorus and ensemble (1968); and just one composition in an extended form, an opera-oratorio, *Human Voices* (1971). Matuszczak's compositions are dedicated to human problems. The composer employs the means of the sonoric palette, and elements of "concrete" music. Such is the score of her *Salmi per un gruppo di cinque* (1972), a vocal cycle on the texts of David's Psalms and Solomon's Song of Songs. The Psalms and the chants are sung in Latin and simultaneously read in a Polish translation. Instrumentation is limited to percussion and harp timbres. Colors, meticulously chosen from the pitched and unpitched percussion group, reinforce the concrete descriptive imagery, and create vivid contrasts. A theatricalized mystery-drama of its own particular kind arises. Moreover, lighting effects were designed to play a part here, creating a type of "light-color music."

A turn toward different systems of contemporary compositional techniques enhanced the sphere of expressive means in opera, and made it possible to enlarge its thematic material. Thus, Krzysztof Meyer wrote the opera *Cyberiada*, using Stanislaw Lem's fantastic narrative. Here, traditional forms are combined with unusual devices and performance apparatus. The heroes of this comic fantasy are—computers! Their "voices" are recorded on tape. Of the three orchestras participating in the opera, two are on tape. "Live" sound interwoven with recorded sound makes it possible to present numerous sonoric stereophonic effects. Sonoristic and aleatoric means are both developed here, and so-called "topophony" is also employed (i.e. spatial and stereophonic music). In addition, different genres of music for theater, ballet and opera, and techniques of stylization are juxtaposed. Along with "usual serious" music, parody, grotesque and "concrete" means are all broadly utilized.

Interesting stylistic fusions arise in the works of Boguslaw Schäffer. An apologist for the avant-garde, a theoretician and historian of music, Schäffer never eschewed a single new technical system. Abstract, graphic music, aleatory, collage—all found their way into his compositions of different genres. Especially numerous and multi-faceted were his experiments with electronic music. Working on synthesizers, recording on one channel over another, combining natural sounds with electronic, the composer's goal was to create a tremendous color scale of sound. This type of technique resulted, at times, in sounds which border on the non-musical; some opuses, especially, have little in common with any established understanding of musical composition.

What is particularly interesting is the direction Schäffer took in his experiments in the area of musical drama. His *Monodram* for reader and magnetic tape (1968) is an unusual psychological poem about a women's life—a general philosophical reflection on her destiny. The composer's idea was to create "a theater of the imagination," which addresses itself to an individual rather than an audience. In the composer's mind this individual is like a radio listener. It is important to cut him off from external impression and direct him to come to grips with the powerful symbolic imagery contained within a special technical system. One actress and orchestra—this combination has been encountered in the more traditional theater of music with narration. Schoenberg's *Erwartung (Awaiting)*, and Poulenc's *La voix humaine (The Human Voice)* come to mind. *Monodram* differs from them, mostly, in its use of technical means: electronic musical material, collage-montage, the placement of sterephonic speakers.

In form, *Monodram* comes close to radio-drama in which the reader's text is supplemented by musical illustration. The similarity, however, is superficial, for the composer takes for his guidelines the laws of musical development. The beginning of the composition is like an overture which leads into the action and creates the needed emotional atmosphere. Later, as the action unfolds, fragments of readings and music are combined or alternated. Contrasts play a big role in the development of the form. Toward the end, as the form is closing, there is a drop in dynamic; a lyric recapitulation of its own sort takes place. This music is rich in carrying concrete associations. Cries, moans, laughter, voices of high and low timbres, simultaneously sounded, rustlings, startling booms resounding in the background—all these sounds, recorded in a radio broadcasting studio, are sounds "overheard," everpresent in ordinary day-to-day life. And although the composer underlines that *Monodram* is neither a concert nor a musical radio-drama, but a "theater of the imagination," built on a foundation of musical development, in actuality the vivid descriptive quality of the images broadens the framework of his intended genre. Much is elucidated by the text. The verse of the modern Greek poets, J. Rizos and J. Seferis, about a woman's destiny acquire a general human significance, and the timeless universal meaning of what is said is emphasized. Associations are evoked, connections made between present, past and future. Symbolism of ancient rites and thoughts of those who are gone are evoked. Stereophonically doubled voices create the effect of echoes reverberating in mountains. And, in this context, it seems neither surprising nor strange that there should burst forth, in collages, isolated fragments of touching lyrical music, quasi-romantic cantilena, stylized romances or nocturnes, the sounds of a sad chorale, solos by various string and wind instruments to pizzicato accompaniements, the sounds of bells, organs and resonant booms.

Edward Pallasz, Bogusław Schäffer. "W.A." 1981.

In another vocal-electronic composition, Schäffer again attained a high level of artistry: *Missa elettronica (The Electronic Mass)* for magnetic tape and a cappella boys' choir was written in 1975. Here, once more, the stylistic sources of the form are varied, though more specific in character. Musical material is drawn from different types of medieval masses. However, the range of borrowed styles, in accordance with the composer's conception, covers a tremendous time span: from the 12th to the 20th centuries so that Romanesque, Gothic, Renaissance, Classic and Modern styles are all included. Choral sections alternate with electronic parts, which are treated as broadly extended instrumental interludes. In spite of some eclecticism, the music is impressive in its power of expression and in its beauty. All the newest technical devices (concrete and electronic music, the sound of the "live" chorus and the one on tape) are organically combined with traditional forms.

Let us conclude our brief survey with a list of premieres which were timed to coincide with the 30th anniversary of the Polish Republic: in the city of Wrocław, two operas were mounted, R. Bukowski's *The Great Lady's Ring* based on Norwid's drama, and Natansons' *Tamango* after Mérimee's novel; in Bytom, J. Świder's opera *Wit Stwosz* dedicated to the great Polish sculptor was presented; also a children's opera by Z. Penherski, *The First*

Day of History; in Lodź, R. Twardowski's *Lord Jim* was mounted, and in Warsaw, W. Rudziński's *Peasants*.

The tendency to synthesize means is also observable in the areas of both cantata-choral works and purely instrumental music. We cite the following cantatas as examples: Górecki's *Ad Matrem*, Z. Rudziński's *Requiem*, E. Boguslawski's *Apocalypse*, T. Sikorski's *Voix humaine*, K. Penderecki's *Magnificat* and *Cosmogony*, T. Baird's *Goethe-Briefe*, K. Serocki's *Niobe*, W. Szalonek's *Beloved Land*, original choral and solo cycles *Solenne* by W. Kilar, *Śpiewy Thakuryjskie (Chants of Thakur)* by M. Stachowski, and *Śpiewy Polskie (Polish Chants)* by K. Meyer. Among these works, one stands out: W. Lutoslawski's magnificent *Les espaces du sommeil (The Spaces of Dream)*.

In vocal-instrumental and symphonic music, there is the start of a dominant trend to re-examine the significance of technical means. Problems of the highest substantive order gain priority. There is a renascence of large forms, and as a consequence, a re-evaluation and reordering of technical means.

Many composers, having shown themselves in the preceding decade to be daringly radical, ready to undermine existing foundations, finally arrive at a wise moderation, limiting the diapason of means, and turning of constructive conceptions into new channels. The trend toward such re-evaluations may be seen in the music of W. Kilar, Z. Bujarski, W. Kotoński, M. Stachowski, Z. Krauze, K. Meyer and many others.

In the following section, we will present several essays dedicated to outstanding contemporary Polish composers.

Grażyna Bacewicz

Chronologically, Bacewicz's compositions belong almost in entirety to the second decade, yet in essence, their evolution speaks of a phenomenon that is characteristic of the third decade, of a synthesis that combines innovations with musical traditions of the 20th century. The beginning of the final period in Bacewicz's music dates back to 1961, when the single-movement symphonic composition, *Pensieri notturni* was written. In it, new tendencies in the composer's music are clearly indicated. Up to that time, the dominant features had been neo-classic, but in certain late compositions, an impressionistic note was sounded, revealing a new approach to form, thematics and development. Specific features of a sonata-symphonic form (for the most part in the Bartók style), were combined with coloristic treatments of the basic elements of composition. This was the period marked by the appear-

Grażyna Bacewicz

ances of: *Concerto for Orchestra* (1962); *Musica Sinfonica in tre movimenti* (1965); *Contradizione* for chamber orchestra (1966); *In una parte* (1967); three concertos for solo string instruments with orchestra—i.e. the *Second Cello Concerto* (1963), the *Seventh Violin Concerto* (1965), and *Concerto for Viola and Orchestra* (1968). In some of the later compositions, an expressionistically sharpened dramatic imagery emerges unexpectedly. Dramatic motifs are often heard there. It may be that they stem from the experiences of the war years. In the extended slow movements in *Music for Strings, Trumpets and Percussions*, in the *Concerto for Orchestra* and especially in *Symphonic Music in Three Movements*, gloomy processions, specific motifs of moaning, ostinato rhythms in mournful marches, all recall the imagery of certain "war and peace" compositions, written for the most part under Bartók's influence. At the height of her powers, as if summing up her experiences, the composer tries to arrive at a philosophical understanding of the path she had travelled. Once more she reviews the treatment of genres and forms, and finds new ways to join traditions of the past with those of the present. Echoes from previous periods remain in the overall formal compositional plans of the cycles, in the affirmative tone of their concluding sections, in certain textural techniques, characteristic of classicism, in types of movements, etc.

However, with all this, Bacewicz presents an individual stylistic concept. For although in 20th century music, the Bartók tradition was the one closest to her, and although she utilized some compositional and structural ideas of the great Hungarian composer (specifically in the organization of modes), yet she transposed them to Polish soil.

The timbre-rhythmic element in Bacewicz's late compositions is most interesting. It fulfills an all-encompassing function, appearing as a thematic, textural, form-generating component of composition, and although generally the contours of the sonata cycle are retained, bearing a resemblance, although distant to traditional forms, the essential aspect of thematics acquires a much modified, original outline, and becomes a sonoric phenomenon. This new direction in Bacewicz's work was displayed in *Pensieri notturni* (*Night Thoughts*, 1961). The title gives grounds to assume hidden meanings. Images in this music evoke thoughts of fantastic and mysterious nighttime landscapes. A flood of kaleidoscopically changing, illusory visions arises. The logic of the form's unfolding is the logic of dreams. The traditional sequence in form building is absent. Instead of the customary melodies, there are structurally unformed constructs, differing in the method of their organization. At times this can be an insistent ostinato repetition of one tone in an eccentric rhythmic pattern, which juxtaposed to pointillistically dispersed material takes on the semblance of a tonic complex.

Especially great is the variety of textural figurational structures: colorful arpeggio fragments (figurations in the harps, celesta, vibraphone), melismatic, rotational and scale types of figurations. Sometimes, at the climaxes, they are gathered into cluster complexes. In spite of their seemingly heterogeneous nature, the musical-textural structures represent timbro-rhythmical variants of the total structural model. Moreover, they fulfill a thematic function. Alternation and juxtaposition of fragments in different timbres, the linking of short structures which form a continuous but uneven fluctuating sequence: such is the new character of the symphonic form.

Pensieri notturni stands out, in the body of Bacewicz's work, because of its experimental approach to form; but in the large cycles which followed, the composer arrived at an organic synthesis of her technical discoveries with laws governing large forms. The *Concerto for Orchestra* and *Musica sinfonica in tre movimenti* are Bacewicz's highest achievements in this vein. Both compositions are modern variants of the concerto genre, always her favorite from her earliest years as a composer. Yet when the *Concerto for String Orchestra* (1948) is compared to the *Concerto for Orchestra* (1962), striking changes in the evolution of style become obvious.

The outer structure of the cycle is traditional. The *Concerto*, like a symphony, has four movements: 1st—*Allegro*; 2nd—*Largo*; 3rd—*Vivo, Scherzo*; 4th—*Allegro non troppo*, Finale. Features which are typical of the concerto form, such as the dialogue of instruments, are retained. At the same time, one discovers here the composer's new approach to thematics. It appears in the sonoric-figurational complexes. On the other hand, the foundations of a conventional form remain stable, due to a functional approach to the structure of composition.

The sharply percussive cluster in the gloomy, low registers (in brasses, tam-tam, piano, tremolo of cymbals) is a variant of a traditional Intrada at the beginning of a classical concerto; followed immediately by the irrepressible pulse of a lively movement. This pulse, however, is inconstant and capricious. Its origins lie in the interplay of a whole network of irregularly accented short phrases in different rhythms which echo and re-echo across a span of time, and enter into complex relationships with each other. This whole network has the same function as a principal theme in an allegro movement. Such original use of rhythmic formulas in a thematic function was first introduced by the composer in *Music for Strings, Trumpets and Percussion*. We are reminded of the continuous impulsive movement themes in the neo-classic opuses of Bartók and Stravinsky. Ex. 23. The development of the theme is made up of continuously varying rhythmic and textural models. The main unit of the rhythmic pulse becomes the sixteenth notes which form the base of a motoric toccata torrent striving toward the culmination.

A different timbre-rhythmical complex takes on the role of the subordinate theme: a dialogue between harsh chords in the strings and the piano struck in its extreme registers. A grotesquely humorous accent is introduced into the expressive character of the music. By means of this dialogue, the concerto principle is again applied. The outlines of the scherzo image,

Example 23

clearly defined in bas-relief, are subsequently dissolved in a torrential layering of contrapunctal lines, in scale-like passages, and in a complex syncopated, polyrhythmic network. A continuous chain of textural transformations forms the development, and not until the recapitulation is the original pulse restored.

It is characteristic that in the recapitulation, the function of a subordinate theme is taken over by a completely new theme: an expressive cantilena in the violas. Forcing its way through a complicated, multifaceted, polyrhythmic system of contrapuntal lines (ranging in the pre-culmination section from 4-5, and climbing to 11 in No. 8), the melody in the violas, which later turns into a duet with cellos, makes up for the absence of a truly melodic, extended theme in the first movement. Entering into a clearly defined relationship with the scherzo-like secondary theme, it directs the development into a new channel of interaction between prolonged melodic lines and motoric figurational types of movement. Thus, by means of constant renewal, through the introduction of unexpected turns into the general, impulse-propelled torrent, through a complex system assembled from short contrasting fragments, this form is constructed: one more example of a contemporary contrasting compound through composition. In an essay on Bacewicz, T. Zieliński expresses an interesting but controversial opinion about composition in her late works: "The formal idea in *Pensieri notturni*, *Contradizione* and other compositions, is the idea of short, freely alternating, passing musical impressions and momentary sound situations, combining elements, which at first glance seem alien to each other in color, figure or structure, and fixing these fleeting moments in the development of the whole—all this is reminiscent of Stockhausen's idea of "Momentform" which demands that the listener's attention be concentrated on a given transient moment."[5] True, Zieliński does underline the fact that Bacewicz aims at achieving the effect of "Momentform" only on rare occasions (in the Second movement of *Contradizione; Pensieri notturni*). In actuality, Bacewicz's very conception of form is opposed ot Stockhausen's intent. The German composer strives to dismember form into short episodes, while Bacewicz proceeds from the opposite point, unifying small fragments into an indivisible artistic whole; a whole in which the displacement of any element or the action of chance is inadmissable. Hence, the affinity between Bacewicz's compositions and the more traditional contrasting-compound form.

Bacewicz displays virtuosic mastery in handling complicated patterns of different rhythms with irregular accents, not only in fast impetuous movements (first allegros and finales) but also in the slow ones. The *Largo* in *Concerto for Orchestra*, after the *Pensieri notturni*, is another example of Bacewicz's sonoric-timbre compositions. Her palette of colors is subtly impressionistic, its imagery tied to fantastic rustlings, fluidly changing spots of color, muted and summoning signals. However, the quietness of the first section is both deceptive and troubling. In the central episode, fanfares become truly threatening. Both the expressive culmination, and the muted, twilight "calm before the storm" in the recapitulation brings up images of war years, at times starkly real, at times veiled by the mists of memory.

The beginning of the *Largo* recalls Webern's pointillistic technique. Each entering tone in the twelve-tone row of the minor 9th's is of a different timbre: vibraphone, celesta, harps, tam-tam, piano in the low register. But, in the next instant, it becomes clear that here is a free sonoric-timbre composition, in which developmental logic of form is subordinate to coloristic problems.

The multiple types of coloristic-timbre thematic texture do not exclude the traditional. Such are the pastoral tunes played by solo flutes. However, the odd design of the melancholy melody, its modal color and textural formation in the developmental process, the distention of strata as they are layered in contrapuntal rhythmic patterns results in the metamorphosis of a simple shepherd's pipe tune into a timbre-textural complex with an irregular accented rhythm which breaks up the motoric figurational background. An original "modulation of genre" occurs; a transformation of one type of genre into another, with a concurrent change in the function of thematicism. The result is a burning intensity in the music, a mounting dramatic tension. Let us compare the beginning of the tune with its transformation as it develops. Ex. 24.

The modal instability here is somewhat reminiscent of Bartók. We must draw attention also to the new harmonic color with its frequently changing inner content. This can be either a heterophony of lines moving along different height levels and spaced at a considerable distance from each other, or

Example 24a

close variants in simultaneity, resulting in an acid, atonal character of sound (*Scherzo*, No. 2). At times, the sound strata are composed of voices entering one by one; a system of imitations, layering, stretti, "catch-up" (No. 3). But more often, there is an aggregate of free, rhythmically different voices which are not doubled (Nos. 1, 4, 5, etc.).

Due to the complicated system of interwoven lines in the polyphonic texture, a semblance of the irregular flow, characteristic of aleatoric texture is created. Bacewicz uses such effects of "aleatory without aleatory" at climactic points in the form. Here we do not speak of true aleatory, for rhythm and pitch are firmly fixed, but rather of colorful effects, resulting from the clash of extremely heterogeneous designs in so many voices. Their number, at the climax climbs to 20-24! (Scherzo, No. 6, 21) Many examples of similar quasi-aleatoric texture can be found in all of Bacewicz's late compositions: *Concerto for 2 Pianos and Orchestra, Seventh Violin Concerto, In una parte*, et al.

Another type of culmination worked out by Bacewicz was the "colorfully quiet." Its effect was based on dialogues in the area of timbro-rhythm (episode of soli bongos, harps, celesta and strings in the low registers in the *Scherzo* of the *Concerto for Orchestra*, Nos. 7, 16).

As we have already stated, with the development of new types of textural thematics, new ways are found to solve the problems of form. Its formations, its development is based on fluid transitions from one coloristic timbre-rhythmic thematic complex to another.

Instead of traditional concepts of form, a new type emerges in the finales of cycles. Impetuous, sparkling in their brilliant virtuosity, these finales inevitably call forth comparisons with finales in the neo-classic works of Stravinsky, Bartók, Lutoslawski and Bacewicz herself. But these similarities concern only the general problem of form and types of movement. Bacewicz's original treatment of finales again flows out of unusual textural thematic types and their development. The fourth movement of the *Concerto for Orchestra, Allegro non troppo*, is a type of toccata. But how different is this toccata from its prototypes in Bacewicz's early works! Its pulse is made up of the uneven beating of irregularly accented, short, syncopated figures which are interrelated in complex polyphonic multiple strata of tutti, creating a scintillating arhythmic effect! Changes in pulsation, contraction and expansion of the voices which comprise it, quickening and relaxation of the pulse—therein lies the essence of the advancement of this "arhythmic in time" toccata.

In this way, the essential development is contained in the inner transformations of the basic thematic-textural line—the linking of different textural segments to form a continuous chain of flowing movement, full of inner oscillations. Hence the never failing renewal in the music, and the fullness of its rich imagery. Harshness of sonority, the extensive use of brass at the beginning, the articulation in the strings of muted and nasal sounds in the middle section (spicato, sul ponticello, No. 7), dour "twilight" episodes, dispersed here and there, once more remind us subliminally of war themes. In the recapitulation, however, the energy of a toccata movement is renewed. This inexhaustible flow, in itself, speaks of Bacewicz's life affirming concepts. The demonic element in the concerto's coda is associated with the powerful, percussive rhythms of Stravinsky's climaxes. Yet a comparison of his *Sacre du printemps* with the *Concerto*'s coda shows that the latter has a different type of percussive-rhythmic texture: impulsive, daring, original, capable of strong affirmative expression.

Much may be said about other compositions of Bacewicz's last years. Each of her works is unique in thematic material, in inventiveness in the sphere of sonoric-timbre transformations, and in the conception of form. Not all have equal merit from the point of view of technical and artistic realization. Nevertheless, vividness, temperament, expressivity and individuality combined with national traditions—the "Polishness" of her artistic palette—all increase the value of Bacewicz's contribution to the music of present day Poland.

Tadeusz Baird

The special emotional world of Baird's music is reflected not only in his art, but also in "his personal musical preferences. Characteristic and consistent,

Tadeusz Baird at a General Convention of the Union of Polish Composers, 1979.

these preferences clarify much. From the past he is attracted by the courtly lyricism of the Middle Ages (troubadours), and by the Renaissance, and by the Romantic period, most of all by two composers, the one who opens and the one who closes this epoch: Schubert and Mahler. Twentieth century neo-Classicism is foreign to Baird. Stravinsky's style is the quintessence of all that he finds unpleasing in music; although objectively he recognizes the worth of his compositions. The composer of this period, to whom Baird feels the greatest affinity, other than Berg, is Szymanowski, who like Baird, is a romantic of the first water, and who was able to find himself through the medium of subtle contemporary colorism. However, Baird was drawn, not to the Szymanowski whose art went under the banner of Góralski music, but to the Szymanowski of that period when the *Third Symphony* was written, and later *Stabat Mater*, Baird's favorite composition. Today, the composer of the *Four Essays* seems to be the only Polish composer, who has an artistic connection to Szymanowski, to his aesthetic and to his type of emotion, and even to the type of melody and receptivity to coloristic expressiveness. Thus, Baird creates for us an important continuity of Polish tradition in the music of the 20th century.''

That was how the music critic, Tadeusz Zieliński evaluated Baird's musical leanings.[6] Baird, himself, does not hide his great respect for Szymanowski: "Szymanowski was, is, and in all probability will remain for me, the central figure in 20th century Polish music, and that, for me, is the only possible means to define my own attitude towards Poland's past; towards its musical tradition. Among all the composers of Poland's musical past, he is the one who is closest to me.''[7]

At a later date, Baird was to comment on this problem at greater length. He emphasized that Berg is related to him, ''. . . because among new-Viennese composers, he was the one closest to romantic tradition. . . . Among Polish composers of the first half of the 20th century Karol Szymanowski was the only bearer of authentic national traditions. . . . Today, I have come to the following conclusion: for a Polish artist the romantic tradition has always been important and meaningful (in my opinion, it is, in fact, the most important one, in all of Polish culture), and I believe that it is precisely by adhering to this path, that I will be able to reveal, emotionally and in full, the essence of my artistic individuality.''[8]

The question again arises in connection with Baird's work, as to what is the character of the continuation of Polish romantic tradition in contemporary music. From the 19th to the 20th century the leading line of succession in Polish music had led from Romanticism to neo-Romanticism. Its influence on contemporary music may be examined in two aspects; first, from the point of view of the composers' emotional and philosophic world; and second, from the standpoint of the stylistic features of the music, the forms and types of structure in compositions.

In Baird's opinion, the specific character of Polish romanticism lies in a combination of vivid expressiveness, highly dramatic in content, and a highly refined delineation of form. In the works of Chopin, Mickiewicz, Slowacki, Norwid, Wyspiański, ''. . . everything, that concerns the emotional side is extremely romantic, yet at the same time, remains strictly classic in form—as if romantic expression were controlled by the intellect.'' This last coexists with ''a typically Polish spontaneous approach to the essence of music.''[9]—a subtle observation, which does much to clarify Baird's own artistic position.

Baird accepted the dramatic structure, the character of expression and imagery, which are inherent in the thinking of the Polish romantics. The romantic traits of Baird's writing style put a special stamp on the works of his first, early classical period; and again on those of his second, dodecaphonic period; and once again on the works of his third and last period, which differs from the preceding two for now there is a merging of classic and romantic tendencies, a greater synthesis, whose dominant note Baird himself identifies as "Polishness." The combination of an individual type of expression with a special colorfulness in the elements of language, is also characteristic. It is a common tendency in Polish music as a whole. Side by side with monumental forms exists a meticulous attention to detail, while from the past, a scrupulous listening for inflection, a highlighting of melody in musical texture still remains, a trait which definitely singles Baird out from among his colleagues.

The composer devoted much attention to vocal music. Two cycles for mezzo-soprano and chamber orchestra (poems by V. Parun and H. Póswiatowska) fall into Baird's last musical period, as does a reorchestrated Shakespearean cycle—a pearl of vocal literature, not only among Baird's own compositions of that time, but possibly in all of Polish music. Baird's turn towards operatic and cantata music (*Tomorrow* and *Goethe-Briefe*) was also characteristic. As can be seen, the bulk of vocal music grew during the last years.

A line of monumental symphonic writing was also continued, while a bent for vivid imagery carried with it an inclination to give compositions literal titles (two symphonic poems: *Psychodrama* and *Elegeia*). Monumental treatment is also adhered to in the concerto genre. During the past years, two beautiful concertos for soloists with orchestra were created (for oboe, and viola: *Concerto lugubre*).

Baird's style during the last period was characterized by a dramatic type of emotion, a purely "Bairdian" kind of bright imagery with flashes of expressive melody at the climaxes. However, its character changed somewhat since the 1960's. The importance of melody, as it is traditionally understood, diminished. More and more, coloristic-figurational complexes carrying a thematic function were used instead. The critic R. Augustyn called this last period in Baird's music, "sonoric-textural," thus underlining the leading role assigned to orchestral texture, which appears in a thematic function, and transforms itself in the developmental process of the composition.[10] Yet Baird rejected aleatory as a way to organize sound fabric, substituting for it textural figurations which resemble those of aleatory music ("aleatory without aleatory.") He attains this kind of effect, for example, in *Five Songs* on the verses of H. Poświatowska (1968). The figurational complex in the third song, based on rotational models, becomes the expressive center of the whole cycle.

In his late symphonic works, Baird continued to develop and evolve many of his techniques from the 1960's. But where before the form was built on homogeneous musical material, the composer now strove towards vivid contrast, creating sharply conflicting situations. A big orchestra, numerous climaxes, the sound of many tutti distinguish the orchestral style of the last period from the refined chamber style of the former years. An example of this late style is the symphonic *Psychodrama*. In essence, this orchestral poem echoes directly the musical drama, *Tomorrow*. The collision of contrasting themes, the juxtaposition of dramatic and contemplative-lyric episodes, impulsive energy, extreme and unstable emotionalism, all have been pushed to the utmost limits. At the center of the concept: a manifestation of various moods, each expressed in an individual way, conveying the psychological complexity of human experience. A special emphasis is put on the expressive melodic lines in solo episodes. In comparison to Baird's chamber works, the dramatic expression here is far more condensed, the tempo of unfolding events quickens, the pulsation of flickering mosaic images speeds up. Yet for all its seeming subjectivity, this concept does not obstruct objective moments.

R. Augustyn calls *Psychodrama* a "particularly melodic" composition; and indeed, in it, Baird paid great attention to the quasi melodic sonoric-textural structures which strengthen emotional intensity, and the romantic-expressive tone of the narrative. At the same time, the thematic material, as the form on the whole, are patterned on the traditional late romantic symphonic style. In this single-movement composition (8–8.5 minutes), it is easy to discern a row of sections, whose functions are analogous to traditional ones.

The opening consists of a row of impulses, attacks in tutti, out of which, gradually miniscule particles form, a recitatival melody in the oboe (No. 10). Out of a row of motifs is born what is, in effect, a theme; an expressive recitative played by strings in unison, typical of Baird (No. 20). An undulant melody, flexible in design, in the dense, low registers of violins and vio-

Example 25

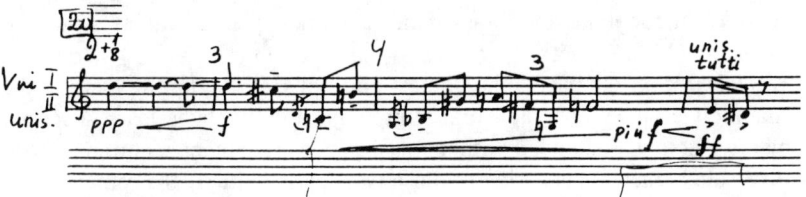

las is the basic theme. Emerging out of the surrounding figurations in the woodwinds and the overtones of unpitched percussion, it serves the same function as a principal theme in a symphonic form. Ex. 25.

An antithesis to the nervous, tempo-rhythmically unstable, impulsive and dynamic "main theme" is the "subordinate theme," a choral episode in a chordal structure in the wind instruments (Poco andante, No. 30). It is followed by soli, alternating repeatedly with tutti, in individualized melodies and deliberately mixed heterophonic episodes. A dense 46-voice texture has a tendency to blend into vertical complexes. The result: a vividly expressed sonorism. Such is the technical arsenal of the expressionistic, sharp climaxes in *Psychodrama*.

The dramatic collision in *Psychodrama* is developed by alternating and transforming contrasting images. In the words of T. Zieliński: "The most characteristic, individual trait of Baird's compositions, perhaps even its most romantic, is the 'flow' of its music, its tempo-rhythmic quality. This creates an impression of maximal 'rubato,' a free, almost improvisational movement of sounds, that seems to exist outside of time, rhythm or bar lines; and this, in spite of the fact that actually, all are precisely marked in the score."[11]

In pace with the unfolding, contrasts grow stronger, expression more condensed. Out of the quasi-development is born a distorted, grotesque "scherzo" (Allegretto ironico, No. 55, soli in woodwinds). The contrasting episode is contemplative, concentrated in mood (*Andante sostenuto*, No. 70). It is an analogue to the slow movement in a cycle, in which an individualized opening solo comes to the fore. A turn has been taken into a personal, meditational sphere.

At the same time, important processes of interaction take place, and one type of dramatic imagery is reborn as another. Lyric, psychological images gradually fuse into generically objective ones. Thus, the summoning fanfare (in the chamber music watercolors of the woodwind trio) find their continuation in the declamatory pathos of a monologue in the strings. This quiet "culmination," a true lyric revelation by the composer of *Psychodrama*, recalls the best pages of Polish chamber symphonies.

A new outburst of dramatic movement in the recapitulation, gives birth to a whole series of recurrent impulsive waves of development. At the end, the sound of the conquering brass fanfare comes like a mighty voice of affirmation.

Psychodrama represents the highest point of Baird's development of the romantic vein in symphonic works. In the music of his later years, a certain objective note was sounded with increasing power; content acquired a broad universal character. The union of these two separate lines, the romantic and the classic, first appeared in the cantata *Goethe-Briefe (Goethe's Letters)*.

The ballad-like narrative and the introduction of choral commentary are timeless, objective features in the cantata. At the same time, intentional analogies to Mahler and particularly to Wagner, (the main motif echoes *Tristan and Isolde*), accentuate the romantic sources of *Goethe-Briefe*.

But in one of the later compositions, *Concerto lugubre* for viola and orchestra (1975), classical traits predominate. Classicism manifests itself in a rare harmony and in the polished quality of the form, in a special "transparency" of its contours, and a clear dramatic plan. The drama of the first movement, the elegiac character of the second and the motoric, aggressive movement of the finale follow the traditional sequence of the thematic conception in a cycle. In this concerto, it is the solo that is the central part. It is extremely rich and steeped in emotion. Often, the orchestra's assigned role is to provide a soft background, performing in solo in climactic episodes. The wave-like development, the restrained but somber character of expression recall the intensely dramatic compositions of Baird, the romantic (Psychodrama, et al).

A unique combination of what is new and traditional constitutes the inimitable individuality of Baird's compositions, whose music opens a new page in lyric-dramatic symphonic writing.

Henryk Mikolaj Górecki

Górecki employs the same methods in large cyclical form compositions that he had evolved in the middle 1960's in single-movement compositions. The line, begun in *Muzyka staropolska*, continues. Affirmation, monumentality, an epic scale, a maximal limitation of means were all carried over into Górecki's later compositions. In many of them, he showed himself to be heir to the traditions of Polish Catholicism, especially in the area of thematic choices and texts. As to genres, vocal-instrumental and choral music stand out: *Ad matrem*, 1971; *Two Sacred Songs* for baritone and orchestra, 1971; the choral work *Amen*, 1975. Some outstanding symphonic pieces should also be mentioned: The *Second Symphony*, (1972) and the *Third Symphony* (1977).

Ad matrem is a composition that is typical of Górecki. Its prototype is a requiem; its performing ensemble: a soprano, mixed chorus and orchestra. Here as in compositions without texts, the performing ensemble is utilized with extreme economy. To be specific: the chorus, used as a means for expressively sharpening the climax, appears only twice, and each time for one measure only. It has already been mentioned that out of the whole liturgical text, the composer chose only the line: "Mater mea, Dolorosa, Lacrimosa. . . ." Correspondingly, both the framework of genres and thematic

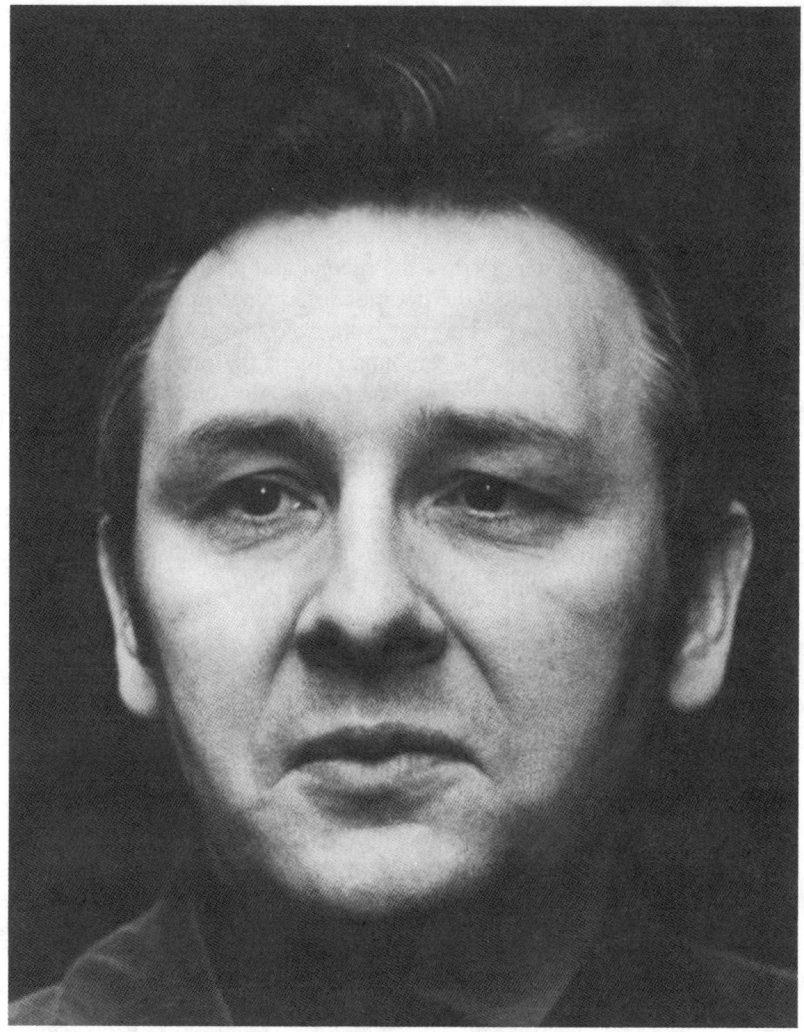

Henrik M. Górecki, 1975.

tendencies are also limited in this original cantata. This one-movement composition falls into several sections. At the base of each section stands a single, well-defined theme. Analogies to traditions may be carried out on all parameters of the musical work: from the point of view of style, thematic structure, form and means. In *Ad matrem*'s construction, an optimal interrelationship of episodes, based on sharply contrasting themes, on various

III. Music of the Third Postwar Decade (1966–1977)

ways of organizing material and on different genre models is found. Such a high degree of emotional and dramatic intensity in the conceptualization of imagery appears for the first time in Górecki's work. An ability to create a mood with a single stroke expressing a concrete meaning, that is the particular character of Górecki's unique style.

In the first section, the basic form-building element is a dynamic percussive-rhythmic-sonoric complex (a regular ostinato pulsation in 16th's in the bass drum). Two timpani and a snare drum, each in its turn, join the bass drum staying in measure with it. As the rate of pulsation increases, the force of the cresting dynamic wave (crescendo from *pppp* to *ffff*) spews out a stark shrieking tritone figure which resembles a desperate wail (in *b*—flat and *e*, ffff, played in unison by woodwinds and brass: clarinets, oboes, trumpets, and trombones). This section is then repeated again and again varying in length. It is an original type of analogue to a Dies irae, depicted by alarming fanfares, signaling the approach of inescapable death. . . . Analogies to this theme may be found in the recent past, in echoes of the war, the horror of Nazi invasion, the furnaces of Auschwitz, in the grotesque grins of the dead in Picasso's *Guernica*.

During one of the repeats of this episode, at the crest of the dynamic wave, as the alarm is sounded, a chorus joins in, in unison, with the words: "Mater mea!" And this fragment, this cry for help, really just a short turn around the second interval, is the culmination of the first episode. Ex. 26.

The contrasting episode has a plaintive theme of quiet sorrow, embodied in a descending 4th, the inflection of a moan (flutes and violins) on a pedal in 3rd (horns, harp, violas and cellos). The tone of the tertian-tritone-quartal harmony is poignantly melancholy. The harmony remains stable. Both the motif of the descending 4th and the means that are used later to fill it, are borrowed from folk practices in lamenting the dead.

The third episode, adjoined to the second, is again contrasting: an in-

Example 26

Example 27

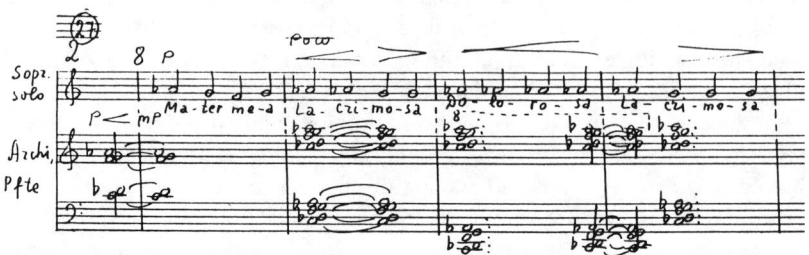

tentedly monotonous psalmody in the low registers of the violas against a pedal background (a major 2nd: *d*-flat—*e*-flat), a conjunct melismatic motion around *d* as its tonal center. In this type of requiem analogies to church psalmody are obvious.

All three episodes alternate, modelled on contrasting-compound forms: ABC —B'C'B"—A'—D. The final episode, which is new, is the dynamic center of the cantata, and fulfills the function of a finale. A minor pentachord pedal in the strings lasts throughout the section. From time to time, the same chord in transparent bell-like tones is struck on the piano. It creates a sense of numb grief and immerses one in the contemplative mood of the finale. The fundamental idea in the soprano ''aria'' is expressed with the same spareness. Only three tones are used: *a*-flat—*g*—*f*: a conjunct tertian scale in different aspects. It is amazing that such ascetic expressive means can lead to such impressive artistic results. The source of the melody in both the ''finale'' and the rest of the composition is a folk lament. It is essential to emphasize that in Poland, folk and Catholic traditions intertwine. Church melodies have long been assimilated into the practices of folk music and now belong to the realm of folklore. Ex. 27.

In *Ad matrem*, Górecki once more demonstrated an approach to genres and forms that was profoundly individual, yet tied to time-honored national traditions. *Ad matrem* is neither a lifeless stylization, nor is it a copy of the external contours of an out-dated model. Rather, it is a way of incorporating great humanistic content by means of living traditions. The composer made use of the most general features of requiem music, and on the base of separate generic formulas created a new kind of funeral song, which combines a deeply personal character (the composition is dedicated to the memory of his mother) with a broader, more general one: a memorial to the martyrs of the war, the fallen heroes of long-suffering Poland and other countries.

H. M. Górecki—The Second Symphony: "Copernican"

While retaining the generic base of the large symphony, Górecki demonstrated a new approach to its material and development in his *Second Symphony*, which he called the *Copernican (Kopernikowska)*. The composition is written for a quadrupled orchestra, with an augmented percussion section (six performers), two soloists (a baritone and soprano), and chorus. The work consists of two movements, unequal in length: the first movement is orchestral, the second—choral. The text is based on two psalms in praise of the creation of the world, and on the text of Copernicus' treatise *On the Revolution of Heavenly Spheres (De Revolutionibus orbium caelestium)*. The symphony was commissioned by the Kościuszko Foundation in New York for the celebration of the 500th anniversary of Copernicus' birth.

The idea of the symphony is not new: celebration of Earth, delight in life and harmony in the world—a theme that has inspired modern artists (Hindemith), no less than the ancients. To some extent the idea is related to certain postulates in Scriabin's work, including the grandiose scale of the cycles. But Górecki's style is quite different from Scriabin's and Hindemith's.

Incontestable analogies also exist between Penderecki's *Kosmogonia* and Górecki's *Copernican*. Yet the individual approach of the two composers to the theme makes itself felt. The marked difference is rooted in the way the artists relate to text. Penderecki "prepares" it, distorts it by layering words on each other. On the other hand, in Górecki's work, all words, whether pronounced by a soloist or scanned by a chorus, are brought out distinctly. The text—only two or three phrases—is usually repeated many times, in order to allow the listener to absorb the meaning. Like Penderecki, Górecki uses a Latin text.

On the stylistic plane, as well, the two works are different. For both composers the keystone of composition lies in sonoristic problems. Yet, the artistic aspect of these two symphonies is deeply individual. A comparison of the two works demonstrates the depth of the differences and the heterogeneous phenomena that can take place within a seemingly similar sonoristic direction.

For Górecki, such principles of traditional classical symphonic construction as the form's large dimensions and clearly defined contrasts are important. On the other hand, it is natural for him to think in aphorisms, make brief formulations. His limited sonorism is tied to this kind of method. Chords and short melodic figures are so extremely expressive that they function as themes. The subsequent ostinato repeats of a metro-rhythmic formula form the content of next section, while the symphony as a whole is made of up several such sections-blocks, which function as the movements of a cycle. Such are the principles governing the structure of both small and large cyclical forms in Górecki's work.

However, this does not imply that the section of a composition—the "block"—is absolutely immobile and remains static. The sonoric material is subject to transformations and inner development. All of which is clearly demonstrated in the *Copernican Symphony.*

In the first movement a fervent affirmation is expressed through numerous reiterations of two clusters related to each other by half tones. In the top layer of the vertical a descending intonation by second (*e* to *d*-sharp) is clearly outlined. An inversion (*e* to *f*) appears in the bass. On each of these tones, a whole-tone vertical is built. Let us call this a binomial sequence, a cluster melodic "figure," analogous to a traditional two-tone motif. The vertical columns seem to literally collapse on the listener: tutti ffff, con massima passione.

The metrical structure is composed of irregular aggregates of rhythmically even beats intensifying in a through continuity. Thus, an illusion of movement, of an unfolding of a theme arises. Moreover, any dynamic change becomes a means of development; for after a prolonged sounding of one pitch, any move is perceived as a cardinal change: a heightened level of emotional intensity. This device is a substitute for melodic development. The principle of transformation is indicated in the repeats of this theme, which acts either as a principal theme or else as the refrain in a rondo form. The result is that the theme acquires the generic features of a march. Ex. 28.

The contrasting theme is analogous to a subordinate theme in a sonata form (Molto lento, precedes No. 6). While the vertical cluster design is retained, there are changes in: 1) the intervallic make-up of the vertical (whole-tone structures, trichords, pentatonic); 2) dynamics (piano sempre); 3) the sound color (calm floating tone colors in the strings, occasionally supported by chorale-like chords in the wind instruments); 4) metrics (prolonged, slowed-down); 5) character (indications: tranquilissimo—cantabilissimo—legatissimo).

Because of its conjunct melismatic circling of the tonal center *C*, a simple

Example 28

melody in the top voice of the whole super-structure recalls Gregorian chants. The generic base of the second subject is a chorale. It is quietly contemplative in contrast to the gigantic power of the "principal theme."

After the refrain, the second contrasting episode is analogous to a scherzo (Tempo ♩ = 98 − 100, inquieto–marcato, precedes No. 16). It is characterized by disturbing harsh signals in the trombones.

By way of contrast, an aleatory episode follows (No. 17). Here a different kind of material is presented: short one or two-tone melodic figures, insistent, willful calls of a fanfaric type, slice through the red-hot "magma" of the aleatory block and form strata of irregular rhythmic patterns. In the progress of the unfolding, the scherzo episode goes through modifications: from fanfares, through a disorganized, turbulently anarchic movement into the framework of an orderly march. A similar process of generic transformations entails the reversal of the expressive means: from aleatory mobility to stable vertical structures in the "principal theme." There is a resemblance here to the way the second movement (*Direct*), unfolds in Lutoslawski's *Second Symphony*.

The sweeping strength in the culminatory zone in Górecki's symphony is astonishing. Here, the dimensions are grandiose, in keeping with the mighty exposition. Its stability, colossal monumentality is contrasted to the activity of the developmental sections. In the chain of the general ascent, one link stands out: it is a new expressive theme, a lyric culmination that foreshadows the dramatic peak of the development (Deciso marcato, precedes No. 27). The typically Slavic broad motion based on a sixth interval with a subsequent circling around its top note creates a lyrico-dramatic song. It is this theme's melodic contour that is memorable and not the acid sonoric setting of the underlying verticals. They only complete the expression, enhance its emotionlly hot "temperature."

The appearance of a new theme on the crest of a swelling wave resembles those *contrasting culminations* which may be seen in Shostakovich's culminations of the development, in whose work melodic heights are connected to a definite clearing in the texture (unisons in tutti follow complex polyphony in the *Fifth*, *Eighth* and other symphonies). This method of melodic emergence is typical of Górecki's compositional technique. It is seen in many works by contemporary composers: Honegger, Prokofiev, Shostakovich, Lutoslawski, Penderecki, et al.

The last stage of the multi-level culmination is a recapitulation of the primary theme (tutti with chorus). The chorus sings in unison, stressing the first verse of the text: "Deus, qui fecit Caelum et Terram. Deus, qui fecit Luminaria magna." In this unison, the top melodic strata of the "principal" theme shines out.

Threads leading to the marvelous finale (the second movement, Lento) stem from some of the lyric themes in the first movement, from the chorale of the subordinate theme, and the culmination of the development. After the gigantic power and dynamism of the first movement, the lyric finale comes as a logical conclusion, the philosophical outcome of the conception of the cycle. Once more, analogies emerge and remind us of Lutoslawski's two-movement compositions, in which the balance of weight is transferred towards the end.

In the development of the finale an important role is played by a falling motif (a cantus firmus on the word "Deus"), the generic nucleus of the chorale. In the process of unfolding, the choral theme turns into a broad melodic wave. It begins as a quietly contemplative cantus firmus by the baritone. At first, the melody appears to be almost static with small up and down off-shoots from e-flat in conjunct motion. The pivotal chord, the harmonic pedal is, in this case, the black key pentatonic-trichord structure on the vertical. A constant hum in the background creates a state of psychic equilibrium. But from No. 3 on, "the harmony of peace" breaks up in a long, scale-like ascending jubilus, with turns, changes, descents and then a reconquest of the heights. The character of expression changes in the culmination from restrained emotion to ecstasy. Analogies to Scriabin again emerge. A special elation in the ringing culmination speaks of divine origin of this rapture.

The inexhaustible prolongation of the expanding wave is realized through the device of changing timbres. At the point when vocal strain in the baritone's high register becomes extreme, his line is taken up by the soprano and carried on with renewed strength. For the first time in the symphony, the dense cluster is resolved into a pure triad (sixth chord in A-flat major). The change of timbre and harmony marks the moment of clearing, peace, reverence and wonder before all creation. Once more, the same words of Psalm 135 are addressed to God. But, in spite of Górecki's deep piety, the breadth of his music's character encompasses more than religious ideology. In this rapturous song of praise, there is a reverence for ever wondrous nature. This is the moment when the musical-image system changes: prayerful (psalmodic), melismatic and Gregorian melodies are relinquished. An undeviating line ascends from the depth to the heights, (low baritone—high soprano) and seems to draw a manifest model of the universe. Ex. 29.

The method for prolonging the theme (and advancing the form) leads to a qualitative renewal of material in the coda: the contrasting coda is the result of the total development of the second movement. Here the composer used the melodics of an authentic chorale from the Miechow Monastery Antiphonarium of the 15th century. However, a quotation from Copernicus was substituted for the original text. The traditional four-voice, white key dia-

Example 29

tonic, deliberately counterposed to the preceding black key orchestral background, the triadic harmonization in natural modes, are all features of Polish Renaissance chorales. They were preserved in that national treasure, the *Psalter* by Mikołaj Gomółka. Here, a direct basis exists for echoing ancient national traditions. The quotation from Copernicus' *On the Revolution of Heavenly Spheres* is stated in a truly concrete way: it is universalized via the genre, and becomes a vivid expression of the central, philosophic idea of the symphony.

Experiencing this Górecki composition as a whole, one is constantly impressed with its simplicity and its economy of means, which the composer used to create clear architectonics in the symphony. The form falls into a fully traditional "scheme," which may be presented in the following way:
1. The statement of the thesis: principal theme in the first movement.
2. The thesis shown from its opposite, contrasting side: subordinate theme.
3. A new level of affirmation: refrain, development of the principal theme.
4. Negation and combat: episode in the development—scherzo.
5. The postulate of the statement triumphs: recapitulation of the principal theme.
6. Finale—recapitulation of the subordinate theme and its new continuation.

Emphatic clarity, extraordinarily succinct means, utmost definition in the construction of formal sound elements, are all particular traits that form Górecki's style. Because of these traits, the *Copernican* is unlike Penderecki's *Cosmogonia* whose theme is similar. Each of the composers resolves this theme according to his own point of view, his conception of form, and the character of his stylistic individuality.

Górecki's experience shows his predilection for large forms, his tendency to draw on various levels of old national traditions and to join them with new expressive musical means. He found his own variant of limited sonorism, was able to incorporate it in a new symphonic form and discovered new possibilities for the future development of the contemporary symphony.

H. M. Górecki—The Third Symphony of Sad Songs

The Third Symphony is an example of that "Górecki paradox" which has repeatedly caused controversy and sharp conflicts of opinion as to the aesthetic value of his music; music in which intentional primitivism is combined with complex sonoric-percussive soundings, in which monumental forms are based on the development of several timbre-textural structures, and where simplicity of expression does not preclude a majestic emotional force.

However, as Polish critics have pointed out, the most significant aspect of "paradox" in Górecki's works is the contradiction between the form and the material on which the form is built. While in Górecki's earlier sonoristic works (*Genesis*, 1963, or *Refrain for Orchestra*, 1965) form grew out of the material and evolved in natural, free exchanges of heterogeneous elements, in the Third Symphony, as in earlier examples of "limited sonorism" like *Ad Matrem*, the composer rejected the freedom of exchanges of material by strictly limiting the structure of the composition.

Yet another creative aspect of form is examined by the critic K. Droba.[12] Proceeding from Max Scheller's ideas on tragedy,[13] Droba postulates that the form itself can predetermine the tragic meaning of a work. In the first movement of the Third Symphony, the unfolding canon becomes such a form.

True, Droba's thesis should not be accepted without further examination. The real problem is not in the matter of priorities, but in the correspondence of form with content and musical material. In our opinion, Górecki employed the forms which convey the accumulation of tragic content in each movement; those forms which are capable of fulfilling the requirements of his musical language, i.e. the system of limited sonorism.

In the *Third Symphony* the form in each of the three movements is different (canon in the first, binary form in the second, varied verse form in the third); each reveals a different facet of the tragic content. The tragic suffering of a mother who has lost her son becomes a universal theme, and takes on a broad humanistic meaning. It is presented in its religious aspect in the first movement. The afflictions and sorrow of the Mother of God who mourns her Son is also a theme of patience, so characteristic of the Christian ethic. However, this meaning of the text is partial, and the sub-text carries a broader implication. The image of the Holy Mother is a symbol for motherhood in general. Moreover, her afflictions and patience may be likened to afflictions of the Polish people who for centuries have been oppressed as their country was subjected again and again to invasions and partitions. The philosophical significance and symbolism are revealed in the following movements. The text of the second movement was taken from a prison cell in a Nazi camp: an inscription scratched on the wall by a young girl about to be executed and addressed to her mother. The text of the third movement comes from a folk song in Adolf Dygacz's anthology.

The different aspects of humanity's problems are reflected less in the texts themselves, than in the way they are related to the music. The unquestionable dominance of the music is firmly established in the generic and stylistic realization of the symphony. When Górecki's ability to extend time and sustain a mood is connected with the methodology of "reduced sonorism" it already predetermines the subservience of poetry in its union with music, and establishes the supremacy of the latter as the moving force in composition.

In terms of musical structure the first movement is of particular interest. As has been mentioned, its basis is a canon. But the theme of the canon is unusual: ascetic and severe, broadly extended, songlike, and long (24 measures). Stated at the beginning in low contrabasses, it is written in the Aeolian E minor. It moves unhurriedly, in a winding, uneven, ledged design. The direction of movement, now ascending, now descending, recalls traditional Mass music, with its "crucifixion themes," although indirectly for this theme is quite songlike; its phrasing is generous in spite of the theme being divided into groups of four, eight, and two measures. The melody of a song from the Kurpian region, collected by Wladyslaw Skierkowski, served as a prototype.

Example 30

The length of the principal theme, written as an eight-voiced canon, caused critics to attack the symphony. This lengthy theme results in the unusual hypertrophic dimension of the entire movement. The composer ignores, as if intentionally, the conventional canon form. The melody of the canon seems ill-suited to its form. Yet it is precisely this canonic form that is so appropriate for the method of recurring material and mood, and for the method of "reduced" sonorism. The first impression is that the music seems to be far from sonorism, yet it is inextricably tied to it, created by the imagery of Górecki's language system.

The manner of construction in the canon is typical: all voices recur and participate, so that a counterpoint in many parts arises. The principle of ostinato is carried out eight times. Entering eight times at intervals of a fifth the rispostas follow a circle of fifths: E, B, F#, C, G, D, A, D, /E, E/. Proceeding through to the point of departure, the propostas merge at the climax in the initial key on an increased dynamic forte, doubling the higher voices. Retaining the natural E minor in a bass ostinato, Górecki employs different modalities in subsequent returns to the theme: a Phrygian B minor, Hypophrygian F sharp, Lydian C, G, D major. The archaic ring of modality is encountered also as a result of harsh chords generated on the vertical by systematically delaying the entrance of each risposta by one measure after the preceding proposta. The combination of archaisms with complicated modern sonoristic chords creates a unique atmostphere, a characteristic Górecki phenomenon. The significance of the repetition of the canon at the climax is purely expressive and not structural. It extends the climax and intensifies the dramatic tension.

The form of the entire first movement is original in terms of the psychology of perception. The canon travels through a full dynamic cycle of development in only 320 measures: crescendo towards the climax (from one to ten voices are involved) and diminuendo on the return (from ten voices to four-voice unison at the end). In the contrasting segment, there follows a typical, Górecki, solo episode: the soprano enters. Her spare motif, limited at first to two or three notes, its gradual evolution into extended scale-like passages, the spontaneous, expansive melody in the high, strained vocal registers and finally the strictly limited orchestral pedal background, in which the verticals gradually "swell" from unison to cluster chords, are all characteristic manifestations of Górecki's "reduced" (limited) sonorism. Also typical is the emotional range of this music: the gamut of its emotional range extends from restrained grief and deep contemplation to dramatic passion. Let us consider the first section of the vocal part as an example: here are combined the traits of chorale and folk lament (Górecki used the "Lament Świętokrzyski" from Lysogor Songs of the 15th century).

Example 31

After a passionate outburst, at the moment of return to hushed melancholy contemplation, the canon is suddenly resumed from that same culminating point at which, in the first section of the movement, the development was left off. (Measure 369, Lento sostenuto tranquillo ma cantabile: #24; ten voices.) Thus, the tableau of a religious procession (like the procession to Golgotha) interrupted earlier by the central episode, is restored, giving the listener a sense of the emotional experiences of participants in the ancient mystery. Such unexpected "straightening out" of the deformed line of development in the recapitulation is the most startling turnabout in the dramatic composition. Analogies with cinematic technique arise here: use of montage and interruptions of chronological sequence. At the same time, Górecki abides by the laws of purely musical architectonics, maintaining the principle of formal symmetry, recapitulation; and preserving the consistency of harmonic-modal language. All of this discloses the system of a "limited," "reduced" sonorism from a new, strictly structural perspective, and broadens the possibilities for unfolding the dramatic composition within the boundaries of the given system. It is essential to emphasize as well the "melodic origin" of this music. Its wide, spontaneous unfolding is realized through the prolongation of the melodic wave, supported, unexpectedly and vividly, by the polyphonic form of the canon. All this reveals the melodic possibilities in the musical system of Górecki, possibilities involving melody as one element of composition in a system of sonorism.

In the next two movements, as well, the melodic material of the *Third Symphony* is songlike. Not by chance is it named *The Symphony of Sad Songs*. But, just as the forms and architectonics of the movements differ from each other, so do both the generic bases of the melody and the qualities of its sonoristic execution. The use of polyphony was a new development in Górecki's music and provoked much discussion of the form of the first movement. The style of the following movements is much more typical for Górecki. As Maria Gąsiorowska writes in her article on the symphony,

"The 'spirit of harmony' predominates over the 'spirit of polyphony.' Górecki's style is focused above all on the chords that he uses; for him the chord is the single most expressive identifying feature, the emblem (signum) of his musical individuality."[14] It is essential to add, however, that these chords are most often of sonoristic, not harmonic, origin. In the first movement, chords encompassing every possible interval are created at points where interweaving melodic lines intersect. In the second and third movements, these chords create a timbre-harmonic sonoric background to the singing and give a special sharpness to expression, supplementing the generic framework of the melody. In the second song (*Lento e Largo*) the arc from the first movement's central episode stretches forward to the beginning of another lament. A typical contrast exists between the initial instrumental passage, (which is like a prelude, an Intrada) and the actual singing. A short melodic figure on the piano, harp and strings creates a serene mood. It should be mentioned that the harp and piano in the Symphony are treated as leit-timbres; their percussive sounding seems to mark the rhythm (central episode of the first movement; second and third movements).

There is beauty and eloquence in the ascending motif E-G# in A minor, and in the harmony which uses spare, "à la Górecki" selected intervals of perfect fifths, a Dorian sixth creating an image of unearthly elevation, spirituality and purity. Ex. 32.

All the darker, then, is the sorrow in the solo soprano passage that follows. Again, a lament begins, this time accompanied by a moaning motif. A mood of anguished pleading is communicated by a short melodic turn. In the severely restrained quality of this sad cry lies the courageous strength and determination of a young patriot about to be executed. This final message to her mother is more exhortation than prayer (which is how Gąsiorowska interprets it). But the implication in the image is definite, made clear by the roughhewn, almost ascetic, expression, so sparse as to be almost miserly. The contrast of color here is especially important: the modal-key and timbre-harmonic progession *A - B* flat, the replacement of the bright major Dorian sixth (statement of a D major triad in an A minor context) by a dark

Example 32

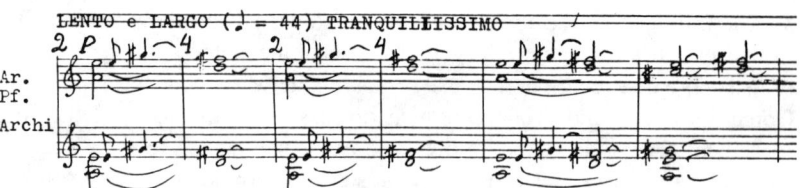

third *b* flat - *d* flat in the low registers of the orchestra (strings, piano, clarinet, French horn). This progression, this change of color has a form-defining significance. Passing beyond the limits of purely modal-harmonic function, it compares and contrasts two diametrically opposed images created by two spare strokes. Thus the realization of this contrast dependent upon maximally limited means.

The movement concludes with an unexpected "genre modulation"—a typically Górecki chorale in the spirit of a psalmody which contains analogies with a prayer of calm resolution. Similar turns of expression in the coda sections, seemingly breaking the form and imparting to it the potential for continuation are frequently encountered in Górecki (*Ad Matrem*, the *Second Symphony*). By introducing a new image in the coda the composer again demonstrates the form-building potentials of sonoristic material and its role as a structural element of form.

The third movement (again *Lento*) is built upon a folk melody from the Opole region found in Adolf Dygacz's collection. This is perhaps the only instance where Górecki has made use of a lyric folk song. This choice for the finale of the symphony is not random, for the composer seeks in the folk world-vision a broad universality in keeping with his sonoristic conception, built on the selection of characteristic elements which relate not only to music but also to his understanding of philosophy and emotion. As Gąsiorowska has observed, Górecki appeals to feelings, addresses himself "to the sources, to the anterior conception of music" and conveys "the essense of folk lyricism." For him, "it is the idea of the attraction of primary expressiveness of music, it is a discovery of the energy of music as a natural form of expression."[15]

The form is based on variations on a couplet from a song. For Górecki, it is essential to preserve the unity of the image over an extended period and, by means of a sudden change in color, to create a situation of conflict that moves with the dramatic composition of the form. The uniting link is the rhythmic-percussive pattern of the accompaniment, which sets a distinctive ostinato pulse of movement. The obsessive repetition of chords is combined with the principle of variation, if only initially and insignificantly: the alternation of duple and triple meter; the stepwise progression of the middle voice in triads; the introduction of coloring effects of other timbres. The harp and piano, acting as the leit-timbre, function as an indicator of the emotional temperature of the symphony. Ex. 33.

The principle of persistence in ostinato is a major principle in Górecki's sonoristic dramatic composition, realized in the form of canon on a persistent basso in the first movement, and in the prolongation of two selected structures in the second. In the third movement, it takes on a new aspect.

Example 33

From a standpoint of dramatic-composition, the combination here of two opposed devices is interesting. While the ostinato pulse of the accompaniment creates a constant image and gives an unified basis to the composition, the vocal part overrides this consistency, never allowing a hint of stagnation to appear through the whole progress of its development. Such an approach is, in this case, related to the composer's ability to capture the essence of the folk music genre, to become imbued with both the mood and the method of its development. Couplet periodicity is overcome by means of variation and prolongation of the musical wave, which gives it a character of through-development from beginning to end. The wave of constant development remains unbroken even by the deliberate pauses which interrupt the course of the song. These pauses emphasize the characteristics of the genre (couplet construction, diverse ways of expression: lyric melody, lament, wail). What is even more important they make way for the coloristic accompaniment, allowing the instruments to predominate, and preserve the connecting uniform background. Ex. 34.

The harmonic shift in the middle movement is typical of Górecki: the modal confrontation of A minor with A major is interpreted as a crucial turning point in the progress of development of the finale. Here is an example of treating a purely sonoric timbre-harmonic coloring as a medium of the dramatic composition: the transition to a new quality marks a structural facet of the form. This transfer to a new phase of development is a shift into a new emotional realm (No. 9, Lo stesso tempo).

Example 34

Although A minor returns in the recapitulation (No. 14, Molto Lento), in the coda it is the major that makes a final and permanent return, affirming the primacy of a (reverently untouchable) elevated ideal. This image is related to the idea of moral purification and catharsis in classical drama.

Such are the numerous aspects of the application of sonoristic dramatic composition in the *Symphony of Sad Songs*. Both the compositional structures and the idea content of the symphony have many roots in various traditions. Górecki drew models from diverse sources. We have already mentioned the ancient stratum of national chorales and hymns. Gąsiorowska draws unexpected analogies between the Third Symphony and Szymanowski's works. Unexpected, because the basis of Szymanowski's art is late romanticism combined with post-impressionism and "colorism." In Górecki there is "the same folk simplicity and severity, the same 'archaization,' although subordinated to his special personal sensibility. The flow of energy in the liturgical works by the two composers is not alike. There is more contemplation, more reflection, time is slowed down in the works of Górecki. Szymanowski is dramatically more external. Here are two worlds, but they originate in the same source."[15]

It is essential to note, as well, that while Górecki creates his tragic images in a completely original manner, he also renders them in accordance with national tradition. There is much in the history of Poland that gives rise to this kind of tradition. (We are speaking of a certain type of content and its realization in terms of genre). Krzysztof Droba writes: "It is a specific kind of tragedy; of a folk and purely Polish variety: mournful and sad (żalosność). And I believe there is no way to give such forceful expression to such mourning, except through the limitation of formal means."[16]

The system of reduced (limited) sonorism is convincingly incorporated in the *Third Symphony of Sad Songs*, for the composer found and exploited means which were adequate to the content. In expressing a conception, the composer attempts to present it each time in a different appropriate formal system. Hence the numerous varieties of structural language realizations in his compositions, and hence also the vitality and the emotional force of Górecki's music.

Krzysztof Meyer—Symphonies

Among composers of the younger generation, K. Meyer stands out because of the significance of his compositional concepts. His music reflects some of the common tendencies of the third period. The composer's search is related to problems of renewal in symphonic and instrumental chamber genres. Meyer's compositions are distinguished by fullness of content, originality in the treatment of genres, and contemporary musical techniques. The composer feels the greatest affinity to the symphonic style of Mahler and Shostakovich. At the same time, the thorough study of 20th century French music, and neo-Classicism left their mark on Meyer's works. A study of K. Penderecki (in Cracow) and Nadia Boulanger (in Paris), Meyer showed himself to be an original artist for whom expressive means were always subordinate to the total concept. He combines various innovations in an organic synthesis that serves his compositional ideas. A distinguishing feature of his music is its strong expression.

For him, a traditional understanding of a tonal center is essential. It is formed by a sound complex grouped around a tonal center. Certain rhythmic-intonational structures also serve as pivotal points for aural orientation. This type of centralization manifests itself differently in each case, and is the cornerstone in Meyer's conception of pitch. An obligatory repetition of separate tones, intervals or cluster complexes serves as a point of support on which the "links", "joints" of the construction rest. These may be sonoric, serial or tonal fragments of the composition.

A remarkable feature of Meyer's compositions is the economy of their material; to draw an image in a few strokes is his special ability. In examples from Górecki's works, we demonstrated that this tendency is not unique in Polish music. It is encountered in the works of many contemporary composers not only Polish but in some Soviet composers as well: Halina Ustwolska, Arvo Pärt, Boris Tishchenko.

However, the conscious selection of just one type of imagery does not lead, in these instances, to a sense of stasis; for these means are connected with an original approach to the unit of measuring time, and are based on overriding a previously established metrical organization. Here the principle is of temporary individualization of duration.

The evolution of Meyer's work shows a path of continuous transformation of the symphonic genre in the first three symphonies. In the fourth, he returns to the basis of a traditional cycle, but on a new level.

Already in the *First Symphony* (1964), there was an essential change in the look of each movement and in its assigned function in the overall plan of the composition. But the very fact that the composer chose to work in the symphonic form shows his interest in preserving the generic foundations of the large form. Nevertheless, Meyer rejected the sonata principle, the juxtaposition of contrasting or conflicting themes, their transformation and subsequent convergence. The kind of movement, which by its weight and dimension could lay claim to the role of a sonata form, does not exist here. The principle of conflict has been substituted by the principle of juxtapo-

Krzysztof Meyer

sition. The title of the symphony is *Four Fragments for Orchestra*. The schematic plans of each of the *Fragments* are ternary. Yet, here is a symphony—not a suite, nor any other cyclical composition, but a symphony—because the movements of the cycle and their components are treated functionally.

The first *Fragment* of Meyer's symphony is a highly instructive example of a theme in its sonoric sense. Its sonoric design is confined to the tonic chord (unison in *C*) and its subsequent growth into an orchestral tutti, followed by a gradual diminuendo, and return to the opening unison. A three-phase schematic design with a contrasting middle section has been formally maintained here. The contrast is created through the juxtaposition of timbre groups, and the realization of a definite dynamic plan (opening *ppp*-crescendo-climax in *ff*-diminuendo-*ppp*). But, as we said before, the whole movement is built on the same material, and is therefore perceived as an exposition within the framework of the cycle. Thus, from the standpoint of a large form, the understanding of its separate movements narrows. The whole first movement of the cycle takes the form of an integral sonoric block. It resembles the exposition of the principal theme. The other movements, due to their contrasting relationship to the first, function in an original way as movements in a sonata-symphonic cycle: scherzo, adagio, finale, and as sections of a sonata form (development, recapitulation). This last is the result of the diminishing role of the movements and corresponds to the expanding dimensions and sphere of influence of the thematic structure itself; that is, the "sonoric blocks" which form over the duration of large section of the cycle. Thus, in the *First Symphony*, Meyer took the first step towards unifying several movements into an integral composition. In the *Second* and *Third* Symphonies, there are no longer any divisions between the "fragments," and a new type of one-part poem has arisen.

The *Second Symphony* (1967) is subtitled *Epitaph in Memory of Stanislaw Wiechowicz*. Formally, this is a single-movement composition, but in reality it falls into several sections, the last of which equals in length the other three combined, and is the basic center and enormous choral finale of the composition. In essence, it is a colorful oratorial fresco. Here, for the first time, the composer goes beyond the bounds of pure instrumental music. Never before had he ventured to work on such a large scale. Now he creates a synthesized genre.

The symphony's primary material is a group of motifs emerging out of the opening melodic figure, a wailing folk lament. The melody is based on a melisma that circles around a central tone, and on a symmetric broadening and narrowing of the intervallic diapason. In the free metrics that override barlines and in the continuous flow of equal durations, there is an element of spontaneous melodic outpouring which grew out of funeral folk songs. Ex. 35.

In the evolutionary process, numerous transformations of thematic structure occur. The motif in the finale, resembling the traditional *Dies Irae* sequence, appears as a kind of generalized folk-epic variant of an epitaph (No. 21). In this composition, based on a juxtaposition of sets of contrasting episodes, sharply expressive moments alternate with moments of detached contemplation. The frequent intense surges of movement are again made

Example 35

possible by strengthening the role of generic formulas. The composer's beloved short fanfare figures acquire the force of pagan invocations; hypnotically repeated, excited outcries which lead to the general climax. Analogous fragments in Stravinsky and Messiaen works had probably served as a prototype for these thematic ideas. Yet, Meyer's way of converting this prototype is his own. It may be that the extraordinary excitement and ecstasy of the culmination is linked with the special poetic imagery of Meyer's chosen text (the poem *Work* from J. Tuwim's collection: *The Gypsy Bible*). The words evoke grief and thoughts about the bonds of death, yet can also call forth frenzied elation, and celebrate life arising from ashes.

In the *Third Symphony—Simphonie d'Orphée* (Op. 20, 1968) dedicated to Nadia Boulanger, Meyer continues the line begun in the *Second* and develops the results of his discoveries in the merging of music with poetry. Like its predecessor, the *Third Symphony*, contains two sections: instrumental and oratorial. Here, however, the latter has the more substantial role, both in size, and in its condensed content. Meyer had turned to symbolist poetry: Paul Valéry's *Orphée*. Hence, the complicated "coded" language of the symphony. Valéry uses original means to interpret the idea of the mighty creative power of an artist-singer. Beauty of word combinations, and the "music" of speech play a large role. All this is reflected in the symphonic conception.

The building material of the composition (an original system of "signs" that unlock the mystery of textual symbols) consists of three elements:
1. Tertian—second chord formations always in the bells; a sonoric-ringing, summoning leit-motif, appearing like a refrain at the opening, at the end, and between of the different sections. Ex. 36.

Example 36

2. A heterophonically-aleatoric mimetic sound element, a chaotic mix of orchestral lines, recalling the sounds of nature.
3. A serial fragment, but not strictly bound by the rules of this technique, and returning frequently to the tonic *A*, as if in a cyclical process of destruction and renewal.

Thus, once more, we encounter Meyer's typical economic and condensed material. A strict periodicity in the alternation of all three elements in the development organizes the form. Here, the dynamic is created by strengthening the colorful timbre-sonoric motif. Besides the thematic refrain, there is another organizing factor: the process of transformation of each element into moving clusters.

What is interesting in this symphony are the stylistic fusions on different levels. Let us start with the lowest level: the material. Here, tonal and serial principles of organization are interwoven, influencing each other in a complex way. The intersection of the new with the traditional leads to a certain synthesized kind of texture in which a heterophonic and cluster fabric are found side by side with clarity and stability (tonal centers, fanfare turns and ringing timbres are constantly emphasized).

At a higher, stylistic level, one senses in the symphony a fusion of expressive features (condensed dramatic material, emotional intensity, multiple climaxes) with the impressionistic, quasi-Messiaen colors and, in the broader sense, merging of an international style with national sources. The Polish critic, G. Michalski, sees in Meyer's work a continuation of a monumental dramatic line of symphonic writing that stretches from Beethoven to Brahms, and in the 20th century, from Mahler to Shostakovich.[17]

In the *Third Symphony*, principles of symphonic and oratorial composition are uniquely combined. Here, we are dealing not only with oratorial factors. Often the literary element is separated from the musical and forms

III. Music of the Third Postwar Decade (1966–1977)

an independent dramatic strand. The influence of French tradition also leaves its mark on the character of the synthesis of the two arts. Expressive potentials of both are exploited, but the laws of musical development are at the head. Let us stress the importance attached to declamation: as the poetic line unfolds, there is a gradual transition from singing to declamation, and then from declamation to speech.

In the climactic episode, the composer injects a new element into the treatment of the speaking chorus. Using the innovative techniques of older colleagues (Lutoslawski's *Trois poèmes d'Henri Michaux*; Penderecki's *St. Luke Passion* and *Dies irae*, et al.), Meyer finds a new noise effect: here in the stretto, 26 voices of a declaming choral mass are layered. The effect arises of verbal heterophony, of mixed sound combinations, while at the same time, mimetic sounds emerge out of illustrational imagery: a depiction of shifting mountains and cliffs.

The French tradition is reflected not only in the generous flow of coloristic sonorism, but also in the inner thematic organization; the prominence of its descriptive, visual, concrete genre images. The inception of a rhythmicized declamation out of fanfares (Nos. 20, 22) was a wonderfully found device: a musical genre giving birth to the non-musical. This kind of transmutation is possible because of the structure of the symphonic material itself: the thematic series are formed into structural models of certain types of summoning signals.

The primacy of the musical element is reflected in the general composition of the symphony. In the coda, the smooth flow of the first fragments is restated in a reverse sequence: i.e. first serial, and then the ringing leit-motif. Meyer's striving for architectonic proportion and symmetry is evident. In the area of dramatic development of the symphony the composer comes up with a wonderful find: after the sonoric declamatory effects, a return to singing in the coda. Here we have the most deeply felt, expressive page of the whole composition. After the complexity of the former development, the language becomes lucid; tonal centers, and tertian-triad formations are stressed. In this quiet contemplative coda, which encompasses all the thematic lines in the symphony, reverence for the singer-artist, a creative genius, is subtly conveyed.

Meyer's talent grows. With each work, he appears as a more mature and wiser artist. The *Cello Concerto* and Concerto for *Trumpet and Orchestra*, the *Fourth*, *Fifth* and *Sixth* symphonies, the *Fourth*, *Fifth* and *Sixth* string quartets, the *Chamber Concerto for Oboe and Orchestra*, and the *Polish Chants* (set to J. Tuwim's verses) for soprano and orchestra, are all landmarks in the artistic evolution of synthesizing new means with traditional forms. Meyer was further enriched as a composer by his work on D. Shos-

K. Meyer with members of the Wilanów String Quartet-Tadeusz Gadzina (violin), Pawel Losakiewicz (violin), Ryszard Duz (viola), Marian Wasiolka (cello). "W.A." 1983.

takovich's unfinished opera, *The Gamblers*, which he brought to completion for production in Wuppertal, West Germany.[18]

Meyer's artistic evolution, not only his changing concept of the cycle and form as a whole, but also the stylistic bases of his music, is best seen in his symphonic works.

In the area of form, the tendency to revise the symphonic cycle continues—a tendency that touched not only Meyer, but other contemporary composers as well. Lutoslawski especially instituted many big changes in the large multi-movement symphonic cycle. To some extent, in his experiments, Meyer emerges as Lutoslawski's follower. The most characteristic feature of the new concept is the transposition of dramatic accents, the sequence of development, the displacement of the principal and secondary movements of the cycle. In other words there is a new kind of direction in the development of the whole, while the fundamental base of the traditional cycle—the large symphonic form, is retained.

Meyer had already found his path of transforming the large symphony when he wrote his *First Symphony*: to call its movements "symphonic movements," or "sonata form" is to stretch a point. However, in the following symphonies, Meyer returned to the contours of a traditional cycle: the *Fourth Symphony* (1975) is a monumental work for a large orchestra. In the *Fifth Symphony*, however, Meyer once more drew away from a cumbersome, orchestral apparatus. This symphony for chamber orchestra comes closer to his quartets while the concept of its five-movement cycle is close to Lutoslawski's ideas: the main accent falls on the finale, where all lines of the previous development are brought into focus. As always in Meyer's works, the connecting link in the symphony is the single leit-motif, a highly dramatic alternative theme.

Most significant is the *Sixth (Polish) Symphony* (1982), in which the composer again returns to the traditional monumental four-movement cycle. Reacting to the historic events which shook Poland at the beginning of the 1980's, Meyer wrote the symphony at the time of the Solidarity "troubles" and martial law. It is an astounding work in its tragic pathos and the intensity of its dramatic tone.

"The *Polish Symphony* is a programmatic work," the composer comments. "It is made up of four movements, containing various quotations, analogies and references . . . In spite of some historical melodies it includes (e.g. *Bogurodzica—The Mother of God*), the composition is about contemporaneousness, the present, the problems that prey on our minds. The *Symphony* is the composer's view of everything we have witnessed and experienced."[19]

The new type of style emerges in its most organic form in the *Sixth Symphony*. It marks all of Meyer's late works, and is most distinct in the *Fifth Symphony* and the *Fifth* and *Sixth Quartets*. Here is a style which could be called contemporary, dramatic, Polish expressionism. It echoes the influence of Shostakovich, Mahler, and Berg, and is reflected through the prism of deeply national traditions. Expressionist sharpness is mirrored here mostly in its themes: gloomy processions, tragic chorales (at times recalling the De Profundis psalm), distorted motifs and timbres. Moreover, the "monologue" manner of statement is absolutely original. It endows the music with a deeply personal character. The whole composition is then perceived as the composer's confession. Slow chorales (first, third movements) alternate with impetuous, "invading" movements (the "angry" scherzo, in the Shostakovich style in the second movement and a march-like finale). Yet, in spite of its tragic intensity, the tone of the symphony is courageous. The chorales, processions and marches have a vivid, national coloration. This truly "Polish" symphony is deeply affecting, astoundingly strong both in expression and imagery. It is a marvelous example of a new, dramatically patriotic symphony.

Kazimierz Serocki—Compositions 1965–1970

In a preceding chapter we discussed the music of Kazimierz Serocki's early, folk-song, and dodecaphonic periods. In the 1960's and 1970's, Serocki showed himself to be an innovator in the area of contemporary techniques in composition. The object of his search, in many instances, was form in composition. Serocki was the first Polish composer to apply aleatory technique to the area of form. *A piacere* for piano (1963), written under the influence of Stockhausen's *Klavierstück XI*, is constructed on a row of segments, whose order the performer may choose freely and change at will. As we can see, Serocki goes much further than Lutoslawski in his understanding of aleatory's influence in the area of composition, and gives the performer equal creative rights—a risky step, which in many avant-garde experiments led to a disintegration of form.

As if sensing the shakiness of his position, Serocki proceeded to mark his scores with a set of directions, whose purpose was to channel the performers' imagination along definite lines. In reality, the composer himself established a plan of possible arrangements of the segments and prefigured the variations in the shaping of the form. In this way, definite limitations are set up, organizing the process of the dramatic unfolding. It is from this same standpoint that Serocki approaches open form even at a later date (*Ad libitum* for orchestra, 1977). But basically, the composer's interests are centered on problems posed by sonorism and particularly by aleatory as a coloristic and formal factor in composition.

Serocki used sonorism as a means for enhancing color timbres and as one of the components in the general sound of the whole, which complements other elements of composition. It is this aspect of sonorism that Serocki employed in a variety of genres: a symphonic cycle (*Symphonic Frescoes*, 1964); a mixed theatricalized cantata composition (*Niobe*, 1966); a concerto genre: *Continuum*—Sextet for Percussion Instruments (1966); *Forte i piano* for two pianos and orchestra (1967); *Swinging Music* for an ensemble (1970); a vocal chamber cycle: *Poezje (Poetry)*, text by T. Różewicz, for soprano and and ensemble.

Gradually, however, the influence of sonorism on the form of composition—that is, on the composition as a whole—became stronger. The form of that kind of composition is realized through a definite sequence of colors from beginning to end. Having mastered segmental composition in the previous period, Serocki remains true to its overall formal concept, and carries over the contours of that form into the area of sonoristic composition, which it could be said, consists of textural-sonoric blocks fulfilling different functions in the general dramaturgic unfolding of the composition. A great mas-

III. Music of the Third Postwar Decade (1966–1977) 143

Kazimierz Serocki, 1968.

ter, with a fine sensitivity to nuances in composition, Serocki feels most at home when he works in a small form. In large forms, he is less successful, since the structure of compositions built on the segmental principle is better adapted to chamber pieces and small-scale compositions. Hence, the vocal cycles succeed better than large works such as *Dramatic Story*, whose form is somewhat loose. And hence also, the composer's predilection for montage techniques and aleatory forms.

Let us stipulate that it is hard to find in Serocki's work supremacy in any one area of compositional or technical principle that belongs to a general system of expressive means. Rather, there is a complex interaction and interweaving of various means that result in an original polystylistic phenomenon. Thus, from 1965 to the late 1970's the serial principle is eccentrically combined with colorful sonorism. For instance, the line that led to the music for T. Różewicz's *Poetry*, obviously stemmed from two cycles written in the 1950's: *Heart of the Night* and *Eyes of the Air*. In *Niobe*, sonorism is directed towards enriching the genre of the theatricalized cantata. As a means of incomparable power for specific imagery, sonorism endows purely instrumental and symphonic compositions with programmatic features. The usual emotional categories—dramatic, elegiac, capricious—acquire new shadings, and are transformed into ephemeral and elusive fairty-tale images of fantasy. The titles of the compositions guide the listeners' imaginations: *Dramatic Story*, *Fantasia elegiaca*, *Phantasmagoria*, *Impromptu Fantasque*. The search for unusual sonoric sound effects leads the composer to the use of unusual instrumental groupings (recorders, mandolins, guitars) and unusual methods of eliciting sounds. But even these measures do not destroy the framework of accepted genres, be they concerto or programmatic overture.

As we can see, although the direction of Serocki's search changed so often, and although he strove to incorporate new means, yet his work was marked by a balance of compositional elements, and achieved an artistic synthesis of the highest order. These are the qualities which bring his work organically into the general musical scene of the third decade.

T. Zieliński made the following comments about the contemporary quality of Serocki's language and his individual style: "He is an artist who is essentially modern and . . . authentic. His receptivity to new sounds, his refined taste and imagination in this area have been recognized for a long time. His impetuous temperament is evinced in the succession and motion of sonoric figures, in the rich and effective . . . and at the same time, aggressive distribution of impulses and contrasts. The meaning of his composition is motivated more by his spontaneous temperament than by any accepted system or program. An instinctive feeling for form, a wonderful mastery and virtuosity in handling contemporary material complete the resultant artistic whole."[20]

Serocki's compostions may be analyzed from the standpoint of the interaction of various technical and aesthetic tendencies. A typical example of this symbiosis is presented in *Niobe* (for two narrators, chorus, and orchestra, set to C. I. Galczyński's poem, 1966). This composition, a cantata with theatrical elements, is a unique kind of drama that carries an atmosphere of ancient tragedy.

Niobe is divided into several parts, which correspond to acts in a classical drama: I-Recitativo, II-Invocazione, III-Lamento, IV-Antifona. Serocki transformed Galczyński's conception successfully into a thoroughly musical stylization of an ancient drama. The Serocki-Galczyński *Niobe* is a musical-theatrical-literary composition with a definite accent on illustrational moments. Music is one of the components of dramatic action. A combination of different aleatory and sonoristic systems served as the means for creating the expressively eloquent side of this work. A graphic type of notation was used in the score and much space was devoted to the composer's remarks explaining the signs and abbreviated symbols of the notated text.

The sonoric conception is revealed primarily in the treatment of the chorus and orchestra. There are many facets to the function of the chorus. It is: 1) an uninvolved commentator: "the voice of the author." 2) a participant in the action—reacting to what is happening, sometimes by singing. 3) a collective speaker—a Greek actor reciting. 4) finally, the chorus provides sound color—as one more instrument of the orchestra. In order to liken the chorus to a narrator reciting in a declamatory style, the chorus is separated into different timbre groups; for instance: six low basses. Two actors, a man and a woman, also take part in the performance.

Declamation in this composition is interestingly treated; stylized in the manner of antiquity. The use of Greek themes, the recreation of a whole set of features typical of that classic drama, the imitation of its dramatic concepts and techniques, revive the forms and aesthetics of neo-Classicism. At the same time, sonorism, the principle of "sound enhancement" in a composition, appears here as an important form-building element.

The form of free-standing segments containing various sonoric-textural complexes provides the impetus for contrasts to arise, for tension to increase and dissolve. At the same time, the composer tries to incorporate distinctive traditional features of classical tragedy, characteristic melodic turns, by employing specific coloristic devices. For instance, the incorporation of genre in Part III—*Lamento* is signficant. The actress who narrates takes on the role of a mourner. Imitating the manner of Greek tragic actors, she chants the declamatory passages, giving her interpretation of Niobe's sufferings and empathizing with her. The inflections of moaning and crying are recreated in the actress's part.

The sonoric noise-producing strand in the music fulfills expressive-illustrational functions. Imitation of the sound of a howling whining wind describes the environment and sets the stage for the action: deserted space, the suffering mother weeping by the rocks (not really rocks, but Niobe's children transmogrified by Zeus). The chorus's part, too, is mimetic, complementing the orchestra (enunciating consonants, howling, rolling glissandi).

The formation of sonoric development of the piece is enhanced by other means as well. The predominant technique is aleatory with its irregular rhythmic network. Changes in pitch and sound color material are implemented within a framework of disjointed segments. The duration of the segments is timed approximately, measured in seconds by a stop-watch. Thematic organization is phono-sonoric, "textural" throughout. Dynamic development is attained by means of distending the mobile cluster mass.

The sonoric conception of the composition is further enhanced by the placement of the chorus, narrator and orchestra in the performance space: basses isolated in a separate group narrators seated at opposite sides of the stage. A diagram which accompanies the score shows the plan of the stage and how the ensemble is located. Thus, a stereophonic type of sound, characteristics of ancient arena theaters, is ensured. All these different components are combined into an elegant, stylistically integrated whole—an impressive performance, convincing in its unusual system of imagery.

While in large theatricalized forms, the techique of sonoric development carries a somewhat external illustrational character, in a vocal cycle made up of small pieces, its role is purely expressive and musical, identified with the musical form of the composition itself. The composer's understanding of sound color encompasses all elements: pitch, timbre, metro-rhythmics. Serocki also developed a new type of unfolding of the form in time. Its distinguishing feature is the constant renewal of sound-color material; i.e. the centrifugal principle, an unceasing advancement of themes. To some extent this resembles the through form, based on continuous renewal and prolongation of the development. Furthermore, through-development in vocal-instrumental music is tied to the logic of the formation of poetic imagery.

As an example, we can take *Poetry (Poezje)* for soprano and chamber orchestra (1969) set to T. Różewicz's texts. Here are four small scenes, each different in mood. Their attractiveness lies in a refinement of nuance and in the multiplicity of complex symbolic imagery.

The form of the composition is constructed via interlocking contrasting segments. The external aspect of the vocal part in the first song is sinuous in outline, like a dodecaphonic series, and resembles pointillistic contours. Yet this likeness is purely superficial. Each phrase is built on the principle of complementary tones in a free development and all color nuances are expressed in intervallic-motivic relationships of the musical phrase. Hence the disjointed quality of the melody as a whole, its fragmentation and partition by rests. Melody is presented as a sonoric impression of verse. Ex. 37.

Example 37

Unlike the first song, the second song is dominated by repetitions of selected tones and intervals against a contrasting generally mobile, active figurational background. Distant analogies to strophic form arise; to a set of openings—"couplets"—with different subsequent continuations, but similar "cadences." Furthermore, the beginning of each "couplet" stands in contrast to its own continuations: the repetition of one tone and intervallically broad, dynamic continuances. Ex. 38.

Sonoric system is reflected not only in the organization of pitch and time in the solo part, but also in its relation to the orchestra. Subtly coloristic, the orchestra is subject to frequent shimmering color changes. Great care was exercised in the selection of the instrumental complement: woodwinds with saxophone, strings (both groups but no basses), celesta, harp, piano and two groups of percussion which include a vibraphone, bells, maracas, marimba, temple blocks and more. Thus a coloristically effective result is attained. The principle of constant renewal extends not only to pitch, but to the whole timbre fabric. Just as within a segment a tone is never repeated, so changes occur at every moment in figurational formations, in the types of sound elicited, and in the orchestration. That is to say, sonorism affects a broad range of expressivity, including the organization of timbre-textural color.

The specific types of textures for the given imagery bring to mind similar ones in other composers' works (for example, Lutoslawski's *Paroles tissées*). Delicate runs in the harps, and the fluid ringing tones in vibraphone, marimba and bells coexist with rhythmic figurations in the piano, a heterophonic whirling stream in the woodwinds, cluster harmonies in the strings. All these alternate and form an incessant current of music.

Example 38

Vivid contrasts within the consecutive order of the songs are given, in accord with analogous sequences in traditional cycles: the first—a lyrico-contemplative opening song; the second—more lively, excited and with a stirring climax; then the expressionistically sharp third song—full of sound effects, and martellato figurations (this is the dynamic peak of the composition, where the concentration of dark colors and the collision of extremes express a soul's anguish) and at last, in the fourth song—balance re-established, tranquillity regained, a "quiet" finale.

Thus, along with all the new and original features in this vocal sonoric cycle, a line is traced that shows continuity in style, logic in form and direction in development.

Similar tendencies may also be observed in symphonic compositions in the late 1960's and 1970's. In a conversation with this author in 1974, Serocki emphasized that his technique is related to his love for the color of sound (barwa dźwięku, kolor): "color is the foundation of the composition. The conception of form is based on it. Changes in sound color create the continuity in time from beginning to end."[21] From the standpoint of this approach to form, any of the big compositions of the 1970's may serve as an example. Let us take *Dramatic Story* (1971). In type, it is a symphonic poem for a large triple orchestra with four percussion sections. The title definitely evokes associations with the dramtic poem. The dramatic quality emerges in the kind of direction that the development takes: a set of "wave-phases," each one growing in intensity, culminates in a disruption at the dense climax, and leads to a tragic resolution at the end. And although this kind of development, according to Serocki's concepts, is realized via a succession of sound colors, yet more objective laws, independent of the sonoric concept, become apparent, speaking of the more traditional origins of the poem. This connection is the result of endowing the sonoric textural complexes in the illustrational background with thematic functions. Such thematic organization possesses an inner logic of development. Its capacity for regeneration, and for continuously revealing the initially hidden strength of impulsive activity is the underlying moving force of, what is in effect sonoric system of development. Although in its overall development, the solutions in this Serocki composition are, as we already said, less convincing than in small forms.

The poem opens with percussion instruments playing complexes in tremolo. Obscure rustlings and waves of rhythmic impulses soon form distinct, ominous sonorities in low register. Cut-off phrases are exchanged between the piano, double bassoon, bassoons, and later low brass. Layered in multileveled rhythmically different figurations, they created the single swell of the first wave.

III. Music of the Third Postwar Decade (1966–1977)

And so, out of the depth of the thick heterophonic mass a certain melodic line clearly drawn in the strings (No. 16), makes its way to the surface. It is composed of short figures progressively growing into longer motifs. Thus, bit by bit, a theme is gathered, whose connecting links are revealed later in the general culmination of the form. Such is the outline of the opening phase of this melodic wave. The upper tones of the cluster band are clear and distinct. Each is harmonized on the vertical. Ex. 39.

The circular or descending direction of melodic figures relates them to the motif of moaning. Another group of motifs has its roots in different traditions, related to the rhythmo-percussive brass fanfare complexes (Nos. 90–100, 250). Their alternations and combinations is what forms the integrated, uninterrupted unfolding continuity. Analogies to traditional forms appear because the sections of the form are so clearly designated: surging augmentations, culminations, disruptions, renewal of movement. The thematic system is characterized by a well-defined genre and vivid expression (fanfares and moaning motifs) hence the title: *Dramatic Story*.

Thus the coloristic sonoric side of the composition coincides with its expressive side.

To enumerate all the sonoric effects is not necessary. There are no extraordinary innovations; but subtle coloristic discoveries appear in inventive combinations of texture and timbre and in the type of figurations, while illustrational effects are not allowed to overshadow expressive imagery. Quick alternations and the layering of segmental frames, do not hinder the unfolding of the single-movement large form.

The preservation of thematic organization and expressive meaningfulness in composition, the distinctness of the motivic—rhythmic structure of music, the conception of development reveal the continuity of Serocki's works of different periods. T. Kaczyński is right when he writes, "While changing his compositional technique, and sometimes even his style, Serocki always remains himself. This ''sameness' shows itself in that he seems to 'adapt' himself to different trends, yet does not lose his own face and avoids any imitation."[22]

Example 39

Boleslaw Szabelski—Fifth Symphony

The path of Boleslaw Szabelski, a representative of the older generation (1896-1979), was marked by repeated shifts in artistic orientation. As we have indicated above, during the first decade romantic and neo-classic tendencies crossed in his music. On the threshold of the 1960's, he turned to serial technique. However, for a man like Szabelski, whose artistry was crystal pure, there could be no question whatsoever of an automatic acceptance of any technique—the technical system had to correspond to his understanding of the aesthetics of music.

Nevertheless, dodecaphonic methods were often at variance with the formal conception in his works. A pull toward monumental forms, a broad stroke in writing, were always characteristic of Szabelski. The compositional material—fanfare motifs—"summons" according to Szabelski's definition,[23] concrete genres—all of this did not correspond to the essential quality of the post-Webern school of serial composition. A romantically eloquent tone was much closer to him. He was an heir to Mahler, and in part to such contemporary composers as A. Honegger and D. Shostakovich. Hence, the natural return to the large symphony in which different lines from former periods are combined.

The stylistic features of his late period are most apparent in his *Fifth Symphony* (1968). In this single-movement composition, the sonata principle remains as a structural base, in spite of the use of dodecaphony, and the free unfolding of the poem form. Most important here are the strong thematic contrasts and radical transformations of thematic organization, methods used in the construction of large traditional forms. The symphonic apparatus also speaks of its monumental proportions: quadruple ensemble, organ, mixed chorus.

Dodecaphonic methods are evident in the construction of themes and in some techniques of their development. Even the appearance of themes speaks of the intersection of various compositional techniques. The theme is formed on the principle of selected and complementary tones, furthermore, a colorful factor is added, as well as a generic-associative factor, stemming from traditions of classical music.

The structural core of the symphony is found in two contrasting thematic elements:

1) A half-tone chromatic complex, grouped narrowly around the bass center *e*. In the first measures it enters in a dense, prolonged pedal in double basses and organ; out of it crystalize melodic turns in seconds; later they are transformed into crying motifs, into Dies Irae theme, and a chorale.

III. Music of the Third Postwar Decade (1966–1977)

Boleslaw Szabelski, "W.A." 1969

Example 40

2) An active rhythmic fanfare theme; a summons, in which half-tone and disjunct intervals are combined. It is played by trombones and horn (No. 1). A purely national symbolism is attached to the fanfare signals, which recall old reveilles. Ex. 40.

The generic contrast between a summoning fanfare and the sounds of weeping is the basis for the dramatic conflict in the symphony. Unity is achieved in the development via numerous variational transformations of themes. Immediately following the warlike reveille, an expressive philosophically focused theme is sounded, first by the organ, and then by the chorus. This is the first transformation of the opening choral motif (No. 2). The chorus is treated as a special timbre, complementing instrumental colors. The text is treated phonically, vowels are sounded by themselves, only occasionally combined with consonants.

In the development of both elements, dodecaphony on both the horizontal and vertical planes is joined with other technical means, particularly those of aleatory means and sonorism.

The fanfare theme is constantly dramatized in the development. The stratification of the orchestral fabric is characteristic. Here, a contrast is maintained between the level, half-tone scale-like passages, and the short rhythmically active fanfares which are isolated by caesuras. Also, characteristic of Szabelski's expressionistic style is the exploitation of the orchestra's extreme registers, the numerous climaxes, the enormous surging augmentation over long durations of time.

The sharpening of expression is attained by alternately condensing and thinning out impulses, and by focusing on characteristic disturbing signals, which saturate and muddy this wave of sound moving in an irregular but progressive manner. The purpose of the development, however, is contained in moments of clarity. Through the viscous mass of sound in the culminations, a definite motif forces its way to the forefront. Its features are clearly defined and associated with visual images.

Szabelski developed a whole system of such thematic signals, which have established generic traits and serve as "guideposts" in the unfolding process of the musical form. Thus, at the height of the vast culminatory zone

III. Music of the Third Postwar Decade (1966–1977)

Example 41

of the first section, insistent dotted rhythms in the brass are brought out, reinforced by a group of percussion (Nos. 9–11), a variant of the grotesque "march of invasion." This impression is created by aggressive passages in the flutes screeching in the upper registers, by cluster chords booming in lower registers of the organ, and by the declaiming chorus' precise rhythmic figures in seconds, a variant on Dies Irae. The "invasion episode" leads inevitably to a catastrophic disruption: an orgy of noise by percussion soli (No. 13). This kind of effect is Szabelski's contribution to sonoristic Polish traditions.

A new transformation of the first theme comes in the next "requiem episode." It appears as a reaction to the raging force of percussion (No. 15). At first a solo fragment, its function in the form is that of a contrasting lyric episode in a development. The timbres are almost personified. In the woodwind trio each instrument is the carrier of one generic formula attached to it; i.e., two second (semi-tone–tone) melodic turns in the 1st flute, fanfare motion in the 2nd flute, one-tone signaling calls in the 1st clarinet. Individualized voices, refined sonorities, prominent melodic patterns differentiate this fragment from the faceless heterophony of the preceding one. Ex. 41.

The requiem episode leads to generic changes in themes in the recapitulation, where the first fanfare theme is sounded in a transparently clear register in the soli violins and violas, and later in the woodwinds (No. 19). The lyric recapitulation, however, is only the first stage in a new chain of generic transformations of the third section of the symphony. Profound contemplation, pastoral arabesques, episodes of withdrawal alternate with energetic outbursts. Szabelski shows an extraordinary inventiveness in creating multiple variations on summoning fanfares. In the process of transformation, the main purpose of the development is attained: the fanfare theme becomes heroic. But this heroism is also not simple. The final outcome appears in the conjunct motion of the last culmination.

In the coda, a modal clarity emerges, unexpectedly and in the mighty sonorities of the trombones and trumpets, a gigantic reveille is heard. A diatonic trichordal structure underlines the tonal center *D* and highlights the national, historically formed, character of this new variant of a fanfare theme.

Example 42

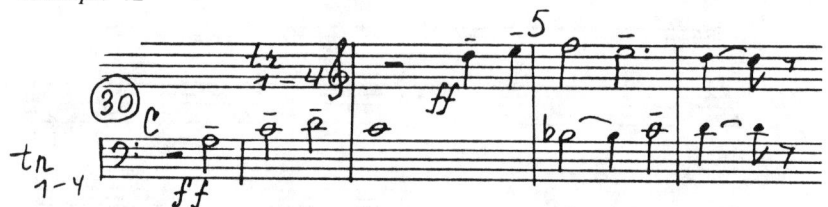

Szabelski's later style crystallizes in the *Fifth Symphony*. This composition contains the best features of the composer's work: great humanistic content, reliance on a heroic national tradition. The impact of Szabelski's individual approach to principles of conflicting musical form and the expressive fullness of his music are felt in the monumental quality of his symphonic writing.

Krzysztof Penderecki—The St. Luke Passion

The appearance of *The St. Luke Passion* was foreshadowed in the evolution of Penderecki's earlier works. The growth of sonoristic tendencies in his music was paralleled by another line of development tied to classical themes and modeled on traditional genres. For instance: *Emanations* (1958) for two string orchestras used new techniques to obtain new sonorities. During the same period came the more traditional *Psalms of David*, a work for chorus and percussion instruments.

In 1960–61, Penderecki took a sharp turn in the direction of sonorism with *Anaklasis, Measure of Time and Silence, Threnody, Quartet No. 1*, and *Polymorphia*. These were followed in 1962 by *Fluorescences* and *Canon* for orchestra and tape. At the same time, *Stabat Mater* appeared, a direct predecessor of *The St. Luke Passion*. It must be noted that after the *Passion* was written, Penderecki continued his prolonged experimentations in search of effective sonoristic composition; i.e. *De Natura Sonoris* Nos. 1 and 2 (1966, 1970).

Still, in Penderecki's work the *Passion* marks a transition toward a new, idea-oriented stylistic position in which a preponderance of weight is given to humanistic, "eternal" concerns, to universal themes. The *Passion* marked the start of a whole series of oratorial frescoes *Dies Irae, Cosmogony, Morning Prayer, Magnificat* and had a considerable influence on other composers, impelling them to work towards synthesizing monumental forms with new technical means.

The St. Luke Passion was commissioned by the West German Radio Corporation for the celebration of the 700th anniversary of Münster Cathedral. While work on this composition was progressing, Poland was preparing to celebrate in 1966 its 1,000th anniversary. It was this atmosphere which gave impetus to the broad treatment of the theme, pushing it beyond the framework of the story of the Passion.

Penderecki engages in a general discourse about suffering and injustice, the cruel scorn for humanity in ancient times—a scorn still present today. This conversation is also about the flagrant crimes of Nazism, its victims, and the violent conflicts of our times. Themes of redemption through suffering, purification through sacrifice, catharsis, as well as motifs of a philosophical religious nature and humanistic themes, have been present in art in all ages. The triumph of spirit over death, good over evil, goodwill over Nazism—these topics are constantly sounded in Penderecki's works during the period of 1960–1970.

Numerous ties with traditional Passion music do not prevent Penderecki from treating this genre in an original contemporary way. L. Erhardt, in his book "Meetings with Krzysztof Penderecki," points out an interesting parallel between this work and J.S. Bach's *St. Matthew* and *St. John Passions*. Penderecki's composition is rooted in older sources stemming back to Schütz and pre-Schütz music of the Baroque era.[24] Schütz developed the old responsorial type of Passion music built on monody, on liturgical singing and medieval modes. Aiming to recount the events of the drama objectively, Schütz minimizes the personal voice of the composer, thus limiting the expressive side of the statement. Besides the responsorial type of Passion music, in which the dialogue between solos and choruses (turbae) was juxtaposed, there also existed the motet type of Catholic Passion music, in which the development of all the parts was subject to complete polyphonic treatment, giving birth to a flexible form and above all, creating a greater mobility and variety in the rhythmic structure, thus replacing the former rigidly measured manner of treatment.

As to the texts of the various Passions—there are cases in which excerpts from all four Gospels exist in the same libretto. (*Summa Passions*, Obrecht-Longaval, 16th century. In the 18th century, Bach developed a different, oratorio type of *Passion*).

The *St. Luke Passion* shows Penderecki's profound knowledge of all these treatments. In his *Passion*, various traditions of both pre-Bach and Bach eras are interwoven. As in the Catholic motet Passion music, one finds here Latin, polyphonic treatment of material, and a fluid development. Some particular features in the use of language peculiar to Penderecki arise in some of his earlier compositions as well, and may stem from Latin prosody and metrics. In some sections, this can be seen in the elongation of certain

Krzysztof Penderecki conducting of his opera *Paradise Lost. Sacra rappresentazione.* "W.A." 1979.

sounds and a flowing psalmody; in others, in metric regularity. Penderecki borrowed the responsorial principle, the antiphonal division of the chorus and the theatrical element of drama from German Passion music. From the Schütz and Bach Passions stems the rich combination of diverse components of dramatic action: the co-existence of different styles, and large sections with a continuous development within individual numbers.

Such are the various sources of Penderecki's neo-baroque style, a style, in which classical treatments are synthesized with more recent ones.

In comparing the content of Penderecki's libretto with those of his predecessors, it can be seen that the elements of action that he chooses to use are different. Dramaturgic accents are transposed. Bach tried to follow the Evangelical texts word for word. Penderecki takes liberties, drawing from different religious sources as the need arises: segments from the Gospels of St. Luke and St. John, psalms used in the Catholic Mass and a whole sequence from the Stabat Mater.

Bach's *St. Matthew Passion* gives the most complete account of Christ's Passion. That of *St. John* is somewhat shorter. Both of them are strictly in accord with primary sources. Penderecki's *St. Luke Passion* is the shortest and therefore the most dynamic. In his chorales and arias, Bach made use of texts by second-rate poets, B. Brockes and Picander. Penderecki uses the texts of the great Lenten hymns and laments (Lamento, Stabat Mater) to fulfill the same function of meditational realization and lyrical commentaries on the events.

In the Bach Passions, the Evangelist's part is recitatival. Penderecki substituted readings for recitatives and thus brought in a new stylistic element: dramatic, theatrical, connected to the contemporary concept of the Passion as an epic musical-drama comparable, for example, to Honegger's mystery *Jeanne at the Stake* in which some thematic elements of the Passion, such as the trial, the betrayal and martyrdom also exist.

Thus, many diverse elements belonging to different genres are woven into *The St. Luke Passion*. Its chief determining stylistic features are:

I. In the text according to St. Luke, the action begins on Mt. Olive and ends with the death of Jesus on the cross; but the trial scene, obligatory in traditional Passions, is omitted in the oratorio. This shortens the action to a great extent and focuses it around the figure of Christ. As in older Passions, there are the figures of the Evangelist, Christ, His mother, Peter, Pilate. Except for Christ, who takes a direct part in the action, all the characters bear a general symbolic significance and are seen through the prism of the composer's attitude in arias, psalms, choruses.

II. Penderecki drew the role of announcer-narrator from dramatic presentations. An actor's voice describes the events tensely, urgently, dynamically, much in the manner of a radio announcer. A critic wrote, "At such moments, the Passion becomes something other than itself: part radio-drama, part theater, part illustrative soundtrack to a film whose images are formed in the imaginations of the listeners."[25]

III. The specific genres of certain forms tell how the Passion, the Mass, and the Mystery are interwoven:
   a. Hymns and Psalms (a cappella)—massive choral oratorio-operatic scenes replacing the traditional responsorial turbae.

b. Arias fulfill their traditional functions. In them, the composer makes his personal statement and conveys different images and moods.
c. A narrative "set to music," a technique for synthesizing the arts, literature, music or film, through the narrator's recounting of events. This last device is analogous to the Evangelist's recitatives. Stylistically, too, there is a resemblance here, for the narrator's voice is accompanied by prolonged pedal sounds in the background although some readings remain unaccompanied.
d. The manifold role of the chorus, sometimes serving the function of commentator (the voice of the composer), sometimes taking on the role of "the people," (turbae) (Nos. 10, 19). The function of the composer's commentaries are embodied in established genres: a hymn (No. 1), Psalms a cappella (Nos. 7, 12, 18, 24), Laments (Nos. 6, 11), and the Stabat Mater sequence (No. 22).

Besides these forms, there is a scattering of choral segments in other sections. These segments are developed polyphonic forms of choral music, such as motets and fugatos in the choruses within the baritone's aria "Deus Meus"—No. 3, which is based on a lament; a chorale built on the ostinato "theme of the cross—B.A.C.H." in the soprano aria No. 12, also in "Stabat Mater" and in the finale.

In addition, the chorus is used as an instrument for color texture, attained through unusual articulations and sonorities. And finally, at times, the chorus becomes a collective reader declaiming along set rhythmic patterns.

All these factors form the concept of "The Passion" as a synthesized genre. According to the composer, his "intention" was to move away from a static description, from a retelling of the Gospel happenings. *The Passion* is intended to be a dynamic and even a bloody experience. It is similar to a medieval mystery, which had no "spectators," emotional impact making participants of all those present. Thus, the chorus in *St. Luke's Passion* does not narrate, but participates in Christ's history.[26]

Penderecki's attitude toward text, his use of it in the *Passion*, as in his other works, is very characteristic of him. He has always preferred Latin and the languages of antiquity. Except for the opera *The Devils of Loudun* (adapted from A. Huxley's original work to German and then translated into Polish) the early composition *The Psalms of David* (1958) is almost the only opus using a Polish text. The translation was by Jan Kochanowski. In a collaboration of the art of music and poetry, Penderecki puts music on the front plane. Still, having realized the power of the word, Penderecki chooses texts from classical languages assuming that the subject matter is generally familiar and needs no word for word translation. Not infrequently, he pinpoints attention on the purely phonetic side of a text. Using it as a sonority and treating the text as a color, he emphasizes certain consonants, sibilants and other phonemes.

But the use of Latin in the *St. Luke Passion* stems from a different consideration. The composer turned to the canonical language found from olden times in religious mysteries and Catholic Passion music. By doing so, he underlined not only the Baroque sources of his Passion, but also its universal human, symbolic character. Moving away from the semantics of language and taking into account that his listeners already know the story, the composer concentrates all the attention fully on the musical composition. Here his approach is much like Stravinsky's in *Oedipus Rex* and other compositions of the same type.

The composition of *St. Luke Passion* is based on a through development of action and a combination of epic and dramatic styles. The epic qualities evince themselves in diverse ways: in the tone of the narration, the slow unfolding of the action, the prolonged dwelling on philosophical contemplation.

However, these moments of deep meditations, in which time seems to slow down, coming almost to a still point—these moments are deceptive. Pregnant with huge force, they erupt, revealing Penderecki's talent for dynamic power and strong dramatic expression.

Outwardly, the architectonic elements of Penderecki's *Passion* resemble in many ways those of traditional Passions: the division into two parts; the structure of individual numbers, the alternating solo, spoken, and choral sections; the co-existence of different genres. The unique quality of the *Passion* lies in its material, in its textural quality, and in the techniques Penderecki used to develop it. Here, we do not find polyphony in its traditional guise—the polyphony that flows through the Passions of Bach and his predecessors. There is no fugue in choral scenes. But there is a passacaglia!— and certain polyphonic methods common to serial techniques: inversion and retrograde.

However, the strict rules of dodecaphony are not observed. Imitations and stretti are widely used but also much modified. Beauty of sonority and unusual textures are Penderecki's prime concern. Moreover, sonorities are used to carry an important dramatical meaning. Their full strength is revealed as the action moves towards moments of greatest tension. Such climactic scenes appear in Part I, No. 10, a mass scene before the high priest, and in Part II, No. 19, the culminating point of the dramatic action—a scene in which the crowd, mocking the crucified Christ, is the chief character. The dramatic canvas emerges through the sequential order of numbers which have a genre character. Moreover, the genre sections and the philosophical-contemplative episodes are not distributed equally between the first and second parts of the Passion. In Part I, the meditational arias and choral episodes are woven into the action. Thus Part I contains:

No. 1	Hymn—a choral exposition for the whole work.
No. 2	The Evangelist's Narrative
No. 3	Baritone Aria, "Deus Meus"
No. 4	Soprano Aria
No. 5	Dramatic Scene—The Taking of Christ
No. 6 & 7	Lamento and Psalm a cappella—a stop in the action, while a meditation on the meaning of events takes place.
No. 8	A scene of action—the Denial of Christ by Peter
No. 9	A short aria for baritone; a commentary on events occurring between the two scenes of action.
No. 10	A scene of action: the mockery of Christ before the High Priest.
No. 11	Lamento—for soprano: a continuation of the meditational line.
No. 12	Choral psalm a cappella.

Part I concludes in a dynamic large-scale scene: Jesus before Pilate; the chorus (the people), the soloists, the evangelist and the orchestra all participate.

In Part II, a short opening "The Way of the Cross" for chorus and evangelist leads into a massive Passacaglia, No. 15. A small episode No. 16, "Crucifixion," for orchestra and evangelist precedes the soprano aria, No. 17. This aria marks the lyric center of the second part.

No. 18—a choral Psalm a cappella—a commentary by the composer coming just before the dramatic climax—the mockery of Christ at the Crucifixion, No. 19. No. 20—Jesus Between the Thieves is a continuation of the preceding scene. In No. 21—the Evangelist tells of the conversation between Jesus and his mother (the baritone in the role of Jesus). No. 22—Stabat Mater. No. 23—a short interlude, The Death of Christ—orchestra, arioso for baritone, and the evangelist's narration which leads into the Finale: a choral Psalm in which both soloists and orchestra participate.

Even this cursory glance at the different sections gives some idea of how the dramatic line evolves and where the emphasis fall. The line of action runs throughout the work; in Part I it dominates: Nos. 2, 5, 8, 10, 13, and draws to a conclusion in the tense scenes of Nos. 19-20. Of the four solo arias in the Passions, three (not counting some fragmentary laments) are in Part I: Nos. 3, 4, 9. Only one, No. 17—the soprano aria stands in the second part. This aria becomes the culminating lyric point of the Passion. The philosophic meditational line is generally more developed in the second part

(Passacaglia, Aria No. 17, Stabat Mater, Finale) becoming more lyric toward the end. While the first part of the Passion is dominated by dynamic, active drama, in the second, there is a sharp turn towards a purely musical development. It is here that the large integrated musical scenes are found: Passacaglia at the beginning of Part II, No. 15, and Stabat Mater, No. 22 nearer the end.

The Passacaglia, because of its dimensions, surpasses all preceding sections and is analogous to Bach's monumental choral fugues. A characteristic detail may be noted; Penderecki turned to the old Baroque polyphonic form and used ostinato variations, rather than a fugue, because the Passacaglia form helps to convey the image of meditation as a philosophic postulate, thus focusing attention on its changeless, non-transformable nature. The Passacaglia stands in the middle of a series of numbers centered around the crucifixion, Nos. 14-19. From the still point where Christ's Passion is contemplated and lamented a gradual disruption of balance begins. It grows and reaches a climax in the scene of that despicable action, the mockery of Christ, No. 19.

The remainder of Part II returns to philosophic contemplation. Penderecki's humanistic ideas are underlined in the progression from a grief-stricken lament to a serene hymn. At the center stands the image of the sorrowing Mother: No. 21, the conversation at the cross between the Mother and John; No. 22, "Stabat Mater," the Lament of the Mother; No. 23, the Death of Christ; No. 24, the Finale, a hymn in celebration of hope and justice. With the advent of light, and in harmony with the general lyric trend as the work nears its end, meditational genres appear with greater frequency; the psalms and hymns, seem to echo the opening hymn, No. 1.

The integrated quality of the composition is made possible to a large extent because the thematic material is unusually sparse. Almost all the main numbers are built on two serial rows stated in the first hymn, which functions as an opening and makes an expository statement for the whole work. The design of the first thematic serial row, ascending but turning, winding and yielding in its climb, is based on sad painfully tight intervals of a diminished 4th. This is the theme of death, symbol of the Way to Golgatha. Ex. 43.

The second serial row, which immediately follows the first, is built on centrifugal movement. Moving out of the center in half-tones, it is reminis-

Example 43

Example 44

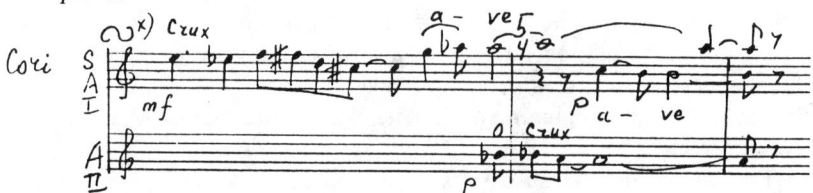

cent of various "themes of the cross." It ends with the symbolic tones B.A.C.H. Ex. 44.

The two serial rows are related through the use of similar intervals. This resemblance becomes obvious in the treatment of the transformations of the series; i.e. inversion, retrograde, retrograde inversion, and the much used diminished 4th and diminished 5th intervals. The character of the transformations draws these two serial rows even closer to the figure of the cross—B.A.C.H. Moreover, at the base of both series lies the same interval, a minor 2nd. In the first row, it is found in inversion, in the second, in its original. The minor 2nd is the building block of most of the themes and numbers, whether in choruses or arias.

The expressive power of this interval is important. That is the reason for its wide use in serial techniques, not only as a minor 2nd, but also in its compound forms as a minor 9th and major 7th.

Example 45

x) ∿ – within the given section the rhytmic values need not be strictly observed.

III. Music of the Third Postwar Decade (1966–1977)   163

The combination of the minor 2nd with a rhythmic fanfare pattern on a single pitch is one of the important motivic conflicts. It is present from the beginning of the work and creates the contrast between the sound of moaning and affirmation. Also characteristic is the development of the chromatic scale which appears almost from the very start. The layering of several lines in their original and inverted forms creates a thick heterophonic texture and eventually leads to cluster formations. Ex. 45.

Besides the treatment of formations of minor 2nd intervals, Penderecki also develops the major 2nd interval, the white-key diatonic, much in the spirit of ancient modes. The first fragment containing a major 2nd appears as a fanfare motif in the quasi-Gregorian Chorale I, a hymn on the text "Fons Salutis." It directly precedes the modal motif of the "Stabat Mater." The major 2nd also lies at the base of the baritone aria "Deus Meus" in which the baritone sings the role of Christ. Ex. 46.

One more motif binds the whole: from time to time, a cadence-like segment on the word "Domine" keeps returning somewhat like a refrain. Its structure resembles an a cappella chorale. Vertically divided into four-parameters, this fanfare-motif moves symmetrically off the central point into a harmonically altered dominant 7th and resolves into a minor triad. The function of this segment is analogous to Bach's chorales, but it is expressed more laconically. It is also reminiscent of the assertive, repetitive ostinato in the finale of Stravinsky's "Symphony of Psalms." Serene hymnology, a tone of devout faith, a sense of completion in the cadence—all mark the chorale "Domine" with universal symbolism and have numerous associations with traditional music. Woven into the narrative seven times, the chorale acts not only as a rondo-like refrain, but serves as a tonal center against a background of atonal music. Ex. 47.

Thus we have the following:
a. intervals of 2nd in fanfares and motifs of moaning;
b. melismatic devices;
c. two serial rows with their usual types of development;
d. monophonic elements, derived from responsorial Passion music;
e. polyphonic elements derived from the German Passions.

The above-mentioned material is developed within a system of contemporary styles in which monody is combined with the most complex

Example 46

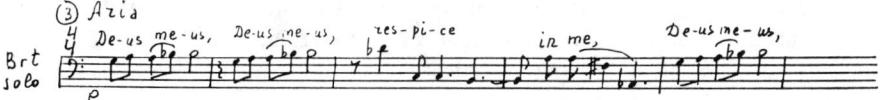

Example 47

cluster-like formations creating the heterophonic tapestry. Such, in short, is the thematic organization of *Passion*.

In contrast to the stepwise melodic content of many choruses, most of the arias are based on a disjunct type of melody. It is characterized by a pointillistic zigzag design and a centrifugal tendency. Here, as in the choruses, despite the thematic contours of dodecaphony, the development of the whole form is not subject to the strict rules of serial techniques. Penderecki employs this technique freely, using only some of the methods for transforming a serial row. For it is the expressive potential in specific models of serial treatment that attracts the composer.

Typically, there is a growing complexity in the relationship of intervals, notably in the solo parts. The composer endows them with a virtuoso character while using a sparse, transparent accompaniment. Such virtuosity has its origin in a specific genre: the improvisational coloratura ''jubilus'', in old arias. But the reason for using these means lies in Penderecki's desire to sharpen as much as possible the picturesque, expressive aspect of the solo parts. Following the Bach tradition, the baritone takes the role of Christ. All the other soloists take on a variety of roles: a woman, Peter, Pontius Pilate, the Thief on the Cross. This may account for the marked stylistic differences in the parts: the Gregorian diatonic of the baritone's part juxtaposed to the expressively convoluted chromaticism of the others. In the soprano part, written with S. Woytowicz's tremendous vocal powers in mind, the contrasts grow, ranging from quarter-tone ornamentations to skips of approximately two octaves. In the conflict between two modal motivic spheres, first one and then the other predominates. But, as a rule, in the end, the tendency is centripetal—steadying, affirmative, an in-gathering force that follows dispersed motion and expressive excitement.

To sum up, in *The St. Luke Passion* we find at least three stylistic tendencies of 20th century music:

1. Neo-Classicism—the revival of classical art in thematics, architectonics, stylistic forms and special language systems, such as modal keys, monodies and others.
2. Expressionistic features, such as extreme sharpness in musical language—a hypertrophy of means used for the purpose of arousing fear, horror, sorrow.
3. Sonorism—if we can say that the first two tendencies are connected to the conceptual side of composition, then sonorism becomes an expressive system serving content. Its arsenal contains orchestral sound effects, speech, and instrumental and percussive type of sounds produced by the chorus.

All these new means connected, for the most part to the color palette, aid in attaining the objective of an organic synthesis of the traditional and the modern.

The fusion of old and the new is demonstrated by both the forms in the composition and by its musical language. At these two different levels of composition, as if in constant counterbalance, two diametrically opposed tendencies are found: centrifugal and centripetal. There is a constant advance, a through compositional technique, not only within the framework of the whole work, but also within particular secondary forms. With this there also exists a pull toward strict organization. Let us note these features: recapitulations, repetitions of themes, leit-motifs, variety as an important form-building element, the principle of common themes, continual transformations. Thus, the ternary form is clearly indicated in the "Deus Meus" and the soprano arias. Recapitulations appear in the finale of Part I. The function of the finale of Part II is to sum up the whole composition. Some critics have even compared it to the Finale of Beethoven's 9th, for in it are gathered all the dramatic threads of the work; basic themes are repeated with a new affirmative meaning. However, mass scenes, large choral episodes in which the crowd is the collective actor in the drama, are structured in a continuous through-composition. Between the dynamics of movement and the stability of general philosophical postulates, there is a complementary and mutually enriching relationship which creates unity and endows the *St. Luke Passion* with universality.

These features are also found at the level of musical language. In the *Passion*, Penderecki decisively moved away from the pure sonorism of the preceding period in his work. He created a flexible, complex system using a wide variety of techniques determined by the expressive potentials of each type of means. The sonoristic effects make their greatest impact in mass scenes. They strengthen the dynamics of the development in the scenes and give a vivid theatrical quality to the action. These representational effects are: laughter, whistles, whispering in the crowd, scanned speech, approaching or receding sounds, spatial stereophonic effects of voices in the crowd, that seem to originate at different points of a city square or the place of execution.

Basically, the means used in the music are both tonal and atonal, yet the pull of the tonal centers is felt throughout the work. Sometimes, these tonal centers take on a unique form, appearing as a wide cluster-stream or as prolonged pedal sounds which are placed at the beginning or end of sections and which hold the development together. In the Passacaglia the function of a tonal center is fulfilled by the thematic series B.A.C.H. in its prime aspect and in its various transformations.

Sometimes the tonic is mobile, changing pitch. This best fulfills the principle of the progress—oriented dynamic movement of Penderecki's forms. The "movable" tonics appear in the large scenes-frescoes, "Stabat Mater" and the finale of Part II. At the beginning of the aria "Deus Meus," the tonality of G-minor is made evident through a prolonged pedal device and an insistent return to the tonal center. The simple epic theme is reminiscent of a Gregorian chant; its nucleus a sequence made up of two motifs of stepwise intervals of 2nds used in a diapason of a minor 3rd. A characteristically recurrent affirmation of the minor 3rd emphasizes the G-minor.

The development in each section, however, often leads away from the tonic, touching on all 12 tones of a broad 12-step atonal scale. The path of these intricate, quasi-dodecaphonic, ornamented solo parts; and the mixed "layering" of the orchestra lead far afield, yet the centripetal tendency always directs the movement back to its base. In the process of development, the tonal center often moves from G to E. Arising first as a temporary tonic in the development and cadences of the choral segment "Domine," the tone E reasserts itself in the reprise, once more affirming the two-fold changeable nature of the tonic.

The theme of "Deus Meus" repeatedly wedges itself into the development of the Passion, preserving its tonal color. But it is typical that the persistent displacements into E leave their mark. In the coda of the Finale, the Passion ends with a stunningly affirmative E-major triad.

The tonal centers of "Stabat Mater" are also twofold since they are changeable and bi-functional. At the beginning, there is a "battle" between two neighboring bases, *A-flat*, the tone on which the progressive movement of the sequence begins, and A, which repeatedly insists on a unison. In the second phrase, the base moves to D, which then disappears in a complex cluster texture. But, in the recapitulation a reversal occurs: a return from complex textures to a D major triad. Ex. 48a,b.

III. Music of the Third Postwar Decade (1966–1977)   167

Example 48

In the *Passion* the strict compositional structure works on all the following levels:

a. architectonics of the total composition;
b. secondary forms in interior sections;
c. tonal development.

Thematic links are at times similar to a leit-motif system. Tonality as a definite emotional color appears gradually, fades, and later reappears. Tonal movement has its own logic; arc links appear paralleling fundamental dramaturgical lines, which exist at the highest compositional level.

Let us remember that even in his early works, Penderecki, an extreme avant-gardist experimenting boldly with musical textures, was already stressing the value of a tonal center, the beauty of the major triad, although in the system of sonorism they stood beyond the pale. Still, we have the concluding tonics of *Polymorphia, Anaklasis*, or other polychords that serve the function of a tonic in *Threnody, Fluorescences*, etc.

The return to big humanistic concerns, to large forms, to classical traditions in the *Passion*, and ultimately, its purely artistic merits, and the depth of its music, all determined the significance and success of this work. The *St. Luke Passion* became an important landmark not only in Penderecki's work, but indeed in all Western music of the 1960's.

K. Penderecki—Dies Irae, Oratorium ob Memoriam in Perniciei Castris in Oświęcim Necatorum Inextinguibilem Reddendam

St. Luke Passion generated a set of compositions of a synthesized type, which were related on one side to oratorial genres, and on the other, to church rites and theatrical genres. Outstanding among the latter are *Utrenya—Morning Prayer* (Russian Orthodox liturgy in two parts, 1970, 1971), and *Magnificat* (1975).

Among oratorios, *Dies irae* occupies a special place. It was a noncommissioned work written as a memorial to the victims of Auschwitz (1967). Penderecki was moved to make this personal statement after reading a news item about the establishment of a monument in Auschwitz to the martyrs of Nazism.

The title, *Dies irae*, has no direct relation to its origin, and is only superficially associated with the corresponding part of the Mass. Penderecki's composition is a modern antiwar work on the same level with such works as Picasso's *Guernica*, oratorios like Honegger's *La Danse des Morts*, Milhaud's *Le château de feu—a Fiery Castle*, and Schoenberg's *A Survivor from Warsaw*. The intense expressivity in *Dies irae* may also be compared to certain Nono and Dallapiccola compositions on related themes. But Penderecki moves away from their styles and takes the direction of sharpening both colorful illustrational and pure sound elements. The style of *Dies irae*, like the *Passion's*, has its roots in a variety of sources. Not only some expressionistic features, but neo-classic traits also may be found here. They appear in the use of some forms specifically related to ancient Greek theater (rhythmicized choral declamation), in the universal type of melody, and in the use of classical languages.

The mixture of textual sources in the oratorio is characteristic. Various verses from the Mass, parts of Psalm 114* and the Apocalypse alternate with sections from Aeschylus' *Eumenides*, Louis Aragon's poem *Auschwitz*, Paul Valéry's *Le cimitière marin*, and verses by the poets of the Polish resistance: Wladyslaw Broniewski—*Ciala (Bodies)* and Tadeusz Różewicz's *Warkoczyk (The Pigtail)*. At the same time, Penderecki remains true to his principle of translating the original texts into a unifying language—Latin—and leaves only a segment from *Eumenides* in the ancient Greek. The translation into languages which are no longer spoken is aesthetically debatable. This point was already under discussion in connection with the *St. Luke Passion*. But the composer was guided by two consider-

---

*Psalm 116 in the King James and other Protestant versions of the Bible.

III. Music of the Third Postwar Decade (1966–1977)   169

ations. First, he believed that in speaking of important human problems of a universal nature, it is necessary to use the language of metaphor and symbol, and that the classic Latin and Greek lend a desirable distance in time.[27] Secondly, he believed that by disengaging the listener from the semantic side of the text, he enabled him to sharpen the focus of his attention on the laws of musical development. Then, too, in many places the text is used as a phonic, color element, while the introduction of "Sprechstimme" in the second part injects a theatrical touch.

In the event, the composer took care to see that during the performance of the oratorio, the listeners were provided with programs which carried complete translations. On the title pages of the score, the text is printed in Polish, English, French, Russian and German. It is quite obvious that Penderecki wanted to leave no ambiguities in the text.

Dies irae, to a far greater extent than other oratorial compositions, originates in the style of the composer's sonoristic period. At the same time, this composition is probably the most vivid example of Penderecki's expressionism, expressionism that corresponds to the aesthetic level of the composition. In comparing *Dies irae* to *St. Luke Passion*, L. Erhardt stresses the contrast in how they were conceived and realized. "The *Passion* is filled to overflowing with expressions of patience and grief, while *Dies irae* appears as a symbolic, apocalyptic image of the triumph of life over death."[28]

In *Dies irae*, as in Penderecki's preceding compositions, connections with traditional generic forms are retained in spite of innovative complexities in the area of means. Above all, such characteristics of oratorial form as universality, laconic statements, a bold placard style of execution are all vividly expressed. In contrast to *St. Luke Passion*, where epic length and a full unfolding of the form dominate, everything in *Dies irae* is compressed to the limit. Each of the three parts of the oratorio has its own system of imagery, its own type of expression, its own specific structure. Each part is prefaced with its own type of epigraph—"a motto"—predetermining the circle of its expressive means. In the center of each part, there is a solo aria, framed by choruses.

Part I is dominated by threnodies. We have already encountered similar generic forms in Penderecki's earlier compositions on the same kind of themes (Threnody to the Victims of Hiroshima; some scenes in the Passion, Utrenya). Part I is titled Lamentatio; its "motto" is "The sorrows of death compassed me" (Psalm 114). Texts from poems by Broniewski, Aragon, Różewicz follow, and form the base of this section. An original refrain appears here, a psalmodic phrase sung in unison by a men's chorus (quasi una litania) on the words "Corpora parvolorum" ("Bodies of Children"). Later the same refrain reappears throughout the oratorio. Sinister scenes of the daily life in concentration camps are depicted by acutely expressionistic means. Choral psalmodies that seem to congeal resemble liturgies for the dead: dark prolonged pedals in low basses increase in volume, as if amplified by echo, and then die out—an effect produced by an open sound changing to a closed one (bocca chiusa). Ominous percussive knocking, funereal bell-ringing, shrieking brass cluster—such are the sonoric-illustrational means of this section.

As in other Penderecki compositions, the instrumental ensemble was selected with great care. Timbres were chosen which would stimulate the visual associative element in the imagination. Not without reason were the clarinets replaced by saxophones with their specific color, or the brass section augmented (two tubas), and the number of low register instruments greatly increased, while the violins and violas were taken out of the string section. The percussion group, too, was augmented (six timpanis, for instance), and special timbres added: gongs, tam-tams. Unusual sound sources of a non-musical type were introduced: siren, lastra (thunder machine), a whip, metal chains; all used to create an impression of grim horror.

The color timbre palette is not the only expressive means; the markedly broken design of the musical themes further strengthens the expression. In spite of the absence of serial technique in *Dies irae*, Penderecki uses his typical pointillistic themes, which either move in disjunct intervals by minor 2nd, minor 9th, major 7th, and tritone, or radiate from the center (centrifugally) in symmetrical motion in the chorus, thus forming cluster layers of prolonged pedaled lines. Ex. 49.

In the soprano aria *Ecce famis*, contrasting devices alternate and further strengthen expressivity. The aria's melodic sphere brings it close to a Lamento. Its typical concrete motifs slide fluidly in half and quarter tones. A

Example 49

III. Music of the Third Postwar Decade (1966–1977)   171

Example 50

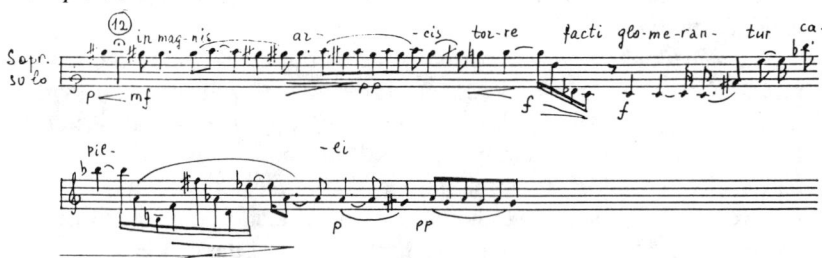

slow trill-like swaying creates the effect of an oscillating reverberation, the sound of weeping multiplied by an echo to which virtuoso passages of decentralized conjunct fiorituras are counterposed. Ex. 50.

Thus the style of Part I, *Lamentatio*, is determined by sharply expressionistic means dominated by unisons and clusters in low, dark registers, heterophonic, floating, phono-type complexes, ominous timpani solos. The wave-like dynamic, the moaning effects, a grief-stricken numbness, the soprano's cries of despair—all make up the character of a requiem.

Standing as a contrast to the monolithic and homogeneous expression of Part I is Part II, the most dynamic and developed in the whole oratorio. Subtitled *Apocalypse*, its "motto" is: "And the pains of hell gat hold upon me" (Psalm 114). Here is a quasi-theatrical fresco, saturated by mimetic and illustrational sound effects. The depiction of apocalyptic visions of the end of the world, comes very close to the tradtional symbolism of Dies irae (day of wrath). In addition, the composer introduces the Hellenic idea of retribution. Lines from the hymn of the Erinyes in the *Eumenides* serve as a refrain. They are delivered by the speaking chorus with oratorial fervor.

All the means in Part II are sharply exaggerated. The harsh intrusion of the choral mass (whole-tone clusters piled one on top of the other), the clatter of percussion (*ff* after *morendo ppp* at the end of Part I)—such a beginning is like a cry of horror in the face of the appalling torments of the ninth circle of hell. Striving to reinforce expressivity, Penderecki employed certain complex devices of his truly virtuoso choral technique. The singing and speaking choruses enter at different points, depending on the character of the imagery. They use unusual articulations. By means of extraordinary textural structures, the composer attains impressive effects of inner mobility, of augmenting and waning dynamics. Such, for instance are the thick cluster blocks in the broadest possible range of registers. The mobility of such a mass (24 voices at times, and sometimes even more), is based on irregular accentuations in each group of parts, although the design in individual voices is simple. Sometimes, however, the whole can be made up of the sum of sinuous, multiple figurations (from 12 to 24 voices) mingled in a heterophonic stream.

The same kind of devices permeate the part of the speaking chorus. Moments of organized rhythmic declamation alternate with irregular rhythms in separate voices (No. 2). Here, the element of mimetic sound is stressed. Rustlings, whispers, sussurations, cries, glissando-slides in the voices are powerfully evocative; while the introduction of aleatoric techniques which free voices in the speaking chorus from time relationships is, in itself, a means that enhances the color-dynamic potential of the chorus.

The *Apocalypse* is composed in ternary form. An aggressive orgy of sounds at the opening gives way to the central bass aria: "Nihil horum timeas" ("Fear none of those things"). Once more motifs of moaning and crying are heard. Quarter to semi-tone moans alternate with scanned fanfares that rise in zigzag fioriituras.

The apogee of violence is reached in the recapitulation. To all the other orchestral elements, Penderecki adds a siren. He had already made use of this non-musical "instrument" elsewhere (*Fluorescences*). In the present context, the siren's whining shriek is associated with real events. It recalls the nightmare horrors of war, and sharpens the humanistic anti-Nazi direction of *Dies irae*.

The crowning wreath of the composition is its third part, *Apotheosis*. The theme takes a new turn, unexpectedly life-affirming. The line of the original dynamic development of the oratorio becomes clear: the bonds of death and lamentation in Movement I; the scene of rampant death in Movement II—a metaphor for the battle against fascist bestiality; and Movement III—an ode in celebration of life and victory. Yet in the coda, the refrain "The bodies of children" returns—a call for vigilance on the part of the living, obligating them to remember the lessons of history. It is this sub-text that gives *Dies irae* its modern sound. This oratorio comes closer to immediate realities than do any of Penderecki's other compositions.

The expressive means in the finale, as in Lamentatio, are extremely laconic. Again the strokes grow bolder: the text concise; a "placard" manner, an accentuation of one particular kind of means. The "motto" in the finale is: "Death is swallowed up in victory" (from St. Paul's epistle to the Corinthians). Dramatic threads which are connected to the solo parts are gathered here. The texture clears, the orchestration is sparse. A striving toward stability, centralization, economy of means is felt. The sonority is reduced basically to unisons and clusters.

A soprano aria stands in the middle of Part I; a bass aria in the middle of Part II. The majority of solos in Part III belong to the tenor. In his fanfare-like calls, a dithyrambic note is sounded. The soloists all sing in high, light registers. Jubilus and broad skips over large diapasons are reminiscent of techniques used by orators to bring out key texts through rising inflections and words shouted with great vocal emphases.

The main thought of the tenor's "speech" is contained in the triumphant line: "Absorpta est mors in victoria" ("Death is swallowed up in victory"). The chorus' words: "The wind rises. Let us try to live" (Paul Valéry) are also accentuated by the use of special techniques. In contrast to the preceding mixed and leveled chords (clusters in the harmonium, long pedaled streams of the heterophonic mass in the chorus in bocca chiusa—No. 21), key words are now underlined, brought out in bright, pointillistically disconnected intonations—a device for creating contrast, whose expressive qualities had previously been tested by the composer. The choral unison, which immediately follows, sounds all the more stable and affirmative as it scans and accents separate syllables of the cry: "Victoria!" (precedes No. 22).

With the words of the concluding refrain, "The bodies of children," the traits of a memorial are restored to the oratorio. This kind of conclusion of form traces invisible arcs from the opening to the coda, and gives *Dies irae* its qualities of balance, symmetry and integration.

Dedicating this musical memorial to the martyrs of the Nazi concentration camps, Penderecki showed that the sonoristic technique, like other techniques, may serve as a most vivid kind of means for musical expression, strengthening the composition's impact and revealing more fully its conceptual content.

K. Penderecki—Cosmogony

An oratorial type of vocal-instrumental fresco, *Cosmogony*, appeared on the occasion of the 25th anniversary of the United Nations Organization (1970). U Thant, the Secretary-General, commissioned Penderecki to write the music, thus honoring the Polish composer's achievements. Of all Penderecki's works, *Cosmogony* shows the greatest consistency in the programmatic realization of both his aesthetic and his techniques of vocal and orchestral writing.

The composition provoked serious debates about the relationship between music and text, for here both components are independent and each follows its own line. In making the dramatic line of the literary text run parallel to the musical development, Penderecki summarized his experiments in this area. However, in a work like *Cosmogony*, where the concept is programmatic, masked semantics are more open to criticism, than when they appear elsewhere. The composition consists of short fragments, heard in the language of their origin: Latin, Italian, Russian, English, ancient Greek. The words are those of Nicolaus Copernicus (The Book of Genesis—De revolutionibus orbium caelestium), Nicolaus de Cusa (De docta ignorantia), T. Lucretius Carus (De rerum natura), P. Ovidius Naso (Ovid—Metamorphoses), Leonardo da Vinci (Sul volo), Giordano Bruno (A i principi de l'universo), Sophocles (Antigone) and astronauts Yuri Gagarin and John Glenn. There is no doubt that the text has merits; however, without an accompanying translation, the public is unable to understand it, not only because it is multilingual, but also because of the unusual "montage" technique where separate fragments are sounded simultaneously on the vertical and horizontal planes. Such a method would have created confusion and deprived the words of meaning, even if the composer had made use of texts that were more familiar and comprehensible to the public.

In L. Erhardt's opinion, the composer "in spite of taking increasingly 'literary themes' was on guard against traditional, conventional combinations of words and sound. Such an approach would inevitably diminish the music, reducing its role to illustration, and lead to the interpretation of sound through meanings foisted on it by the text."[29]

Text interests Penderecki as an important component of sonoristic composition. Without attempting to reflect the text in any detail, he tries to convey through music its general meaning, the main idea. This idea is of prime importance to the composer, and his effort to mask semantic meaning is related to his desire to highlight the music. The specific nature of his titles elucidates the philosophically conceived set of compositions and determines the general expression of the musical imagery. For Penderecki, work on a text as the foundation for composition always becomes the point of departure for purely musical architectonics.

The cornerstone of the dramatic conception in *Cosmogony* rests precisely on the interrelationship of separate fragments of the text to each other, and on the musical and literary plan. In contrast to the indistinct fragments, key words which accentuate the basic idea are deliberately sounded, clearly scanned, and emphasized in culminatory sections: i.e., 1) Copernicus' words that the sun is the center of the universe—the culmination of Section I (*Arché*), marked by a brilliant triad in E-flat major; 2) Sophocles phrase from *Antigone*, about the power of the man in Section II (*Apeiron*). This phrase is scanned by the chorus. It appears as a contrast to the heterophonically mixed fragments which border it.

In this way, central ideas are emphasized and elucidated. Let us compare this technique also with an analogous technique in Lutoslawski's composition: his heterophonic mixed masses which compose the fabric of pre-culminatory and post-culminatory moments, serve to emphasize the clear, definite generic aspect of the culminations themselves.

Cosmogony is a single-movement composition, in which the elements of symphonic and oratorial forms are kept in balance. Its philosophic-literary plan calls for two sections. They bear Greek titles: *Arché* (*Genesis, Origin*) and *Apeiron* (*The Infinite Universe*). But the division into sections is purely formal; the second part follows the first with no pause.

The choral and orchestral parts are tightly interwoven, inseparable, since the chorus is used for the most part as an instrumental color. But the solo parts are brought out in vivid, musically differentiated segments whose material differs from the other parts.

Erhardt discerns four contrasting groups of soundings in *Cosmogony*:[30]
1. Static (prolonged sounds, or else multiple sound collections of the cluster type) in chorus and orchestra.
2. Dynamic (fragments of choral and orchestral figurations changing dynamically from *sf* to *subito p* and *f*; the sound elicited in various ways: pizzicato, staccato, legno battuto).
3. A group of noises sound effects produced by unpitched percussion instruments elicited from the orchestra and chorus by various methods.
4. Singing in its traditional sense in the solo parts, and occasionally in the chorus.

Such classifications of sound texture are perfectly acceptable. From the point of view of sonorism, even more detailed classifications exist.[31]

In short, it is possible to distinguish: 1) blurred textures leveled by various means. These appear where semantic meaning is not essential. (In Lutoslawski's works, they occur also in certain types of episodes: preparations for culminations, or post-culminatory fragments); and 2) clear textures with definite contours. Expositional moments belong here (the formation of themes, "static" prolonged pedals, which are layered at the beginning and the ending of sections), and climactic moments where dramatic threads are gathered into the whole and the texture is organized.

Let us analyze the composition of *Cosmogony*. First exposition—Arché. Prolonged "static" soundings of the pedalled type, banding into clusters in extreme registers. They create a sense of infinite space. A primordial environment suggests the genesis of world harmony.

The evolutionary tendency from a center to a diverse mix, creates a second, dynamic type of themes, saturated by rhythmo-percussive elements and mimetic sound effects, as if the whole were shattered and dispersed into particles. In the unfolding process multi-layered bands appear, heterophonic masses ("magma," in Lutoslawski's own vocabulary). These are transitional moments in the development. At times, they appear as leveled episodic fragments; at other times, they become more dramatic. Such dynamic surges, achieved by combining cluster and figurational bands (in No. 10), prepare the way for the colorful culmination in the "purely" orchestral, first section of the composition. A resolution follows—a withdrawal. The basses enter, and the texture clears. These means are analogous to a traditional orchestral diminuendo (No. 12).

The chorus' entrance in phonically heterophonic leveled complexes appears as a second, this time choral, exposition (No. 13). Inner mobility is attained through irregular rhythmics; attacks on phonemes are spaced unevenly. The flow of color changes in the heterophonic magma, the play of percussive-rhythms, the occasional unexpected sound effects—all create a cosmic image. This variegated illustrational mix serves as a preparation for the central culmination in Movement I: Copernicus' words about the sun. Figurations are gathered into compact masses and united in a triumphant, ringing pure triad in E-flat major (No. 20). Next, the soloists enter. Tenor and soprano cry out exultantly in the highest registers: "And there was light!" The means in the culmination are directed towards clarifying textures, accentuating fanfare motifs.

After the culminations, the process reverses itself: decentralization, disruption; again, figurations in different rhythms (a "dynamic group" according to Erhardt). The conflicting elements in the mixture of two different types of materials in the post-culminatory section is characteristic: mixed heterophonic masses alternate with the soloists' clear song-like melody (on Ovid's words from Metamorphoses: "The rising sun shines forth; the darkness has vanished."). This transitional moment marks the turn in the form of *Cosmogony*. Thus, imperceptibly, through the introduction of new thematic groups, begins Movement II: *Apeiron*.

The constant change in contrasting elements creates dynamic transformations reminiscent of the development sections in traditional forms. This type of dynamic method had already been developed by Penderecki in earlier sonoric compositions.

The types of melody in the solo parts are also characteristic of Penderecki. The melodic line is built on extreme contrasts: transitions of the most fluid kind (half and quarter tone, and sometimes, simply a prolonged straight line—one long sound), and on disjunct, angular, pointillistic lines. *Cosmogony* demands a greater virtuosity in the vocal parts than do other compositions with their more common type of difficulties. Here, we see melismas, coloratura passages and figurational fanfare fragments. The thought suggests itself, that the complicated geometric designs of the parts symbolize the ancient Pythagorean concept of the harmony of spheres (see terzetto, Nos. 25-27). The numerous fanfare turns, moreover, speak of

Example 51

brightness, and announce the elevated, oratorial tone of the statements (a celebration of the Universe, in the bass solo, No. 29). Ex. 51.

A terzetto culminates the solo line of the development. What follows is analogous to a traditional recapitulation: registers are lowered; the bass' monologue takes the place of the terzetto. The movement slows down; the clear inflection in the soloist's aria gives way to leveled heterophonic figurations.

Next, come Gagarin's words in Russian ("The flight is progressing well. I can see Earth"), and then Glenn's in English (". . . Oh, the sun is coming up behind me . . . a brilliant, brilliant red!"). Actually, these words dissolve in the choral magma. In this section, it is easy to see how Penderecki, fully aware that the whole text cannot be understood, illustrates the general content in bright colors, and at the same time molds the image contained in the words. At the highest point in *Apeiron*, the chorus scans Sophocles' words on the powers of man ("There exist many potent powers, but nothing is more powerful than man."—No. 35). Here is a purely theatrical device, stressing the combined culmination of musical and literary dramatic strands.

A continuous surge of sound, the introduction of a percussive element, an undeviating ascent in the strings in broad bands of glissandi, all this unites the different stages of the dynamically prolonged culminations and leads into the rich post-culminatory zone (the dynamic recapitulation of the work). The heightened tone towards the end of a composition, is a characteristic which Penderecki's recapitulations share. But, while in compositions related to religious themes, an ecstatic tone indirectly answered to a liturgical expression and mood, in *Cosmogony*, as in early sonoristic symphonic pieces, what is felt, is an elevation of the human spirit, a state of oneness with nature. Recalling the programmatic titles of the early poems (*Anaklasis, Fluorescences*, and others), it is possible to conclude that even then, the "cosmic" theme enticed the composer. Sonorism became the powerful expressive means which corresponded to the symbolic imagery of his chosen theme. From this point of view, one can question the opinion of those critics, who emphasize the influence of Catholicism on the aesthetic of the composer of the *St. Luke Passion*, and assume that there is a narrow philosophic premise in his work, while actually it reflects life in its broadest aspect.

The crystallization of a sonoristic technique attained during his early and mature periods, and at the same time a complete, thematically substantive line, all define the significance of Penderecki's *Cosmogony*.

Witold Lutoslawski—Preludia i Fuga

For Lutoslawski, 1965–1975 was a period of a synthesis of the highest order; a merging of the best features of music written at different stages of his development. All achievements of the past, his findings in the technique of textural, or limited aleatorism, were subjected to revision from the standpoint of a judicious balance of all stylistic components within the ordered form of a large classical symphony. This was not a return to his earlier classical period. The composer of *Trois Poèmes* and *String Quartet* had travelled too far from that first high point of achievement, the *Concerto for Orchestra*. Yet, unquestionably, the aesthetic premises of that period reappear, although on a new level. They are best seen in Lutoslawski's persistent search for his own particular variant of the large form, and for the type of means which would adequately serve its expression. Lutoslawski develops and polishes his stylistic conceptions over a period of several years. The first sign of a new turn on this path comes in the form of *Three Postludes* (1958–60). This rather small cycle of separate orchestral pieces was an inconclusive attempt to create a multi-sectional composition whose parts, definitely coordinated, each with its own textural, thematically selfstanding imagery, would yet be functionally dependent on the others within the framework of a single large composition. In the *Postludes*, this concept had not yet been completely realized. The composer had limited himself to creating three independent small pieces. The large concluding fourth piece, that was conceived as a summation and finale of a whole cycle, was never completed. Nevertheless, this incomplete cycle is interesting because it became a "laboratory" for new technical devices, the object of a search for new material and its corresponding principles of form-building. Here, for the first time, the type of thematics changed. Intricate complexes of rhythmo-textural, harmonic-timbre, colorful elements began to appear functioning as themes.

The next landmarks on the path of formulating a new conception of large forms were *Venetian Games* (1961) and *String Quartet* (1964). The *Games* is an original instrumental concerto in four movements, whose importance

III. Music of the Third Postwar Decade (1966–1977)   179

Lutoslawski conducting his *Double concerto for Oboe, Harp and Chamber Orchestra*. "W.A." 1980.

lies in its declarative statement that here is a new way of playing: in collective ad libitum. The thematic structure is realized as a process of establishing a theme; the growth of harmony out of the sum of melodies. But despite the novelty of this colorful thematic texture and its unfolding, the movements on the whole, retain the same functions as those in a traditional cycle.

In the conceptions of form the transposition of the center of gravity to a concluding movement, is an idea which is realized in different ways in the *Venetian Games*, *Quartet*, *Symphony No. 2*, *Livre pour orchestre*, the *Concerto for Cello and Orchestra*, and the *Preludia i fuga*.

The *Second Symphony*, a most complex work for large triple orchestra, states the principles of the composition of the extended "closed form" whose theory and practice Lutoslawski developed. He counterposes it to the "open form" extant in modern music, which he calls an "anti-form," or "a collection of events following each other in any sequence."

The concept of a large form at the base of which lie themes, "key ideas," and where the structural plan is founded on various relationships of functionally understood sections, is, in practice, incorporated in all his compositions of that period.

When the *Second Symphony* is compared to compositions of the previous period, it can be seen that something new has appeared in its style. This is also true of the compositions which followed: *Livre pour orchestre* and the *Cello Concerto*. While in *Trois poèmes* and *Quartet*, Lutoslawski tested numerous potentials of aleatory counterpoint in relation to complicated symbolic imagery and found unusually rich color effects, in the *Second Symphony* controlled aleatory technique proved to be inadequate for incorporating the large concepts inherent in the extended form. The composer came to certain conclusions about the natural sphere of influence of textural-aleatory techniques, of the separation of its functions, and the more traditional technique of the common pulse.

Moments that express moods of uncertainty and unformed thought are strictly differentiated from activity, clarity and collectedness.

Correspondingly, two different techniques are combined in the symphony's style: washed out contours produced by non-coinciding rhythms in the voices of the aleatory texture are counterposed to simple, generically defined motifs, which push their way through the unstable magma of this fabric. In *Hesitant* (first section), Lutoslawski exhibits fanfares, trichordal ascetic motifs, lament motifs, grotesque scherzo elements and other themes which evoke powerful associations. This kind of twofold entity lying in the very method of expositional themes already anticipates the closeness of the two dramatic lines: that of veiling the basic idea of the composition in aleatory episodes, and that of making it concrete in climactic episodes (in *Direct*) in the traditional manner of simultaneous playing.

III. Music of the Third Postwar Decade (1966–1977)

At the base of the unfolding of the form lie the transformations of a single timbre-motivic element. It appears in the first segment as an energetic fanfare in E-flat major in the brass. Dissolving soon in the unstable magma of the aleatory texture and losing its vivid summoning character, it is subsequently reborn in the broad unfolding of the finale's cantilena. Acquiring a new continuation in the form of a rhythmic, syncopated figure, the theme gains energy, mobility and provides the stimulus for the ensuing generic transformations. The wave of unswerving augmentation generates active rhythmic march formulas. Gradually the turning point is reached; from colorful sonoristic complexes (lengthy aleatory layers at the start of the finale) via dynamic rhythmo-percussive and tempo shifts during the process of augmentation to the decisive march (a battuta, a return to strict meter at the culmination of the finale).

The transition at the climax of the finale to a traditional kind of playing creates a stunning effect. That talented dramatist, Lutoslawski, was able to calculate exactly how forceful the impact of the contrasting traditional technique would be, and foresaw the impression that the juxtaposition of the two technical systems would create. The return to aleatory anarchy, the shattering of the common pulse in the ensuing moment, bears witness to a catastrophic breakdown, the disruption of the positive element. Thus, thanks to the ability to distribute and balance all the components of the form, thanks to the functional approach to various technical systems, Lutoslawski creates an organically integrated large form capable, in its music, of giving voice to the complicated problems and collisions of our time. From the standpoint of the means found, this symphony points to new possibilities for the development of this genre.

In the next symphonic cycle, *Livre pour orchestre—Book for the Orchestra*, Lutoslawski would consolidate and perfect the principles of form-building and the new relationship between the techniques of common and ad libitum rhythms. In this laconic and concentrated four-movement composition, the idea of alternation and interaction of two different methods of playing, is even more convincing than in the *Second Symphony*. The first three movements—"chapters"—are shorter than the large finale, which, as usual, forms the core of the symphonic conception. The collective ad libitum method of playing is employed in sections which function as episodes, and also at moments that are transitional in character, or represent sharp turning points.

It is worth nothing that in *Livre pour orchestre*, Lutoslawski returns to the expressive side of music, to the broad range of emotion representative of his early works, especially the vocal pieces. The whole tone and the very character of the music now changes. Never before in the works of this period has the thematic material appeared in such a polished aspect. It becomes possible to talk of melody almost in the traditional meaning of the term. It is a melody of process, constantly changing, internally mobile. Its source is vocal cantilena; but its texture distinguishes it from the usual classical melody: the heterophonic voluminous polychromatic fabric is melodic throughout, as though a bunch of melodies were stereophonically layered one on top of the other. The constant unfolding, the progression of these "bundles" generates the form of this expressive, thoroughly gripping work. *Livre pour orchestre* marks the turn towards a new dramatic fullness of style, in which romanticism, expressionism, and impressionism all combine to form a new and amazing character.

This line is continued in the large form works that followed: *Cello Concerto* (1970) and *Preludes and Fugue* for 13 solo strings (1972). In this last work, a certain autobiographical reference to earlier works may be detected. The thematic material is abundant and varied. In many places the themes of previous compositions are almost identically repeated. The conception of form is fully embodied in the given cycle. It is a conception which Lutoslawski had already presented in many variants. The present work is a two-part cycle, in which dramatic weight is unevenly distributed. Seven preludes make up the first part, whose function is analogous to the function of *Hesitant* in the *Second Symphony*: seven preludes—seven impulses to the act, an exposition of numerous contrasting images. The fugue, however, is a large finale, counterbalancing the multi-partite opening half. The extent of the fugal unfolding is unusual. The enormous exposition carries six themes. A great surge of movement leads up to the central climax and then gradually subsides. This type of dramatic structure summarizes the trend in the area of form in Lutoslawski's works of the 1960's and 1970's.

The title, *Preludia i fuga*, is associated with the classic form. Yet, Lutoslawski's composition is substantially different from the usual two-part Prelude and Fugue polyphonic cycle. Instead of one prelude, Lutoslawski introduces seven consecutive pieces; moreover, they are multi-sectional with interior contrasts. The structure of the fugue itself is also unusually free. The sixfold fugue begins with an introduction; numerous transitional episodes have a great importance; the fugue itself concludes in a free contrasting coda. All this moves Lutoslawski's cycle away from the Baroque form. Yet analogies remain, resulting from the assigned roles of the sections. The opening postulate is stated in the preludes. They are characterized by thoughts left half said—a search for the main idea. The fugue is the base, the gravitational center of the form. It is the culmination of the cycle.

But, most of all, Lutoslawski's composition differs from what is traditional in the texture of its music. In it, the composer returns to textural aleatorism, to heterophonic lays. If we are to compare it to polyphony in the usual sense of the term, then we could say that here is the polyphony of complexes: bundles of voices. The multi-rhythmic relationships inside such complexes, however, strengthen the stereophonic divisions, and the distensions of bands. These are characteristics of heterophony rather than polyphony. It is this kind of texture that lies at the base of the preludes as well as the fugue.

The richness of sonority in the strings is extraordinary. Making use of nothing but the usual means of eliciting sound, the composer finds in the new types of texture alone, a tremendous scale of color-hues. A special kind of vibration in the rhythmical network, arising when rhythmically different voices are layered, is combined here with other devices, such as unusual intervallic structures in the material. Every prelude and fugal theme has its own intervallic relationship, its own articulation, its own dynamic plan, its own imagery. Lutoslawski demonstrates the highest mastery in the creation of the extended, through-composed form: the pitch organization at the end of each prelude and the start of the new one is designed in such a way that any prelude may follow any other without detriment to the overall conception. This kind of device makes it possible, under certain performance conditions, to leave out some preludes. But it gives no grounds for comparisons with open form compositions. Chance has no place here. It cannot deform the integrity of the composition. The exact adjustment of interval-sound relationships and the logical succession of the parts determines the constant dramatic unfolding of the whole. However, nothing in this music creates the impression of an artificial intellectually arrived at construction. So great are the music's emotional intensity and expressive qualities that for a listener to remain indifferent or uninvolved is impossible.

On further examination of this work, we see that the thematic material in the preludes is a preparation, made well in advance, for the basic themes of the fugue; a set of arcs in the form is drawn. The opening prelude is an exponent of energetic images, fanfares of the old Polish reveille type. The the-

Example 52

matic developmental process is formed by layering lines on the vertical and, at the same time, unfolding them along the horizontal. The breadth and fluidity of intervallic motion, the volume of dense bands, the undeviating current of sound—all give the feeling of stable strength, of the affirmative quality of the opening theme. After the energetic single fanfares, the music changes, gaining momentum (figurations in the 16th notes); but the broad, bold intevallic motion remains (7th–5th–major 2nd). Ex. 52.

The development motion in the prelude grows out of a row of unfinished beginnings; a striving towards increasingly higher points with accompanying breakdowns. From the first theme of the prelude an arc stretches across to the first transitional episode of the fugue. The contrasting second material is made up of sighing laments, a theme of weeping (see segment *E*), based on fluid glissando slides. It anticipates the third theme in the fugue, *Lamento*. Before us is one of the many Lutoslawski melodies which possess the truly expressive quality of speech. Towards the end of the prelude contrasts appear with greater frequency. A rousing martellato, impulsive and harsh (a 12-tone cluster encompassed on the vertical) arises; but disappears quickly, scattered into staccato fragments, as if the theme had disintegrated into nothingness before one's eyes. The fabric thins out, but the coda is the forerunner of the fugue's scherzo segments.

The variety of the thematic material in the following preludes is also abundant. In the second prelude, another pair of contrasting themes is expounded. The first is a fantastic scherzo, a rotation of somewhat dry scattered pizzicatos; on the second plane: the laments, extremely fluid, gliding in quarter-tones. Lutoslawski considers the quarter-tone system to be complete; a system in which the integrity of each sound and all pitch relationships is retained, and where the nature of the quarter-tone is purely melodic (never harmonic), originating in a vocal source. It is a system which enables the composer to make the smoothest kind of changes from one pitch to another, and heightens the expressive qualities of melody.

Two opposite ways of playing, two dissimilar types of articulations are deliberately combined in the second prelude. And that is exactly what makes it possible to maintain the clarity of the voice-leading, the principle of pure timbre. Both lays can be heard distinctly. Each one anticipates the two corresponding themes in the fugue: the scherzo-like II (*grazioso*) and the lamenting IV (*misterioso*). Ex. 53.

An abrupt break interrupts the full swing of play (see segment *C*). The capricious "dance of the masks" is disrupted, movement fractured and scattered in ringing sounds. The scherzo theme is transformed into an aggressive march, reminiscent of analogous types of fragments in the *Second Symphony* and *Livre pour orchestre*. But even this impulse leads nowhere.

Rhythmic impulses intrude into the Prelude 3. A tremolo-martellato on

III. Music of the Third Postwar Decade (1966–1977)

Example 53

one tone anticipates the VI theme in the fugue. The same method is in effect here as in the preceding preludes: the function of timbres changes. The first material is soon pushed back to the secondary plane, and a broadly unfolding contrasting cantilena, resembling declamatory speech, takes its place. This cantilena foreshadows the fugal transitional episodes. The development follows the same pattern that appears in all the other preludes. There are three stages: 1) an ascent toward the culmination; 2) an expressively intense culmination (an aleatoric group of figurations in high registers); 3) and finally a post-culminatory break-up.

The style of this prelude is characterized by odd flourishes that surround single tones. They resemble the arabesque ornamentations of the Baroque period (see segment *D*). In this instance they appear as a variation on the intoning of a moan. The constant renewal of themes that results from the dramatic unfolding is combined with the principle of economy of material with its obligatory continuation and transformation in the course of subsequent development.

In Prelude No. 4, the ensemble plays together in measure. What is more important here is the vertical harmonic structure. In its fluid collective cantilena lies the half-hidden fantasy of shimmering mirage-like collonnades of quiet chords. This illusory image, borrowed from *Livre pour orchestre*, is destroyed gradually by intruding signals, appearing at first singly, and later in mass. The density of the pulse increases. This serves as a preparation for the incandescent climax (*F*): an aleatoric feverish tremolo played by the whole ensemble, the forerunner of the 6th fugal theme, *furioso*. The climaxes within the preludes form their own particular line of development. Each climax is stronger than the one before; all of which also anticipates the subsequent fugal development.

In Prelude No. 5, a new genre appears: an arioso solo played by the dou-

Example 54

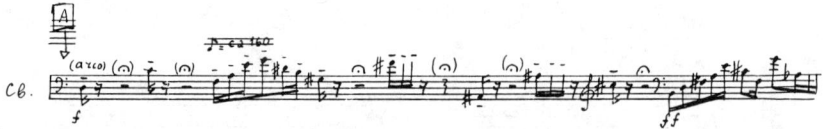

ble bass against a background of light, sparkling pizzicatos in the high strings. Everything in this arioso is unusual: the choice of timbre for the solo, and the type of cantilena; declamatory, fervent, emphasizing broad intervals; a fanfaric motion on harmonic chordal notes: a rare happening in Lutoslawski's works. A special kind of expression, again associated with an orator's declamatory manner of speech, arises. Its effect may be ascribed to the rise and fall of inflections, the speeding up and slowing down of tempo, and to the force of conviction in the delivery of its intonational design. The idea of the juxtaposition of a solo and these specific timbres was carried over from the *Cello Concerto*. Ex. 54.

Once more the dramatic line takes a tragic turn. Suddenly, impassioned speech changes to piteous moans sliding in quarter-tones, and divided by pauses. So expressive are these lamentos in the double bass's highest registers that they almost seem to imitate the sound of human weeping. At the same time, the background of high strings is impressionistically refined, illusively muted and unreal (flageolets, sul ponticello). An arc will stretch from both lines of the corresponding themes in the 3rd fugue, *lamentoso*, and the 4th *misterioso*.

The three last preludes serve as the developmental area for the whole first part. Interrelatedness and a through type of unfolding grow. Prelude No. 6 may be said to be far more evolved than the preceding one. Following the long double bass solo, new voices join: cello and later solo viola and some single violins. Already, we see here grouped solos, a new type of cantilena line made up of multiple, separate voices of the ensemble. Compared to preceding heterophonic "bundles" of melodies in which one main melody was doubled and redoubled, the individual character here is much stronger, the differences between parts much greater, and cantilena (melodic fluidity) is stressed.

Example 55

III. Music of the Third Postwar Decade (1966–1977)

As before, a contrapuntal band in high registers is juxtaposed in contrast to this theme: a row of sharply rhythmic fanfares, conducted in measure. The insistent pulse becomes more agitated and leads to the culmination, *a battuta*. In the course of evolution, the change in development becomes more marked, moving from song-like melodics to percussive rhythms. The final stage of the long culmination is an unexpected generic episode: a strange, grotesque dance in an ostinato rhythm played by 2 celli on a low *c*-sharp. Ex. 55.

There are few themes in the score so obviously associated with concrete images. The composer tries to prolong the theme by a method that in this score is unusual: the fragment is echoed by an aleatory passage, again in the cellos. It is the only passage in the score where the pitch is not fixed but appears merely in graphic outline: thus comes the post-culminatory breakdown.

Prelude No. 7 is launched immediately in a flow of aggressive figurations: an "angry" demonic scherzo. The collective motoric movements and the onslaught of the agitated passages raise tension to a new level and anticipate the most dynamic themes in the 5th and 6th fugues, *estatico* and *furioso*. The combination of a sweeping motoric movement with an *ad libitum* texture (12 voices at once), creates the effect of a rousing martellato: a wild dance. There is no lessening of tension, due to the rotating oncoming waves of passages, and a variety of ostinato figurational models. All this is incorporated in asymmetric simultaneous rhythms.

The final stage of the culmination is again a definitely formed generic episode. Out of the chaotic torrent, reiterative multiplied fanfares enter in 4th's (*J*). The greater the level of activity, the greater the crash that follows. Movement decelerates suddenly. Short fragments, some sounds of weeping and snatches of signals from former episodes, appear as from a distance. It is thus that the synthesized coda of this gigantic, unhomogeneous section of the composition is molded. In its music lies wisdom and philosophic contemplation.

Let us summarize what has been said. Because of the functions assigned to them, the seven preludes form the single large unit of the cycle's first part. Despite its variety, there is a tight fusion of elements arrived at through the inner logic of development and structure. Moreover, all the preludes follow similar compositional models. The overall concept is related to the increase of tension as the cycle draws to a close.

While in the first preludes, expositional type of statments of large scale dominate, in later preludes it is the developmental element that is strengthened; the expression becomes more impassioned. At the same time there is "a modulation of genre" from lamento and cantilena to dance and a scherzo-like element (in Preludes Nos. 6 and 7). The choice of tones at the end of each prelude and at the start of the next is finely calculated. The sum of the tones is usually six (half of the total twelve steps). Thus, an uninterrupted transition from one prelude to the next is realized, and the needed continuity in the type and quality of sonority is secured.

In addition, arcs are drawn on other levels of composition. A crooked graphic line connects the highest points of the preludes, and demonstrates the gradual rise in tension. Also characteristic is the time line: the transition from a deliberate, slowed-down unfolding to a tightened pulse.

Numerous ties exist between the preludes and fugue, not only of thematic imagery, but also of the compositional kind. They are evinced in the consecutive order of the unfolding: the logic of construction in the whole cycle.

As we said before, the differences between this fugue and the classical fugue are vast. In the first place, Lutoslawski's fugue functions as the large finale of a multi-part cycle. Secondly, in its structure the significance of transitional episodes is heightened. They provide the framework for the fugue and serve as connective-transitions between themes and sections. These thematically stable, homogeneous transitional episodes cement the form, link the contrasting themes, and enhance fluidity in the transitions from one sphere of imagery to another. The six themes in the fugue appear as an independent thematic-imagery system. They stand in contrast to each other in the first half, and in the second flow into the constant stream of the unfolding. Actually the model of development of Part I is, to some extent, doubled in the fugue. Indicative titles appear correspondingly in the following order: *cantabile, grazioso, lamentoso, misterioso, estatico, furioso.*

The continuity of the development is also furthered by intervallic-motivic unity of the themes.

The introductory episode appears as a broad stream of fluid cantilena. The full sound flows over a large gamut of registers. The arc here stretches from the 1st Prelude. The themes in the Introduction as in the following episodes of the fugue are all based on a 12-tone row. At the same time, thanks to a deliberate avoidance of chromaticisms, the introductory theme immediately distinguishes the fugue from the material in the preceding preludes.[32] A great sense of space and balance has been created due to the choice of intervals of row: 4th, 5th, 7th. The wide diatonic "white-key" intervals endows this theme with a certain resemblance to the opening march-like theme of the Second Symphony. But in the fugue, the introductory episode is devoid of the symphonic theme's summoning fanfare character. The motion sweeps in the same direction over several intervals, traveling along a broad path that encompasses all the registers. It then ascends to a narrow cluster. The sharply expressive sonority in a high register with no basses recalls

Example 56

Mahler and Shostakovich's expressive timbre techniques. Here, the orchestra plays in a common pulse.

The first theme (No. 1, *cantabile*), continues the same full singing line. However, intervallic content alters its character substantially. The line is constructed like a free twelve-tone series and is prolonged by the repetition of certain groups of tones. What is most important here is that only two intervals are combined: tritone and minor 2nd. A similar structure lies at the base of the theme in *Musique Funèbre*. The similarity between the types of expression in the two themes, both steeped in the elegiac imagery of grief, is emphasized by their common intervallic material. But again how different is the style of the last composition from that of *Musique Funèbre!* Subject, answer, counter-subject—all the voices are doubled or tripled by the bundles of lines. The inner oscillating meter (irregularly accented rhythmic organization) endows these bundles with a sinuous contour, and a stereophonic quality, which further strengthens expressivity. A constant movement is created via canonic imitations, and overlapping stretti. We will compare the fugue's themes (top voice given) to those in *Musique Funèbre* (see Example 15): Ex. 56.

Despite the changes in genre and character, the first four themes continue to present variations on the same tritone and semi-tone intervallic sequence.

A soft dance-like quality, a light, delicate articulation (staccato) marks the second theme (*grazioso*). Its refined fragmentary character bears a light imprint of the New-Viennese school.

The grieving mood of the third theme puts it into the lamento genre. Let us call attention to the increased number of descending minor 2nds; they follow one upon another. This theme echoes one of the saddest episodes in Lutoslawski's compositions: *Funèbre*, in the coda of the *Quartet*. The present theme, encompassing a great mass of voices, is internally more mobile.

The fourth theme introduces changes in the intervallic, structural and articulatory aspects: tritones are filled by narrow quarter-tone intervals. Rhythmically the theme is grouped in a new way: all sounds are repeated twice, and each twofold group (32nds) is separated from its neighboring groups by rests. The spasmodic rhythms, the mysterious, flickering (*misterioso*), seem to dance, but the dance is gloomy and grotesque. The movement is initiated by cellos and a double-bass.

As thematic-imagery moves away from cantilena, contrasts between sections sharpen. Even in transitional episodes, the breath quickens; movement achieves a higher level of activity.

This emotional change provides the impetus for the fifth theme, *estatico*. The furious excitement of the tremolando motoric motion intermingles with rousing scale passages. The basic intervallic "exponent" in the thematic texture is a sharp skip over a major 7th. It is subsequently filled by a brilliant technique of repeated 16th notes, and returns to the starting point. Beginning with the fifth theme, a change takes place in the leading intervallic line. The tritone, as the voice that expresses deep contemplation, or a graceful dancing quality, no longer dominates. Instead, the major 7th becomes the means for stressing emotion. Lutoslawski attaches great significance to intervallic motion and endows it with emotional weight. Here, intervallic motion is tied to textural types, motoric and impetuous, a torrent of miniscule durations. The continuity of progressive movement also increases. It encompasses the sixth transitional episode, where in a new way and in a fast tempo declamatory fanfares are sounded.

The voluminous current flows into the crushing avalanche of the sixth theme (*furioso*). Here is the culmination of the surging wave of all the themes and transitional episodes in Preludes Nos. 4–6. The furious tremolando, the impetuous jumps in tritones and major 7ths, all are swept into the seething avalanche of aggressive movement. High registers with no basses, dynamic *fff*, and articulations are all means that serve the growth of expression. Ex. 57.

Example 57

The developmental section begins as a contrast to elemental fury. It is one of the most deeply felt monologues of the transitional episode (No. 24). After the anarchy of irregular rhythms, here is an episode which is conducted in the usual way. The exciting melody flows in a broad, rounded wave, full of inner oscillations, splashings, alternating progressive movement with stops.

The extensive developmental area travels through several stages. Like transitional episodes, themes are subject to change, their expression enlivened and heightened. Various kinds of stretti are developed. At first, the themes are introduced one by one. Muted, fantastic images predominate. The mood is reflective, contemplative. There is a withdrawal from impulsive motion, and an immersion in deepening meditation.

An outburst of energy marks the start of the expressive culmination (No. 47). A dynamic second stretto (No. 50) is located here. Intruding themes, separated by short intervals, are layered on top of each other on the vertical; the most dynamic types predominate. For the most part, they contain quarter-tones, in both regular rhythm and augmentation. The unfolding progresses from disparity to unity. The importance of the individual elements grows: thirteen independent parts are sounded in the general mass.

The next stage is a quiet, contemplative high point of the whole cycle (No. 54). Against a trichordal, oscillating pedal background, a solo violin is heard playing in a high register. The expressive quality of this pure, singing cantilena is extraordinary. Again a lamento genre appears, but now expressed in a more personal, individual manner. The expressivity of the descending major 7th is sharpened. It is surrounded by sliding quarter-tones; the purely recitatival repetitions of sounds are enveloped in highly fluid transitions. Ex. 58.

The theme of lamentation is developed further here than when it appeared before. The melodic line thickens, and becomes a whole-tone cluster band.

Example 58

The sonority acquires a choral hue. Registers are slowly lowered; the number of voices comprising a "bundle" lessen, and the texture becomes more sparse. Tension slackens. Everywhere the main voice is brought out, dominating in the trichordal and whole-tone oscillating texture. The registers drop to the lowest depths: for the last time, the cellos sound the lament on the 7th (No. 58), which finally dies out in a gloomy whole-tone-tritone complex (No. 59 and 60). Thus ends this large coda episode in sad reflection and funeral song.

But the real conclusion is yet to come. After all sound dies out—a pause—then, unexpected by force of contrast, a postscript: an energetic outburst of affirmation. Constructed along the melodic tones of chords, the declamatory phrase is drawn precisely and concretely. Its intervallic make-up endows it with the character of a resounding fanfare (it moves over the tones of a major six-four chord and ascends to a 7th, 5th). This rather small fragment is the organic summation of the line of the first Prelude and its transitional episode. In this way, the composition is enclosed within a firm, structural framework.

Preludia i fuga once more demonstrates Lutoslawski's extraordinary mastery in constructing large forms. In it the innovative individuality of his style is combined with a classic balance in construction, while philosophic wisdom and depth exist side by side with stirring emotional content.

The music of Lutoslawski and other major contemporary composers of Poland is authentic and valuable, and shows many progressive tendencies. Compositions written since 1965, bear witness to an increasingly artistic understanding of the syntheses of various expressive means, and of the potentials inherent in certain musical forms. The solutions found were convincing to greater or lesser degrees, but on balance enhanced contemporary concepts of form. The composers' deepening interest in the rich world of Polish and European classical traditions can be observed. This trend is evinced in the many ways that composers exploited the forms and genres characteristic of Polish and international heritage. Such an intelligent attitude has appeared in the history of Polish music more than once, giving birth to fruitful solutions and setting a direction to experimentation.

The music of Poland is a phenomenon that is constantly evolving. In it a great significance is attached to the development of new expressive means, which in practice are vividly interpreted. Asserting their artistic ideas, Poland's leading composers of today find a deeply personal, impassioned note. Their devotion to artistic ideals and adherence to unchanging humanistic values unites them and distinguishes their art.

Since this book was completed, new evolutionary processes continue to take place. Outstanding symphonies, operas, oratorios, and chamber music are being composed. During a difficult transitional period in the life of their country, the spontaneous energy, creative strength and personal courage of the Polish composers is reflected in the continuing development of their own particular traditions and the pursuit of their own individual vision in music.

Notes

Chapter III

1 Józef Maria Chomiński, "Przemiany techniki kompozytorskiej w trzydziestoleciu PRL," *Muzyka*, No. 3, 1975, p. 17.
2 A quotation from A.D. Hogarth's preface to program notes for Penderecki's *Diably z Loudun* (Warsaw: Teatr Wielki, 1974).
3 Tadeusz Kaczyński, notes on album cover of the recording of Tadeusz Baird's *Tomorrow*, Muza SXL 1057.
4 Bloch also wrote: the ballets *Voci* (1962), *Bulls* (1965), *Mirror*—a ballet pantomime, music recorded on magnetic tape (1975). His compositions: the musical *Pan Zagloba* (1971) and the cantata *Salmo gioioso*, were produced in a ballet version by the Warsaw Grand Theater (Teatr Wielki, 1972).
5 Tadeusz A. Zieliński, "Grażyna Bacewicz," in: *Spotkania z muzyką wspólczesną*, opus cit., p. 25.
6 Tadeusz A. Zieliński, *Tadeusz Baird* (Kraków: PWM, 1966), pp. 38-39.
7 Janusz Cegiella, "Tadeusz Baird," in *Szkice do autoportretu Polskiej muzyki wspólczesnej* (Kraków: PWM, 1976), p. 24.
8 Tadeusz Baird, "Ya vsegda staralsia byt' chestnym v svoiem iskusstve" ("I have always tried to be honest in my work"): interview with Irina Nikolskaya, *Sovetskaya Muzyka*, No. 10, 1978, p. 127-128.
9 Ibid., p. 128.
10 Roman Augustyn, "O melodyce utworów Tadeusza Bairda" *Ruch muzyczny*, No. 8, 1975, p. 13.
11 Tadeusz Zieliński, "Tadeusz Baird," in Bulletin *Muzyka v Pol'she*, opus cit., pp. 35-36.
12 Krzysztof Droba, "Droga do sensu tragicznego," *Ruch muzyczny*, No. 15, 1978, p. 3.

13 Ibid., see: Max Scheller, "O zjawisku tragiczności," in *O tragedii i tragiczności* (Kraków, 1976).
14 Maria Gąsiorowska, "Symfonia pieśni żalosnych," *Ruch muzyczny*, No. 3, 1978, p. 3.
15 Ibid., p. 5.
16 Krzysztof Droba, "Królewstwo pieśni i księstwo Tansmanii," *Odra*, 6/78, p. 56.
17 Grzegorz Michalski, "Symfonie Krzysztofa Meyera," *Ruch muzyczny*, No. 18, 1971, p. 10.
18 Shostakovich began composing *The Gamblers* during World War II (1942), and completed only a third of the opera. Meyer took on the difficult task of completing the rest of the opera in Shostakovich's style, a task which he fulfilled successfully.

Krzysztof Meyer is author of several monographs on Shostakovich. See: Krzysztof Meyer, *Szostakowicz* (Kraków: PWM, 1973); Krzysztof Meyer, *Dymitr Szostakowicz. Z piśm i wypowiedzi* (Kraków: PWM, 1979); Krzysztof Meyer, *Dmitri Schostakowitsch* (Leipzig: Verlag Philipp Reclam jun., 1980).

K. Meyer after the 1st performance of the Opera *The Gamblers*. Wuppertal, West Germany, 1983.

19 See: Meyer's comments on the *Sixth Symphony* in *Warsaw Autumn* program (1984), p. 181.
20 Tadeusz A. Zieliński, " 'Continuum' Kazimierza Serockiego," *Spotkania z muzyką wspólszesną* (Kraków: PWM, 1975), p. 183-184.
21 In his article, Lyn Davis coins the term "spatial sonoristics" and offers an original interpretation of Serocki's sonorism. See: Lyn Davis, "Serocki's spatial sonoristics," *Tempo, a Quarterly Review of Modern Music*, No. 145, (June 1983).
22 Tadeusz Kaczyński, "Kazimierz Serocki" in *Muzyka v Pol'she*, opus cit., p. 45.
23 *Muzyka v Pol'she*, opus cit., p. 47.
24 Ludwik Erhardt, *Spotkania z Krzysztofem Pendereckim*, opus cit., pp. 78-79.
25 Ibid., p. 84. Erhardt cites here an article: A. Kijowski, "Proby czytane. Sluchając 'Pasji' wedlug Pendereckiego," *Dialog*, No. 1, 1967.
26 Erhardt, opus cit., pp. 77-78. Erhardt cites here an article: R. Wasita, "Awangarda i dziedzictwo," *Polska*, No. 7, 1966.
27 Erhardt, opus cit., pp. 101-102.
28 Ibid., p. 104.
29 Ibid., p. 161.
30 Ibid., p. 163.
31 See: Krzysztof Bilica, " 'Ofiarom Hiroszymy'—Tren Krzysztofa Pendereckiego. Proba analizy jednego z aspektów utworu," *Muzyka*, No. 2, 1974.
32 S. Stucky uses this row as an example in his book (6.23, p. 181).

APPENDIX I
MUSIC AND MUSICAL LIFE IN CONTEMPORARY POLAND

MUSICAL EXAMPLES

No. 1 Tadeusz Sygetyński. March of Peace.
No. 2 Boleslaw Woytowicz. Cantata *The Prophet*.
No. 3 Tadeusz Szeligowski. Opera *The Students' Rebellion*.
No. 4 Ibid.
No. 5 Ibid.
No. 6 Andrzej Panufnik. *Lullaby* for Strings and 2 Harps. Mm. 5-11.
No. 7 Boleslaw Woytowicz. Symphony No. 2 (*Warsaw*).
No. 8 Kazimierz Sikorski. Symphony No. 3 (*Concerto Grosso*).
No. 9 Kazimierz Serocki. Symphony No. 1, Mvt. 1.
No. 10 Ibid., Mvt. III.
No. 11 Kazimierz Serocki. Symphony No. 2. Scherzo: (2) 1st theme
No. 12 Witold Lutoslawski. *Concerto for Orchestra*, Mvt. 2 (theme of *Arioso*).
No. 13 Ibid., Mvt. 3 (theme of *Passacaglia*).
No. 14 Tadeusz Baird. *Four Essays*, Mvt. 2.
No. 15 Tadeusz Baird. Cantata *Egzorta*.
No. 16 Witold Lutoslawski. *Funeral Music*: Prolog.
No. 17 Henryk M. Górecki. *Epitaph*.
No. 18 Henryk M. Górecki. *Scontri* for Orchestra.
No. 19 Krzysztof Penderecki. a) *Polymorphia*; *Fluorescences* (Codas)
            b) *Threnody* (Coda)
            c) *Anaklasis* (Coda).
No. 20 Zygmunt Krauze. *Folk Music*.

Appendix I

No. 21 Witold Lutoslawski. *Three Poems by Henri Michaux*.
No. 22 Ibid.
No. 23 Grażyna Bacewicz. *Concerto for Orchestra*, Mvt. 1.
No. 24 Ibid., Mvt. 2 (Largo).
No. 25 Tadeusz Baird. *Psychodrama*.
No. 26 Henryk M. Górecki. Cantata *Ad Matrem*, 1st theme.
No. 27 Ibid., solo soprano.
No. 28 H.M. Górecki. The *Second Symphony "Copernican"*, Mvt. 1.
No. 29 Ibid., Mvt. 2, solo baritone.
No. 30 H.M. Górecki. The *Third Symphony of Sad Songs*, Mvt. 1, 1st theme.
No. 31 Ibid., Mvt. 1, 2nd theme.
No. 32 Ibid., Mvt. 2.
No. 33 Ibid., Mvt. 3.
No. 34 Ibid.
No. 35 Krzysztof Meyer. The *Second Symphony*, Mvt. 1, main theme.
No. 36 K. Meyer. The *Third Symphony (d'Orphée)*. Motive of chimes (campane).
No. 37 Kazimierz Serocki. *Poetry* by T. Różewicz, No. 1.
No. 38 Ibid., No. 2.
No. 39 K. Serocki. *Dramatic Story*.
No. 40 Boleslaw Szabelski. The *Fifth Symphony*, 2nd motive.
No. 41 Ibid., a development of the 2nd motive.
No. 42 Ibid., Coda.
No. 43 Krzysztof Penderecki. The *St. Luke Passion*, 1st serial row.
No. 44 Ibid., 2nd serial row (with the motive:*B-A-C-H*).
No. 45 Ibid. An example of the choral heterophonic texture.
No. 46 Ibid. The Baritone's aria: *Deus Meus*.
No. 47 Ibid. A choral: *Domine*.
No. 48 Ibid. *Stabat Mater*: a) the beginning
b) the development.
No. 49 K. Penderecki. Oratorio *Dies Irae*. A sample of the choral theme.
No. 50 Ibid. The soprano part.
No. 51 K. Penderecki. Oratorio *Cosmogonia*, Terzetto (in a development).
No. 52 Witold Lutoslawski. *Preludes and Fugue*, the theme of the 1st Prelude.
No. 53 Ibid. The theme of the 2nd Prelude.
No. 54 Ibid. The 5th Prelude. The solo for a double bass.
No. 55 Ibid. The 6th Prelude. A section in the development.

No. 56   Ibid. The themes of the Fugue: (1) cantabile
                                          (6) grazioso
                                         (10) lamentoso
                                         (15) misterioso.
No. 57   Ibid. (19) estatico. (21) furioso.
No. 58   Ibid. The Fugue, No. 54.

APPENDIX II
List of the Works of the Polish Composers*

Grażyna Bacewicz (1909-69). *Orchestral Works*: 4 Symphonies ('45, '51, '52, '53); *Overture* ('43), *Partita* ('55), *Variations* ('57), *Music for Strings, Trumpets and Percussion* ('58), *Pensieri Notturni* for Chamber Orch. ('61), *Concerto* for Great Orch. ('62), *Divertimento* for String Orch. ('65), *Musica Sinfonica in Tre Movimenti* ('65), *Contradizione* for Chamber Orch. ('66), *In Una Parte* for Symphony Orch. ('67).

Concertos for Solo Instruments and Orchestra: 7 for Violin and Orch. (II-'46, III-'48, IV-'51, V-'54, VII-'65); 2 for Cello ('51 and '63); 1 for Piano ('49); for 2 Pianos and Orch. ('66); for Viola ('68).

Stage Works: *Peasant King*, Ballet with libretto by A.M. Swinarski ('53); *The Adventure of King Arthur*, Radio Comic Opera with libretto by E. Fischer after Sigrid Undset ('59); *Esik in Ostende*, Comic ballet in 1 act with libretto by L. Terpiowski ('64); *Desire*, Ballet in 2 acts with libretto by M. Bibrowski after the burlesque play by Pablo Picasso "Desire Trapped by the Tail" ('68).

Works for Choir, Soli and Orchestra: *Olympic Cantata* for Mixed Choir and Orch. to the text from "Ode" by Pindar ('48); *Cantata for Mixed Choir and Orch*. after the drama "Acropolis" by S. Wyspiański ('64).

Chamber Music: 7 String Quartets ('38, '42, '47, '51, '55, '60, '65); 2 Quintets for Piano and Strings ('52, '65); *Quartet* for 4 Vno ('49), *Quartet* for 4 Cellos ('64), *Trio* for Ob., Harp and Perc. ('65); Sonatas and other pieces for different solo instruments; Songs.

Tadeusz Baird (1928-81). *Orchestral Works*: *Sinfonietta* ('49), 3 Symphonies ('50, '52, '69); *Concerto for Orch.* ('53), *Cassazione* per Orch. ('56), *Four Essays* for Orch. ('58), *Variations Without A Theme* ('62), *Epiphany Music* ('63), *Four Novelettes* for Chamber Orch. ('67), *Sinfonia Breve* ('68), *Psychodrama* for Orch. ('72), *Elegeia* for Orch. ('73), *Canzona* for Orch. ('81).

Works for Solo Instruments and Orchestra: *Piano Concerto* ('49); *Colas Breugnon*, Suite in the Old Style for String Orch. and Fl. ('51); *Espressioni Varianti* per vno e orch. ('59); *Four Dialogues* for Ob. and Chamber Orch. ('64); *Concerto* for Ob. and Orch. ('73); *Concerto Lugubre* for Viola and Orch. ('75); *Scenes* for Cello, Harp and Orch. ('76).

Works for Voices and Orchestra: *Lyric Suite*, Four Songs for Soprano and Orch., to the words by J. Tuwim ('53); *Four Love Sonnets* for Baritone and Symph. Orch., to the words by W. Shakespeare ('56, 2nd version '69); *Exhortation* for Reciting Voice, Mixed Choir and Symph. Orch., to old Hebrew texts ('60). *Love Songs*: Six Songs for Soprano and Symph. Orch., to the words by M. Hillar ('61). *Etude* for Vocal Orch., Perc. and Piano ('61). *Four Songs* for Mezzo-Soprano and Chamber Orch., to the verses by Vesna Parun ('66). *Five Songs* for Mezzo-Soprano and Cham. Orch., to the words by H. Poświatowska ('68); *Voices from Afar* for Baritone and Orch. to poems by J. Iwaszkiewicz ('81). *Goethe-Briefe*, Cantata for Baritone, Mixed Choir and Orch., to the words by J.W. Goethe and Charlotta von Stein, selected by the composer ('70).

Chamber Music: *Divertimento* for Fl., Ob., Cl., and Bassoon ('56). *String Quartet* ('57); *Play* for String Quart. ('71). *Variations in the Rondo Form* for Quart. ('78). *Chansons des Trouveres* for Contralto with the Accompaniment of 2 Fl. and Cello, to old French texts ('63).

Works for Piano and Solo Instruments with Piano.

Stage Works: *Tomorrow*, Musical Drama in 1 act for Baritone, Mezzo-Soprano, Bass and Actor. Libretto by J.S. Sito, based on a story by J. Conrad, "Tomorrow" ('66).

Zbigniew Bargielski (b. 1937). *Stage Works*: *The Little Prince*, Chamber Opera after A. de Saint-Exupery ('66). *Danton* after G. Büchner ('68–'69). *Ghosts Do Not Lie*: Tragicomic Opera after S.I. Witkiewicz "The Little Haunted Manor" ('72, 2nd version—'79–'80). *Alice in Wonderland*, Opera for the young after L. Carrol ('71–'72).

Orchestral Works: *Sinfonia* ('56), *Parades 1970* ('70), *Concerto* for Perc. and Orch. ('75), *Concerto* for Vno. and Orch. ('75), *Polish Rhapsody* for Wind Orch. and Perc. ('76), *And They Both Will Flame Up, and No One Will Suppress It* for String Orch. ('78). *Reconstruction of a Picture* for

Orch. ('80), *Nocturne in Blue* for Vno. and String Orch. ('81).
Vocal and Instrumental Works; Chamber and Solo Music.

Augustyn Bloch (b. 1929). *Stage Works*: *Voci*, Ballet in 1 act for Soprano, Baritone, and Chamber Orch. ('62). *Awaiting*, Ballet in 1 act, also a concert version ('63). *The Bull*, Ballet in 1 act ('65). *Ayelet, Jephtah's Daughter*, Mystery-Opera with libretto by J. Iwaszkiewicz after the text from the Bible ('67), *Gilgamesh*, Ballet and Music in the concert version for Symph. Orch. and Men's Choir ('69). *Very Sleeping Beauty*, Opera-ballet-pantomime in 1 act afer Ch. Perrault's fairy tale ('73). *Pan Zagloba*, the Musical ('71). *The Looking Glass*, ballet-pantomime, music for tape ('75).

Works for Orchestra: Dialoghi per Vno ed Orch. ('64). *Enfiando* per Orch. ('70), *Layers of Time* for 15 Strings ('78), *Oratorio* for Organ, Strings and Percussion ('83).

Works for Solo Voice with Orch., including: *Espressioni* per Soprano ed Orch. ('59); *Meditations* per Soprano, Org., and Perc. ('61); *Salmo Gioioso* per Soprano e Cinque Fiati ('70); *Wordsworth Songs* for Baritone and Chamber Orch. ('76). *Just So Music* for Sopr. and Orch. ('76). *Carmen biblicum* for Soprano and Chamber Orch. ('80).

Works for Choir and Orchestra, incl.: *Impressioni Poetiche* for Men's Choir and Orch. ('59); *Warsaw*, Poem for Reciting Voice, Mixed Choir and Orch. ('74); *Anenaiki* for 16-part unaccompanied Mixed Choir ('79).

Works for Solo Instruments (Piano, Organ, Clarinetto, etc.)

Edward Boguslawski (b. 1940). *Orchestral Works*: *Signals* for Symph. Ensemble ('66); *Intonazioni II* for Symph. Orch. ('67); *Concerto per Oboe*, Oboe d'amore, Corno Inglese, Musette e Orch. ('68); *Capriccioso Notturno* per Orch. ('72); *Pro Varsovia* per Orch. ('74); Piano Concerto ('81); *Symphony concertante* for Violin and Ch. Orch. ('82); *Musica Concertante* per Sax. alto e Orch. ('83).

Works for Choir, Soli and Orchestra: *Apocalypsis* for Speaking Voice, Mixed Choir and Instr. Ens. ('65); *Canti* per Soprano e Orch. Without Words ('67); *Sinfonia* per Coro e Orch. ('69); *L'Être* for Soprano, Fl., Cello and 2 Pianos, text by J. Prévert ('74); *Evocations* for Baritone and Orch. ('74).

Chamber Music, incl.: *Metamorphoses* for Chamber Ens. ('67); *Musica per Ensemble MW-2* for Fl., Cello and 2 Pianos ('70), etc. *Beelzebub's Sonata*—chamber opera ('79).

Zbigniew Bujarski (b. 1933). *Orchestral Works*: *Zones* for Symph. Ens. ('61); *Kinoth* for Orch. ('63); *Contraria* for Great Orch. ('65); *Similis Greco I* ('79).

Works for Voice, Choir and Orchestra: Burning Bushes, Vocal Cycle for Soprano and Piano ('58, 2nd version for Voice and Chamber Ens.); *Chamber Composition* for Voice, Fl., Harp, Piano and Perc., 2 Microphones, Amplifier, Loudspeakers ('63). *El Hombre*, Oratorio for solo Voices, Choir and Orch. ('73); *The Birth* for mix. Choir and large Orch. ('83).

Chamber Music: Musica Domestica per Archi ('77); *Concerto* per Archi ('79); *Quartet for the Opening of the House* ('81); *Quartet on the Advent* ('84), etc.

Florian Dąbrowski (b. 1913). *Vocal-Instrumental Works*, incl.: *Litany to the Blessed Virgin Mary* ('47, new version '76). *Frederic's Withdrawal*, Cantata ('49); *Lyrical Cantata* ('66); *Hymn to the Black Madonna* ('81).

Orchestral works; 2 Piano Concertos; Symphony; Children's music.

Andrzej Dobrowolski (b. 1921). *Symphonic Works*: Symph. No. 1 ('55); *Music for Orchestra* No. 1 ('68), No. 2 (*Amar* '70), No. 3 ('73), No. 4 (*A-La* '74), No. 5 (*Passacaglia* '79), No. 6 ('83). Also, music for different instrumental ensembles with orchestra, and solo voices, choir and orchestra.

Music for Tape and Electronic Music, incl.: Music for Tape and Ob. Solo ('65); Tape and Piano Solo ('72); Tape and Dbl. Bass Solo ('77); Tape and Bass Cl. Solo ('80); *S for S* for Tape ('73).

Jan Fotek (b. 1928). *Orchestral and Vocal-Instrumental Works*, incl.: *Epitasis ('67); Musica Chromatica* for String Orch. ('82); *Ode* for Mixed Choir, Soloists, and Orch. ('63); *Verbum* for Mixed Choir, Org., 2 Pianos and Perc. ('67); *Hymne de Sainte Brigitte* for dramatic Mezzo-Soprano and 7 Instruments, after the early medieval Irish texts ('71); *Cantata Copernicana* in the Old Style ('73); *Apostrophes* for Baritone and 2 Pianos ('66).

Vocal works for Choir a cappella (*Anecdotes* for mix. choir, '79); Chamber works; Radio-Operas (*Vir sapiens dominabitur astris*, '73); Stage Works: *Galileo*, Musical Drama, '69; *Spoons and the Moon*, Opera-grotesque, '75; *A Forest Queen*, Opera-ballet for Children's Ens., '77; *Everyman*, Opera-misterium, '83.

Henryk Mikolaj Górecki (b. 1933). *Symphonic Works: 3 Symp.: No. 1 1959* ('59), No. 2 *Copernican* ('72), No. 3 *Symphony of Lamentation Songs* ('76); *Scontri* per Orch. ('60); *Three Pieces in Old Style* for String Orch. ('63); *Choros I* per strumenti ad arco ('64); *Refrain* for Orch. ('65); *Canticum Graduum* ('69); *Old Polish Music* ('69); *Three Dances* for Orch. ('73).

Vocal-Instrumental Works: *Epitaph* (Choir, Orch., '58); *Ad Matrem* (Soprano, Choir, Orch., '71). *Two Sacred Songs* (Baritone, Orch., '71). *Euntes*

Ibant Et Flebant (Choir à cappella, '72). *Amen* (Choir à cappella, '75). *Beatus Vir* (Bar., Choir, Orch., '79). *Miserere* (Choir à cappella, '80).

Chamber and Concerto Music, incl.: *Songs of Joy and Rhythm* for 2 pianos and Orch. ('56); *Concerto* for 5 Instr. and String Quartet ('57); Five pieces for 2 Pianos ('59); *Monologhi* per sopr. e tre gruppi di strumenti ('60); *Diagram* No. 4 for Fl. solo ('61); *Genesis* (I—*Elementi*, II—*Canti strumentali*, III—*Monodrama*, '62); *La Musiquette*, Nos. 1, 2, 3, 4 for different ens. ('67, '67, '67, '70); *Concerto* for Harpsichord and String Orch. ('80). *Lerchenmusik* for Cl., Cello and Piano ('85).

Wojciech Kilar (b. 1932). *Orchestral Works*: 2 Symph.: No. 1 for String Orch. ('55), No. 2 *Sinfonia Concertante* for Piano and Orch. ('56); *Oda Béla Bartók in Memoriam* (Vno Solo, Ottoni and Perc., '57); *Concerto* for 2 Pianos and Perc. ('58); *Riff 62* per Orch. ('62); *Générique* for Orch. ('63); *Springfield Sonnet* for Orch. ('65); *Prelude and Christmas Carol* for Strings and Oboes ('72); *Krzesany*, Symph. Poem for Orch. ('74); *Kościelec 1909*, Symph. Poem for Orch. ('76).

Vocal-Instrumental Works: *Diphtongos* for Mixed Choir and Orch. ('64); *Solenne* per 67 Esecutori (Soprano solo con microfono, Batt., Piano, Archi, '67); *Upstairs—Downstairs* for 2 Boys' Choirs and Orch. ('71); *Bogurodzica (Mother of God)* for Mixed Choir and Orch. ('75); *Grey Mist* for Baritone and Orch. ('80); *Exodus* for Choir and Orch. ('81).

Chamber Music, incl.: *Training 68* (Cl., Tromb., Cello, Piano).

Stefan Kisielewski (b. 1911). 4 Symph. incl.: *Symphony for 15 Performers* ('61), *Symphony in a Square* ('78), and other Symph. and Concertos Works. Vocal Works for Choir and Orch. and for Voice and Piano. Chamber Works. Music for Theater and film. Light Music.

Stage Works: *The System of Doctor 'Tar' and Professor 'Feather'*, Ballet-Pantomime in 1 Act ('62). *Amusement Grounds*, Ballet in 1 Act ('67).

Włodzimierz Kotoński (b. 1925). *Orchestral Works and Concertos*: *Musique en Relief* for 6 Orch. Groups ('59); *Canto* per complesso da camera ('61); *Musica per Fiati e Timpani* ('63); *Concerto per Quattro* for Harp, Harpsichord, Guitar, Piano, and Chamber Orch. ('65); *Music* for 16 Cymbals and Strings ('69); *Concerto* per Oboe (Oboe electrically amplified, also Oboe d'amore, 6 Winds and Orch. '72); *Wind Rose (The Compass Card)* for Orch. ('76); *Bora* for Orch. ('79); *Sirocco* for Orch. ('81); *Terra incognita* for Orch. ('84).

Works for Instrumental Theater with scenario: *Multiplay* for 6 Brass Instr. ('71), *Musical Games* for 5 Players ('73).

Music for Tape: Study on One Cymbal Stroke, Concrete music ('59); *Aela* ('70); *Euridica* ('70); *Herbstlied* for Harpsichord and Tape ('81); *Textures*, Computer music for tape ('84).

Eugeniusz Knapik (b. 1951). *Orchestral Works*, incl.: *La Flute de Jade* for Soprano and Orch. (Chinese texts, '73); *Psalms* for Soprano, Alto, Baritone, Mixed Choir and Great Orch. (Latin texts, '75); *Le Chant* for Soprano and Orch. (P. Valery poem, '76); *Concerto Grosso No. 1* for Chamber Orch. ('77); *Islands* for String Orch. ('83).

Zygmunt Krauze (b. 1938). *Works for Orchestra*: 3 *Pieces for Orchestra* (No. 1-'69; No. 2-'70; No. 3-'82); *Folk Music* ('72); *Piano Concerto* ('76); *Fête Galante et Pastorale* (Orch. and Folk Instru., '75); *Suite de Dances et de Chansons* for Harpsichord solo and Orch. ('77); *Violin Concerto* ('80); *Tableau Vivant* ('81).

Works for Instrumental Ensembles: *Polychromy* for Cl., Tromb., Piano, and Cello (specially for the "Music Workshop" Group formed by Krauze in '63**); *Voices* for 15 Optional Instr. ('72); *Aus Aller Welt Stammende* for 10 Strings ('73); *Idyll* for Folk Instr. and Tape ('74); *Soundscape* (Folk instr. with amplification and tape, '75); *Automatophone* for 6 (3) Mandolins, 6 (3) Guitars, and 1-6 Music Boxes ('74); *Blanc-Rouge, paysage d'un pays* for 4 Brass Orch., 2 Accordion Orch., 2 Mandolin Orch. and 6 Perc. ('85).

Spatial Music Compositions No. 1 (for 6 tapes, '68) and No. 2 (for 2 tapes, '70): for simultaneous and continuous performance with T. Kelm, architect, and J. Morel, sculptor.

Chamber Music, incl. pieces for prepared Piano; 3 String Quart. *Arabesque* for Piano and Chamber Orch. ('83).

Stage Work: *Die Kleider*, Chamber Opera ('81).

Witold Lutoslawski (b. 1913). *Symphonic Works: Symphonic Variations* ('38); 3 *Symphonies*: No. 1 ('47), No. 2 ('67), No. 3 ('83); *Overture* for String Orch. ('49); *Little Suite* for Orch. ('51); 5 *Folk Melodies* for String Orch. ('52); *Concerto for Orchestra* ('54); *Musique Funèbre* for String Orch. ('58); *Three Postludes* for Orch. ('58–'60); *Venetian Games* ('61); *Livre pour Orch.* ('68); *Concerto* for Cello and Orch. ('70); *Mi-Parti* for Orch. ('76); *Novelette* for Orch. ('79); *Preludes and Fugue* ('72). *Double Concerto* for Ob., Harp and Orch. ('80). *Chain 1* for Chamber Orch. ('83), *Chain 2* for Violin and Orch. ('85). *Chain 3* for Orch. ('86).

Vocal-Instrumental Works: *Silesian Triptych* for Soprano and Symph. Orch. ('51); *Children's Songs* for Voice and Instr. ('52); *Five Songs* for Female Voice and 30 Solo Instr. after the poems by K. Illakowicz ('58); *Trois*

Poémes d'Henri Michaux ('63); *Paroles Tissées* for Tenor and Orch., after the poems by J.F. Chabrun ('65); *Les Espaces du Sommeil* for Baritone and Orch. to the words by R. Desnos ('75).

Chamber Music incl.: *Bucolics* for Viola and Cello ('62); *String Quartet* ('64); *Sacher Variation* for Cello solo ('75).

Works for Solo Instruments, incl.: *2 Studies* for Piano ('40–'41); *Variations on a Theme of Paganini* for 2 Pianos ('41); *Folk Melodies* for Piano ('45); *Bucolics* for Piano ('52); *Epitaph* for Ob. and Piano ('79); *Grave* for Cello and Piano ('81); *Partita* for Violin and Piano ('85).

Works for Voice and Piano (Organ), incl.: *Lacrimosa* ('37); 20 *Polish Christmas Carols* ('46); *Children Songs* ('47–'53), etc.

Juliusz Luciuk (b. 1927). *Stage Works*: *Niobe*, Ballet-pantomime in 1 act ('62); *Marathon*, Pantomime for Prepared Piano ('63); *Battleship "Potemkin"*, Ballet-Pantomime in 1 act ('67); *Brand-Peer Gynt*, Mimeodrama ('67); *Death of Euridice*, Ballet in 1 act ('72); *L'Amour d'Orphée*, Opera-ballet in 2 parts ('73); *Medea*, Ballet in 1 act ('75); *Demiurgos*, Opera in 1 act ('76).

Vocal-Instrumental Works, incl.: *Floral Dream* for Voice and 12 Instr. ('60); *Pour un Ensemble* for Speaking Voice and 24 String Instr. ('61); *Poeme de Loire*, 5 French Songs for Soprano and Orch. ('68); *The Mass* for à cappella Choir ('74); *Portraits Lyriques* for Mezzo-Soprano, 2 Vns., Cello and Piano ('74); *St. Francis of Assisi*, Oratorium ('76), and others.

Orchestral Works: Concertos; Chamber Music; Works for Prepared Piano, for Soli and Piano.

Jan Maklakiewicz (1899–1954). *Stage Works: Cagliostro in Warsaw*, Ballet ('38); *The Golden Duck*, Ballet ('50).

Symphonic Works and Concertos: 2 Symph. (No. 2—*Holy Lord* for Bar., Mixed Choir and Orch., '27); 2 Vno. Concertos (No. 1, '30, No. 2—*Mountaineers*, '52); *Concert Overture* ('39); *Grunwald*, Symph. Poem ('39–'44).

Vocal-Instrumental Works, incl.: *Polish Mass* ('44); *Silesia Works and Sings*, Folk Suite ('48); *Suite from Lowitz* ('48), etc.

Artur Malawski (1904–57). *Symphonic and Chamber Music*: 2 Symph. (No. 1–'43, No. 2—*Dramatic*, '56); *Toccata* for Orch. ('47); *Symphonic Etudes* for Piano and Orch. ('47); *Overture* ('49); *Toccata and Fugue in the Form of Variations* ('49); *Hungaria*, Symph. Poem ('56); 2 String Quartets; Trio, Sonatas, Pieces for Solo Instruments, Songs.

Stage Works: Wierchy, Ballet-pantomime ('44–'50)

Bernadetta Matuszczak (b. 1937). *Vocal-Orchestral Works: Septem Tubae* for Mixed Choir, Orch. and Organ ('66); *Rilke's Songs* for Bar. and Orch. ('71); *Elegy of a Polish Boy* for Soprano, Reciting Alto, 2 Women's Choirs, and Orch. ('74); *Canticum Canticorum* for Soprano, Baritone, Alto, Basso, and Orch. ('79).

Voice and Small Ensemble, incl.: *Gitanjali* for Recit. Male Voice, Soprano, Fl., and Bells, to the texts by R. Tagore ('63); *A Chamber Drama* to T.S. Eliot's poem "The Hollow Men" for Baritone, Tape-recorded Baritone, Reciting Alto, Bass-Cl., Cello, Dbl-Bass, and Perc. ('65); *Salmi per uno Gruppo di Cinque* for Baritone, Reciting Male Voice, Harp, Dbl-Bass, and Perc. ('72).

Stage Works, incl.: *Juliet and Romeo*, Chamber Opera in 5 scenes for Actors, Dancers, Mimes, Mezzo-soprano, Baritone, Women's and Men's Choirs and Orch. ('67); *Humanae Voces*, Opera-Oratorium ('71); *The Mystery of Heloise*, Opera ('74); *The Diary of a Fool*, Opera-Monodrama according to N. Gogol ('76); *Apocalypsis*, Opera-Oratorium ('77).

Krzysztof Meyer (b. 1943). *Orchestral Works and Concertos:* 6 Symph.: No. 1—*Four Sections* ('64), No. 2—*Epitaphium Stanislaw Wiechowicz in Memoriam* for Mixed Choir and Orch. ('67), No. 3—*Symphonie d'Orphée*, for Mixed Choir and Orch. ('68), No. 4 ('73), No. 5 for Chamber String Orch. ('79), No. 6—*Polish Symphony* ('82); also *Symphony* in D major in Mozartean style ('76). 8 Concertos: for Violin and Orch. ('65), for Cello and Orch. ('72), for Trump. and Orch. ('75), *Piano Concerto* ('79), for Fl. and Orch. ('83), *Concertos da Camera* per Fl., perc. e archi ('64), per ob., perc. e archi ('72), per v/cello ed orch. ('84), per arpa, v/cello ed orch. d'archi ('84); *Fireballs* for Orch. ('76); *Hommage a Johannes Brahms* for Orch. ('82).

Vocal-Instrumental Works, incl.: *Polish Chants* for Soprano and Orch., words by J. Tuwim ('74); *Lyric Triptych* for Tenor and Chamber Orch., words by W.H. Auden ('76); *Lyrics* for Soprano and Chamber Ens. ('63–'67).

Chamber Music, incl.: 7 String Quart., 5 Piano Sonatas, Piano Trio, *24 Preludes* for Piano, Sonatas and other pieces for solo instr.

Stage Works: Cyberiada, Fantastic comic Opera in 3 acts ('67–70, 2nd version '85); *The Countess (Hrabina)*, Ballet in 1 act on the motives from S. Moniuszko's opera ('80); *The Gamblers*, a completed version of D. Shostakovich's opera, according to N. Gogol ('80–'81).

Krystyna Moszumańska-Nazar (b. 1924). *Orchestral and Vocal-Instrumental Works*: 2 Overtures for Orch. ('54 & '56); *Hexaedre* for Orch.

('60); *Exodus* for Orch. and tape ('64); *Variazioni Concertanti* per Fl. e Orch. da Camera ('66); *Pour Orchestre* ('69); *Rhapsody* for Symph. Orch. ('75); *Intonations* for 2 Mixed Choirs and Orch. ('68); *Bel Canto* for Soprano, Celesta and Perc. (2nd version with Cello, '72); *Polish Madonnas*, poem for Mixed Choir and Orch. ('74); *Challenge* for Baritone and Chamber Ens. ('77).

Chamber Music, incl.: *Music for Strings* ('62); *Interpretations* for Fl., Tape and Perc. ('67), *String Quartet* ('74), *Variants* for Piano and Perc. ('80), and others.

Zygmunt Mycielski (1907–1987). 5 Symphonies: *Polish Symphony* ('51), No. 2 ('61), No. 3—*Sinfonia breve* ('67), No. 4 ('73), No. 5 ('77); *5 Symphonic Essays ('45); Silesian Overture* for Orch. and 2 Pianos ('48); *6 Songs* for Orch. ('78); *Variations* for String Orch. ('80).

Vocal-Instrumental Works, incl.: *Portrait of a Muse* for Reciting Voice, Mixed Choir and 15 Instr. ('47); *New Mazovian Bard* for Soprano, Bar., Mixed Choir and Orch. ('55), *Psalms* for solo Baritone, Choir and Orch. ('82).

Stage Work: Merrymaking at Lipiny, Ballet in 1 scene ('53).

Tadeusz Natanson (b. 1927). 7 Symphonies (No. 3—*John Kennedy in Memoriam*, '65), 2 Piano Concertos, a number of Concertos for other solo instr. Vocal-instr. works; Chamber music.

Stage Works: Quo Vadis, Ballet-Pantomime ('70); *Tamango*, Opera in 3 acts ('72).

Tadeusz Paciorkiewicz (b. 1916). 2 Symphonies ('53, '57); 2 Piano Concertos, also Concertos for Violin, Organ, Clarinet, Trombone, Harpsichord with Orch.

Vocal-Instrumental Works, incl.: Cycles songs for Soloists or Choir with Orch. (*Fatherland*, '62 and others); oratorio *De Revolutionibus* ('72); cantata for Choir a cappella *Chopinesque* ('48); songs for choir from the Kurpie, Mazovia and Silesia regions.

Stage Works: Warsaw Legend, Ballet ('59); *The Maiden from the Dormer Window*, Opera in 4 acts ('64).

Edward Pallasz (b. 1936). *Orchestral Works: Four Old-Fashioned Polish Dances* ('73); *Three Kaszubian Folk Tales* ('75); *Symphony 1976; Violin Concerto* ('78). *TV Opera: Where the Devil Can't,* or *Red Shoes* ('72).

Vocal-Instr. and Choir Works: Fragments to Sappho's Texts ('67); *Lada, Lada* for Lute or Guitar and 24 Voices ('73); *A Black Cloud Near the Forest* for Mezzo-Sopr. and Cham. Orch. ('74); *Pastor ed Magister* for mix. Choir ('79); *St. Barbara's Day* for Solo Voices, Choir and Orch. ('81); *Supplicatio* for Solo Voices, Choir and Orch. ('83); *De Beata Virgine Maria Claromontana* for Mix. Choir ('84).

Chamber Works; Piano Works; Songs for Children, and others.

Roman Palester (b. 1907). *Orchestral Works*: 5 Symphonies ('35, '42, '51—revised '71; '72); *Passacaglia* for Orch. ('53); *Variations* for Orch. ('55); *Metamorphoses* for Orch. ('66).

Vocal, Choir and Stage Works: Requiem ('48); *Sonnets for Orpheus* for Voice and Cham. Orch. ('52); *Songs* after Milosz for Sopr. and Chamb. Orch. ('76); *Te Deum* for 3 Choirs and Instrs ('79). One-act opera *La Mort de Don Juan* ('60).

Concertos and Chamber Works: Concertino for Piano and Orch. ('42); *Serenade* for 2 Fl. and Str. Orch. ('47); *Concertino* for Harpsichord and Instr. Ens. ('55); *Viola Concerto* ('78); String Trios; Piano Sonatas; Works for different solo instr. and ens.

Andrzej Panufnik (b. 1914). *Orchestral Works and Concertos: Tragic Overture* ('42, revised '55); *Nocturne* for Orch. ('47), *Lullaby* for Str. and 2 Harps ('47); *Divertimento* for Str. ('47, rev '55); *Sinfonia Rustica* ('48); *Old Polish Suite* for Str. Orch. ('50, rev. '55); *Concerto in modo antico (Gothic Concerto)* for Trumpet and Orch. ('51); *Symphony of Peace* for Choir and Orch. ('51); *Heroic Overture* ('52); *Rhapsody* for Orch. ('56); *Polonia* for Orch. ('59); *Landscape* for Str. Or. ('62); *Autumn Music* for Orch. ('62); *Piano Concerto* ('62); *Sinfonia Sacra* ('63); *Jagiellonian Triptych* for Str. Or. ('68); *Epitaph for the Victims of Katyń* for Woodwinds, Strings and Timp. ('68); *Violin Concerto* ('71); *Sinfonia Concertante* for Fl., Harp and Str. ('73); *Sinfonia di sfere* ('75); *Sinfonia Mistica* ('77); *Metasinfonia* for Organ, Strings and Timp. ('78); *Concerto Festivo* for Orch. ('79); *Sinfonia Votiva* ('81); *A Procession for Peace* for Orch. ('82); *Arbor Cosmica*, 12 Evocations for 12 Str. ('84); *Metasinfonia* ('85); *Concerto* for Bassoon and Orch. ('85).

Vocal-Instr. Music: Hommage a Chopin for Sopr. and Piano, or for Fl. and Str. Orch. ('49, rev. '55); *Five Polish Peasant Songs* for Treble Chorus and Instr. ('40, rev. '59); *Song to the Virgin Mary* for Chorus a cappella ('64, rev. '70); *Universal Prayer*, cantata ('69); *Thames Pageant*, cantata for young players and singers ('69); *Winter Solstice* for Solo voices, Chorus and Instr. ('72); *Invocations for Peace* for Treble voices and Instr. ('72); *Dreamscape* for Mezzo-Sopr. and Piano ('77).

Chamber Works; Ballets (*Miss Julie*, '70); Piano pieces, and others.

Krzysztof Penderecki (b. 1933). *Orchestral Works: Emanations* for 2 String Orch. ('58); *Epitaphium A. Malawski in Memoriam* for String Orch. and Kettle-drums ('58); *Anaklasis* for String Orch. and Perc. ('60); *Threnody to the Victims of Hiroshima* for 52 Strings ('60); *Polymorphia* for 48 Strings ('61); *Fluorescences* for Orch. ('62); *De Natura Sonoris*, No. 1 ('66) and No. 2 ('71); *Pittsburgh Overture* for Wind Orch. and Kettle-drums ('67); *The Awakening of Jacob* for Orch. ('74); *Intermezzo* per 24 Archi ('78); 2 Symphonies: No. 1 ('73) and No. 2 ('81).

Vocal-Instrumental Works: Psalms of David for Mixed Choir and Perc. ('58); *Strophes* for Soprano, Speaking Voice and 10 Instr. ('59); *Dimensions of Time and Silence* for 40-part Mixed Choir, Perc. and Strings ('60); *Stabat Mater* for 3 Choirs a cappella ('62); *Cantata* in honorem Almae Matris Universitatis Iagellonicae . . . for 2 Mixed Choirs and Orch. ('64); *Passio et Mors Domini Nostri Iesu Christi Secundum Lucam* ('65); *Dies Irae*, Oratorium ('67); *Cosmogony* ('70); *Utrenia*: The Entombment of Christ ('70); *Utrenya II:* The Resurrection ('71); *Canticum Canticorum Salomonis* for 16 Voices and Chamber Orch. ('73); *Magnificat* ('74); *Te Deum* ('79); *Agnus Dei* ('83); Polish Requiem ('84).

Instrumental Solo with Orchestra: Fonogrammi per Fl. e Orch. da camera ('61); *Sonata* per Cello and Orch. ('64); *Capriccio* per Oboe e 11 archi ('65); *Capriccio* per Vno. e Orch. ('67); 2 *Concertos* per Cello e Orch. ('72, '82); *Partita* for Harpsichord, Electric Guitar, Bass Guitar, Dbl-Bass, and Chamber Orch. ('72); *Violin Concerto* ('76), *Viola Concerto* ('83).

Chamber Music: 2 String Quartets ('60 & '68); Solo pieces.

Music for Tape: Psalmus 1961 for Tape ('61); *Canon* for 2 String Orch. and 2 Tapes ('62); *Brigade of Death* for Tape ('63).

Stage Works: The Devils of Loudun, Opera in 3 acts ('69); *Paradise Lost*; Sacra rappresentazione in 2 acts ('78); *Die schwarze Maske*, Opera in 1 act ('86).

Zbigniew Penherski (b. 1935). *Orchestral and Vocal-Instr. Works: Incantationi I* for 6 Perc. players ('72) and *II* for 7 performers ('76); *Mazurian Chronicles II* for Symph. Orch. and Tape ('73); *Radio Symphony* for 2 perf. ('74); *Anamnesis* for Symph. Orch. ('75); *String Play* ('81); *Ostinata* for Mixed Choir and Orch. ('60); *Contrasts* for String Orch., Selected Instr. and Vocal Ens. ('62); *Musica Humana* for Bar., Mixed Choir and Symph. Orch. ('63); *Missa Abstracta* for Tenor, Reciting Voice, Mixed Choir and Orch. ('66); *Cantatina* for Choir and Children's Symph. Orch. ('69); *Hymnus Laudans* for Choir and Chamber Orch. ('70).

Operatic Music: Samson Put on Trial, Radio-opera ('67); *Peryn's Twilight*, Opera ('72); *Edgar, Walpor's Son* ('82).

Music for Unaccompanied Choir, Chamber music, Music for Tape.

Piotr Perkowski (b. 1901). *Orchestral Works and Concertos* (selection): 2 Symphonies ('25, '55); *Sinfonia Drammatica* ('63); *Warsaw Overture* for Orch. ('54); 2 Violin Concertos ('32, '59), Cello Concerto ('78).

Choral and Vocal-Instrumental Works: Cantata *Vistula* ('51); *Epitaph for Nicos Belojannis* ('52); *Wedding Suite* for Soprano, Ten., Mixed Choir and Orch., based on folk Mazovian music ('52); *Cantata 1962; Ode to a Soldier* for Baritone, Reciter and Orch. ('73).

Ballets: Swantewit (1930, new version 1945); *Rhapsody* ('49), *Balladyna* ('60); *Clementine* ('64).

Bronislaw K. Przybylski (b. 1941). *Orchestral Works*, incl.: *In Honorem Nicolai Copernici* ('72); *Guernica—Pablo Picasso in Memorian* ('74); *Sinfonia Polacca* ('78); *Sinfonia da Requiem* ('76); *Sinfonia-Affresco* ('82); and others.

Concertos, Cantatas (incl. *In Memoriam*, '82), Chamber and Solo Works (incl. pieces for Accordion).

Marta Ptaszyńska (b. 1943). *Symphonic Music: Improvisations* ('68); *Crystallites* ('73); *Spectri Sonori* ('73); *Concerto* for Perc. Quartet and Orch. ('74); *La novella d'inverno* for Str. Orch. ('84); *Concerto* for Marimba and Orch. ('85).

Chamber Music and Ensembles with Percussion, incl.: *Spacial Model* for Perc. solo ('71); *Madrigals* for Chamb. Ens. ('71); *Siderals* for 2 Perc. Quintets and Light Projection ('74); *Mobile* for 2 Percussionists ('75); *Quodlibet* for Double bass with tape ('76); *Epigram* for Female Choir and Ens. ('77); *Un Grand Sommeil Noir* for Sopr., Fl. and Harp ('77); *Synchrony* for Perc. Trio ('78); *Two Sonnets to Orpheus* for Mezzo-Sopr. and Chamb. Orch. ('80); *Dream Lands, Magic Spaces* for Vno, Piano, Perc. ('81).

Oscar of Alva, TV spectacle ('72); *Soirée snobe chez la Princesse.* Instrumental Theatre ('79).

Music for Children, incl.: *Colorful World of Percussion*, A book in 5 volumes for Fl., Recorders, Voices and Perc. (Co-author: B. Niewiadomska, '70–'78).

Witold Rudziński (b. 1913). *Operatic Works: Janko the Fiddler* ('51); *The Commander of Paris (Jaroslaw Dąbrowski)* ('57); *The Dismissal of the Grecian Envoys* ('62); *Shulamite* ('64); *The Yellow Nightcap*, Musical-comedy ('69); *The Peasants* ('72); *The Rose and the Ring*, Children's opera ('82).

Orchestral Works, incl.: *Pictures from the Holy-Cross Mountains* ('65). *Oratorios*, incl.: *The Roof of the World* ('60); and *Gaude Mater Polonia* ('66).

Vocal-Instrumental, Chamber Music, etc.

Zbigniew Rudziński (b. 1935). *Orchestral Works: Contra fidem* ('64); 3 *Moments Musicaux* (I—'65, II—'67, III—'68); *Night Music ('70).*

Vocal-Instr. Works, incl.: *4 Songs* for Barit. and Chamb. Ens. ('60); *Epigrams* for Fl., 2 Women's Choirs & Perc. ('62); *3 Songs* for Tenor and 2 Pianos ('68); *Symphony* for Men's Choir and Orch. ('69); *Requiem for War Victims* ('71, 2nd version '73); *Tutti e Solo* for Soprano, Fl., Fr. Horn and Piano ('73).

Chamber Works, incl.: *Impromtu* for 2 Pianos, 3 Cellos and 3 Perc. ('66); *Quartet* for 2 Pianos and 2 Perc. ('69); *Campanella* for Perc. ('77); *Tritones* for Perc. ('79).

Trios; Sonatas for different solo instr.

Stage Works: 2 Chamber Operas—*Antigone* ('80); *Mannequins* ('83).

Boguslaw Schäffer (b. 1929). *Orchestral Works*, incl.: *Little Symphony: Scultura* ('60); *Tertium datur* for Harpsich. and Cham. Orch. ('58); *Topofonica* for 40 Instr. ('60); *Codes* for Cham. Orch. ('61); *Musica Ipsa* for Orch. of Deep Instr. ('62); *Collage* for Cham. Orch. ('64); *Cantata (Audiogram)* for 60 Vocal Voices and Orch. (66); *Experimenta* for 2 Pf. and Orch. ('72); Symphony in 9 Movmnts ('73); *Warsaw Overture (Harmonies and Counterpoints I,* '75; *Romuald Traugutt (Harmonies and Counterpoints II,* '76); *Gravesono* for Wind and Perc. Orch. ('77).

Electronic Music: Symphony: Electronic Music ('66); *Concerto for Tape* ('69); *Bergsoniana* for Fl., Soprano, Piano, Horn, Dbl-Bass, and Tape ('72); *Missa Elettronica* for Boys' Choir and Tape ('75); *Theme: Electronic Music* ('78); *Proietto simultaneo* for Sopr. and Ens., electronic media ('84); *Voice, Noise, Beuys, Choice* for Sopr. & Ens. ('84).

Stage Works: TIS MW-2 for Actor, Mime, Ballerina, and 5 Musicians ('63); *Howl*—Monodrama for Reciter and Ens. ('66).

Chamber Music (incl. 3 Str. Quartets, Trio); Concertos (incl. Concerto for Vno with Orch., for Harpsichord, for Alto Sax.); Instr. Solo Pieces; Jazz Compositions.

Kazimierz Serocki (1922–81). *Symphonic Works and Concertos:* 2 Symphonies: No. 1 ('52), No. 2—*Symphony of Songs* ('53); *Sinfonietta* for 2 String Orch. ('56); *Concerto* for Tromb. and Orch. ('53); *Musica concertante* for Chamber Orch. ('58); *Episodes* for String and 3 Perc. Groups ('59); *Segmenti* for Orch. ('61); *Symphonic Frescoes* ('64); *Continuum* for 6 Perc. Groups ('66); *Forte i piano* for 2 Pianos and Orch. ('67); *Dramatic Story* for Orch. ('71); *Swinging Music* for the "Music Workshop" Ensemble ('70); *Phantasmagoria* for Piano and Perc. ('71); *Fantasia elegiaca* for Organ and Orch. ('72); *Impromptu fantasque* for Recorders, Mandolins,

Guitars, Perc. and Piano ('73); *Concerto alla cadenza* per fl. a becco e orch. ('74); *Ad libitum* for Orch. ('77); *Pianophonie* for Piano with electrically transformed sound and Orch. ('78).

Vocal-Instrumental Music: The Heart of Night for Baritone and Orch. ('56, 2nd version with Piano); *The Eyes of the Air* for Soprano and Piano ('57, 2nd version with Orch.); *Poetry* for Soprano and Orch. ('69); *Niobe* for 2 Reciters, Mixed Choir and Orch. ('66).

Chamber Music, incl.: *A piacere* for Piano ('63); *Arrangements* for 1–4 Recorders; pieces for Piano, Trombone and others.

Kazimierz Sikorski (1895–1986). 6 Symphonies: '19, '21, III—*in the Form of Concerto Grosso*, '55, '69, '79, '84; *Popular Overture* ('54); *Stabat Mater* for Solo Voices, Choir and Orch. ('50); *Four Polonaises of Versailles* for Orch. ('74); *Tre Canoni su un Tema Unico* for String Orch. ('81).

Concertos with Orch.: for Cl., Horn, Fl., Tromb., Oboe; also *Concerto* for Trumpet, String Orch., 4 Kettle-drums, Xyl. and Tam-tam ('60); *Polyphonic Concerto* for Bassoon and Orch. ('65).

Vocal works, Chamber music, Arrangements of compositions (mostly Polish) from 17–19th Centuries, etc.

Tomasz Sikorski (1939–88). *Orchestral Works: Sequenza I* ('66); *Holzwege* ('72); *Other Voices* for 24 Winds, 4 Gongs, and Chimes ('75); *Music in Twilight* for Piano and Orch. ('78); *De Autoritratto* for 2 Pianos and Orch. ('83); *Strings in the Earth* ('80); *Paesaggio d'Inverno (Winter Landscape,* '82); *Sickness unto Death* for Reciter and Ens. ('76); *Self-portrait* for Orch. ('83); *La notte* for String Orch. (*Night, Omaggio a Friedrich Nietzsche*, '84).

Vocal-Instr. Works, incl.: *Prologues* for Fem. Choir and Ens. ('64); *Vox Humana* for Mix. Choir and Ens. ('71); *Music from Afar* ('74).

Concertos, Chamber music, Solo works, Music with Tape (incl. *Echoes II*, '63; *Afar a Bird*, '81); Electronic Music.

Radio-Opera: The Adventures of Sinbad the Sailor ('72).

Stanislaw Skrowaczewski (b. 1923). *Orchestral Works:* 4 Symphonies: No. 1 ('40), No. 2 ('45), No. 3—*Symph. for Strings* ('48), No. 4 ('54). *Overture in Classical Style* ('34); *Preludium—Fuga—postludium* for Orch. ('46); *Overture 1947*; *Music at Night* ('49–'51, new vers. '77); *Concerto* for English Horn, and Orchestra ('69); *Ricercari Notturni* for Sax. and Orch. ('77); *Concerto* for Cl. and Orch. ('80); *Violin Concerto* ('85); *Concerto for Orch.* ('85).

Vocal-Instr. Works incl. *Peace Cantata* ('53); *Anczar*, Cantata à capella; *The Song of Songs* for Sopr. and 23 Instr.

214   Appendix II

Ballet: Ugo and Parisina ('49).
Chamber Music incl. 4 Str. Quartets, Trio for Cl., Bassoon and Piano; 6 Piano Sonatas, Songs; *Fantasie a Quattro* (Vl., Vc., Cl., Piano, '84). Music for Theater and Cinema.

Michal Spisak (1914–1965). *Orchestral Works: 2 Symphonies Concertante* ('47, '56); *Serenade* ('39); *Aubade* for Small Orch. ('43); *Suite* for Str. Orch. ('45); *Toccata* ('47); *Divertissement* "Musique légère No. 1" ('50); *Three Miniatures* for Chamb. Orch. ('51); *Allegro de Voiron* ('43; 2nd version—'57).
Works for Solo Instr. and Orch.: Concertino for Cl. and Orch. ('41); *Concerto* for Bassoon and Orch. ('44); *Concerto* for Piano and Orch. ('47); *Divertimento* for 2 Pianos and Orch. ('48); *Sonata* for Vno and Orch. ('50); *Andante and Allegro* for Vno and Str. Orch. ('54).
Vocal-Instr. Work: Pedrek Wyrzutek, Cantata for Sopr., Bass, Reciting Voice, Boys' and Men's Choirs.
Chamber Music.

Marek Stachowski (b. 1936). *Orchestral Works: Musica con una battuta del Tam-tam* ('66); *Sequenze Concertanti* for Orch. ('68); *Irisation pour Orch.* ('70); *Musique Solennelle* for Orch. ('75); *Poéme Sonore pour Orch.* ('75); *Divertimento* for String Orch. ('78); *Choreia* for Orch. ('81); *Capriccio* for Orch. ('83).
Vocal-Instrumental Works: Five Senses and the Rose for Voice and Ens. ('64); *Neusis II* for 2 Vocal Ens. and Instr. Ens. ('68); *Chant de l'Espoir* for Soprano, Bar., Reciter, Mixed Choir, Boys' Choir, and Orch. ('60); *Words. . .* for Soprano, Bass, Mixed Choir, and Orch. ('71); *Thakurian Songs* for Mixed Choir and Orch. ('74); *Birds* for Soprano and Instr. ('76); *Amoretti* for Tenor, Fl. and Viola da gamba ('81); *Madrigali dell'estate* for Voice and Str. Trio ('84); *Sapphic Odes* for Mezzo-sopr. and Symph. Orch. ('85).
Chamber Works incl. 3 Str. quartets, pieces for wind quintet, piano, etc.

Boleslaw Szabelski (1896–1979). *Symphonic Works and Concertos*: 5 Symphonies ('26, '34, '51, '56, 68); *Concerto Grosso* ('54); *Concertino* for Piano and Orch. ('55); *Sonnets* for Orch. ('58); *Verses* for Piano and Orch. ('61); *Preludes* for Cham. Orch. ('63); *Concerto* for Fl. and Orch. ('64); *Concerto* for Piano and Orch. ('78).

Vocal-Instrumental Works: Heroic Poem for Mixed Choir and Orch. ('52); *Improvisations* for Mixed Choir and Chamber Orch. ('59); *Mikolaj Kopernik*, symphonic poem for Soprano, 2 Mixed Choirs and Symph. Orch. ('75); *Redoubt 56*, Cantata ('76).

Chamber Works, incl.: 2 String Quartets and *Aphorisms "9"* ('62).

Jadwiga Szajna-Lewandowska (b. 1912). *Stage Works*: Ballets for Children: *Pinocchio* ('56); *Kidnapping in Tuturlistan* ('66); *Thais* ('70); *Peau d'Âne*, Musical for Children ('74); *The Blue Cat*, Musical Fairy-tale with Ballet ('76); *The Magic Tailor*, Historical-Fantastic pageant with ballet ('77).

Vocal-Instrumental Works: Cantatas, Vocal Cycles. Chamber music. Educational works.

Witold Szalonek (b. 1927). *Orchestral and Chamber Works: Toccata Polyphonica* for String Orch. ('54); *Symphonic Satire* for Orch. ('56); *Les Sons* for Symph. Ens. ('65); *Mutazioni* per orch. da camera ('66); *Connections* for 10 Instr. ('72); *Concerto for Strings* ('75); *Musica Concertante* per violbasso e orch. ('77); *Little B-A-C-H Symphony* for Piano and Orch. ('81).

Music for winds (soli and ens.), for percussion, for diff. solo instr.

Vocal-Instr. Works, incl.: *Suite from Kurpie* for Contralto and 9 Instr. ('55); *Confessions*, Triptych for Speaker, Mixed Choir, and Cham. Orch. ('59); *O, Pleasant Earth*, Cantata ('69); *Nocturne* for Bar. and Cham. Orch. ('80).

Tadeusz Szeligowski (1896–1963). *Stage Works: The Peacock and the Maiden*, Ballet ('48); *The Scholars' Revolt*, Opera ('51); *Krakatuk (The Nutcracker)*, Opera ('54); *Teodor the Gentleman*, Opera ('60); *The Lamenting Forsaken Odysseus*, Opera-Oratorium ('62).

Orchestral Works and Concertos, incl.: *Piano Concerto* ('41); *'Lublin' Suite* for Small Orch. ('45); *Nocturne* for Orch. ('47); *The Comedy Overture* ('52). *Epitaph* for String Orch. ('56).

Choral Works, incl.: *Lublin Wedding* ('48); *The Charter of Hearts*, Cantata ('52); *The Angels Sang Sweetly*, Motet ('54).

Chamber Music (2 Quartets, Trio, etc.)

Józef Świder (b. 1930). *Stage Works*, incl.: *Magnus*, Opera ('70); *Wit Stwosz*, Opera ('74); *A Ball of Fairy-Tales*, Opera-musical ('77).

Concertos: Piano Concerto ('55); *Concerto* per Sopr. and Orch. ('56). *Concertino da Camera* per 5 gruppi concertanti ('61); *Concerto* for 4 Wind Instr., Strings and Perc. ('62); *Little Symphony* for Wind Orch. ('75).

Instr. Works: Symphony ('58); *Little Symphony* for Wind Orch. ('76).

Vocal-Instr. Works, incl.: Cantatas (*Eternal Summer*, '62; *Song about the Homeland*, '64; *Steel Poem*, '76); Oratorios (*Insurgent Triptych*, '71); Chamber and Piano Music.

Zbigniew Turski (1908–79). *Ballets: The Grand Opening* ('61); *Titania and the Donkey* ('66); *The Bird* ('71).

3 Symphonies: II—*Olympica* ('48); III ('53); *Sinfonia da camera* ('47); 2 Violin Concertos ('51, '63); 2 Quartets, Cantatas (incl. *Earth*, '52, and *Canti de Nativitate Patriae*, '69).

Romuald Twardowski (b. 1930). *Stage Works: The Naked Prince*, Ballet-pantomime ('60); *Cyrano de Bergerac*, Opera ('62); *The Sorcerer's Statues (Sculptures of Master Peter)*, Ballet-pantomime ('63); *Parable*, Pantomime ('64); *Tragedy or Story of John and Herod*, Morality play ('65); *The Fall of Father Suryn*, Musical Radio-drama ('69); *Lord Jim*, Musical Drama ('73); *Maria Stuart*, Musical Drama ('78); *The History of St. Catherine*, Mus. Morality Play ('81).

Vocal-Instrumental and Choral Works: Trittico Fiorentino: I—*Tre Studi Secondo Giotto* per orch. da camera ('66), II—*Sonetti di Petrarka* per tenore solo e due cori a cappella ('65), III—*Impressioni Fiorentini* per quattro cori strumentali ('67); *Little Orthodox Liturgy* for Vocal Ens. and 3 Instr. Groups ('68); *Ode to Youth* for Reciter, Mixed Choir and Orch. ('69); *Three Farewell Sonnets* for Bass and Cham. Orch. ('70); Also works for unaccompanied choir.

Orchestral Works, incl.: *Antifone* per tre gruppi d'orch. ('61); *Nomopedia*, 5 movimenti per Orch. ('62); *Studium in A* ('73); *Two Landscapes* for Orch. ('75); *A Spanish Fantasy* for Vno & Orch., etc.

Adam Walaciński (b. 1928). *Orchestral Works: Composizione "ALFA"* for Orch. ('58); *Horizons* for Chamber Orch. ('62); *Sequence* per Orch. con Fl. Concertante ('63); *Concerto da Camera* for Violin Solo and Str. Orch. ('67); *Refrains et Reflexions* pour Orch. ('69); *Torso* for Orch. ('71).

Chamber Music incl. Str. *Quartet* ('59); *Canto Tricolore* for Fl., Vno and Vibraphone ('62); *Epigrams* for Chamb. Ens. ('67), *Dichromia* for Fl. and Piano ('67); *Notturno 70* for 24 Str. Instr., 3 Fl. and Percussion ('70); *Divertimento Interroto* for 13 Players ('74).

Music for Voice and Small Ens.; Graphic Music.

Piotr Warzecha (b. 1941). *Orchestral Works: Evolutions* ('66); *Interpenetration* ('67); *Ripetizioni* ('69); *Arcades* ('70); *Concerto* for Orch.

('72); *Concerto* for 4 Soloists and Orch. ('78, Soli: Fl., Violin, Vc., Batt.); *Poem-Fantasia* for Violin and Orch. ('80); *Metamorphoses* ('82).

Chamber and Solo Works: Music by Night for Guitar Ens. ('79), *Metamorphoses* for Harpsichord ('79); *Str. Quartet* No. 1 ('82), etc.

Stanislaw Wiechowicz (1893–1963). *Orchestral Works: The Hop*, Wedding Dance for Orch. ('26); *Kate (Kasia*, Folk Suite, '46); *Old Town Concerto (Staromiejski)* for String Orch. ('54).

Vocal-Instrumental Works, incl.: *Romantic Cantata* for Soprano, Mixed Choir and Orch. ('30); *On a Little Clay Pot*, Children's Cantata ('48); *The March of the Times. The Masses Paying Tribute to Chopin*, Rhythmic Onomatopoeia (Paraphrase of Chopin's Etude Op. 10, No. 12): Mass Recitation for Great Mixed Ens. and Perc. Instr. ('49); *Letter to Marc Chagall*, Dramatic Rhapsody for Soprano, Mezzo-Soprano, 2 Reciters, Choir and Orch. ('61).

Works for Unaccompanied Choir, incl.: *Kujawiak-Ballad* (Folk Tune from the Lublin region, '44); *Harvest Cantata* (to the folk text, '48); *Passacaglia e Fuga* (to the folk text, '60); *Mizkiewicz Songs* ('50); *Ten Silesian Songs*, and others.

Boleslaw Woytowicz (1899–1980). *Orchestral Works*, incl.: 3 Symphonies: No. 2—*Warsaw* ('45), No. 3—*Piano Concertante* ('63), *Poème Funèbre "In Commemoration of Marshal Pilsudski"* ('35).

Vocal-Instrumental Works, incl.: *Cantata in Praise of Labor* ('48); *The Prophet*, Cantata ('50); *Three Silesian Folk Songs* for Unaccompanied Mixed Choir ('53–'58).

Chamber works: 2 String Quartets and others.

Foonotes for Appendix II

*The translations of the titles and the dates in the Appendix are those given by the PWM editions, Sole Exporter of Polish Music in their booklets, and in the index (of composers, compositions, performers) attached to the "Warsaw Autumn '84" program.

The translations of titles in the text are not always identical to the translations in the list. This list of works includes compositions that belong to a later period than the periods covered in this book.

**The leader of this group was the composer, Krauze. He was also the piano-soloist. The "Music Workshop" was concerned with the performance of modern music and worked directly with composers.

A Selected Bibliography

I. GENERAL WORKS

A. Books

Marek, T. *Współczesna muzyka polska (1945–1956)*. Kraków: PWM, 1956.* *La musique polonaise contemporaine 1945–1956*. Varsovie: "Polonia," 1957.
Kultura muzyczna Polski Ludowej 1944–1945 [The musical culture of the people Republic of Poland 1944–55]. Kraków: PWM, 1957.
Kisieliewski S. *Z muzyką przez lata* [Through the years with music]. Kraków: WL, 1957.
Mycielski Z. *Mazowsze*. Warszawa: "Arkady," 1958.
Biegański K. *Filharmonia Narodowa* [National Philharmonic]. Kraków: PWM, 1960.
Marek T. *Wielka Orkiestra Symphoniczna Polskiego Radia (WOSPR)* [Polish Radio Symphony Orchestra]. Kraków: PWM, 1960.
Mycielski Z. *Notatki o muzyce i muzykach* [Notes on music and musicians]. Kraków: PWM, 1961.
Polska współczesna kultura muzyczna 1944–1964 [Polish contemporary musical culture 1944–64]. Ed. E. Dziębowska. Kraków: PWM, 1968.
Drobner M. *Wspomnienia o początkach życia muzycznego w Polsce Ludowej 1944–46* [Memoires of the Beginnings of Musical Life in Poland 1944–46]. Kraków: PWM, 1985.
Polish music. Ed. S. Jarociński. Warszawa: PWN, 1965.
Erhardt L. *Contemporary music in Poland*. Warsaw: "Polonia," 1966.
Hanuszewska M.; Schäffer B. *Almanach polskich kompozytorów współczesnych* [Dictionary of Polish contemporary composers]. Kraków: PWM, 1956; 3rd ed. 1982.

Chomiński J.M. *Muzyka Polski Ludowej* [The music of Polish Republic]. Warszawa: PWN, 1968.
Lissa Z. *Music in People's Poland. Sketches and Monographs*. Warsaw: Polish Interpress Agency, 1973.
Schäffer B. *Maly informator muzyki XX wieku* [Small Encyclopedia of 20th Century Music]. 3rd ed. Kraków: PWM, 1975.
Zieliński T. *Spotkania z muzyką wspólczesną* [Encounters with contemporary music]. Kraków: PWM, 1975.**
Cegiella J. *Szkice do autoportretu polskiej muzyki wspólczesnej* [Sketches for a self-portrait of Polish contemporary music: interviews with the composers]. Kraków: PWM, 1976.***
Maciejewski B. *Twelve Polish composers*. London: Allegro Press, 1976.
Entelis L. *Vstreči s sovremennoj pol'skoj muzykoj* [Encounters with contemporary Polish music]. Leningrad: "Muzyka," 1977.
Zieliński T. A. *Style, kierunki i twórcy muzyki XX wieku* [Styles, directions and composers of 20th century music]. Warszawa: 1972.
Helman Z. *Neoklassycyzm w muzyce polskiej XX wieku* [Neoclassicism in Polish music of the 20th century]. Kraków: PWM.
Michalski G., Obniska E., Swolkień H., Waldorff J. *Dzieje muzyki polskiej* [History of Polish music]. Warszawa: Interpress, 1983.
Stan badań nad muzyką religijną w kulturze Polskiej [Research materials of the all-Poland musicological symposium on Polish religious music on June 22–23, 1971]. Warszawa: ATK, 1971. (See articles: Piotrowska M.: "Polska muzyka religijna po II wojnie światowej" [Polish religious music after World War II]. Przybylska K.: "Muzyka religijna w polskich nagraniach plytowych po roku 1945" [Religious music recorded on Polish disks after 1945].
Hanek L. *Wroclawscy kompozytorzy, muzykolodzy i publicysci* [The Wroclaw composers, musicologists and critics, 1945–1985]. Wroclaw: Akademia Muzyczna, 1985. (Among others: Tadeusz Natanson).

B. Periodicals

Jarociński S. "Polish Music after World War II." *The Musical Quarterly*, V. LI, No. 1 (1965), pp. 244-258.
Dibelius U. "Polnische Avantgarde." *Melos*, No. 1 (1967), pp. 7–16.
Marek T. "Contemporary Polish Composers: in Retrospect of the last 30 years." *PM* No. 3–4 (1973), pp. 4–17.
Zieliński T. A. "La création musicale dans les trois décennies de la Pologne Populaire." *La Musique en Pologne* (1975), No. 1(13), pp. 3–17; No. 2(14), pp. 3–18.

Lissa Z. "Główne nurty stylistyczne w muzyce polskiej 1944–74" [The main stylistic directions in Polish music '44–74]. *Muzyka*, No. 3(78) (1975), pp. 5–15.
Chomiński J. M. "Przemiany techniki kompozytorskiej w trzydziestoleciu PRL" [Changes in compositional techniques in Polish music 1945–75]. Ibid., pp. 16–27.
Dobrowolski A. "Wpływ festiwali 'Warszawska Jesień' na rozwój życia muzycznego w Polsce" [The influence of the festivals 'Warsaw Autumn' on the development of Polish musical life]. Ibid., pp. 58–63.
Gojowy D. "Avantgarde in Polen." *Die Musikbildung* (1975), No. 12, pp. 618–621; *Das Orchester* (1976), No. 1, pp. 5–11.
Chomiński J. M. "The Contribution of Polish Composers to the Shaping of a Modern Language in Music." *Polish Musicological Studies*, v. 1 (1977), pp. 167–215.
Tarnawska-Kaczorowska K. "Composers About Themselves: Krystyna Moszumańska-Nazar, Zbigniew Bujarski, Krzysztof Meyer, Marek Stachowski, Józef Rychlik." *PM*, No. 3–4 (1983), pp. 36–45.****
Węcowski J. "Polish Religious Music (outline history)." #9: "Contemporary Times." *PM*, No. 3–4 (1983), pp. 21–35.
Baculewski K. "In statu nascendi: o muzyce nowej generacji kompozytorów" [On music of the new generation of composers]. *RM*, No. 8 (1984), pp. 3–5; No. 9, pp. 8–10; No. 10, pp. 17–18.

II. WORKS ON COMPOSERS

BACEWICZ Grażyna

Kisielewski S. *Grażyna Bacewicz i jej czasy* [Grażyna Bacewicz and her times]. Kraków: PWM, 1964.
Zieliński T.A. "Grażyna Bacewicz." *Spotkania* . . . pp. 7–30.
Gąsiorowska M. *Grażyna Bacewicz*. Kraków: PWM.
Malawski A. " 'Uwertura' Bacewiczówny" [Overture]. *RM*, No. 17 (1947).
Chomiński J.M. " 'Koncert' na orkiestre smyczkową Grażyny Bacewicz" [Concerto for Strings]. *SM*, v. V (1956).
Helman Z. "Problem stylizacji muzyki dawnej w 'Sonacie da camera' G. Bacewicz" [The problem of stylization of old music in the 'Sonata da camera' by GB]. *SM*, v. V (1956).
Erhardt L. "Telewizyjna 'Przygoda króla Artura' " [The adventure of King Artur for television]. *RM* No. 15 (1960).

Zieliński T. A. " 'VI Kwartet' G. Bacewicz." *RM* No. 18 (1960).
Gorczycka M. " 'Pensieri notturni' G. Bacewicz." *RM* No. 21 (1961).
Kański J. "'II Koncert wiolonczelowy' G. Bacewicz" [II Cello Conterto GB]. *RM* No. 22 (1963).
Schiller H. "Ze studiów nad muzyką G. Bacewicz" [Study of the Music GB]. *M* Nos. 3–4 (1964).
Marek T. "Grażyna Bacewicz." *PM* No. 1 (1969).
Ruch Muzyczny (1969), No. 7: Bacewicz' issue.
Zieliński T. "Ostatnie utwory G. Bacewicz" [The late works of GB]. *RM* No. 12 (1972).
Cisowska B. " 'Pożadanie'—ostatnie dzielo G. Bacewicz" [Desire—the last work of GB]. *RM* No. 13 (1973).
Zieliński T. A. "Grażyna Bacewicz (1913–1969)."*PP* No. 10 (1974), pp 20–26.
Kisielewski S. "Grażyna Bacewicz 1913–1969." *PM* No. 2 (1975), pp. 11–15.
Rosen J. *Grażyna Bacewicz—her life and works*. Preface by Witold Lutoslawski. Los Angeles: Friends of Polish Music, University of Southern California (1984).
Thomas A. *Grażyna Bacewicz. Chamber and Orchestral Music*. Los Angeles. Ibid. (1985). (See: Select Bibliography).

BAIRD Tadeusz

Zieliński T. A. *Tadeusz Baird*. Kraków: PWM, 1966.
——— "Wokól problematyki ekspressji (T. Baird)" [About the problem of expression]. In: *Spotkania* . . ., pp. 30–38.
Cegiella J. "Tadeusz Baird." In: *Szkice* . . ., pp. 18–30.
Augustyn R. "O melodyce utworów T. Bairda" [On melodics in the works of TB]. *RM* No. 8 (1975).
Marek T. "Grupa 49" [Group 49]. *M* No. 5/6 (1953).
Gorczycka M. " '4 Esseje' T. Bairda." *RM* No. 15 (1960), p. 5.
Prosnak A. " '4 Esseje Bairda i perspektywy techniki serialnej" [4 Essays TB and perspectives of serial technique]. *M* IX/3–4 (1964), p. 26.
Gorczycka M. "Przed prawykonaniem 'Egzorty' T. Bairda" [For the premiere of Egzorta]. *RM* No. 18 (1960).
Malinowski W. " 'Muzyka epifaniczna' T. Bairda." *RM* No. 22 (1963).
Kański J. "Dramat muzyczny T. Bairda" [On 'Tomorrow']. *RM* No. 23 (1966), p. 4.
Nikol'skaja I. "O tvorčestve T. Bairda" [On the works of TB]. *Sovetskaya Muzyka* No. 7 (1974), pp. 105–110.

Wightman A. "Tadeusz Baird at 50." *Musical Times* CXIX (1978), p. 847.
Baird T. *Rozmowy, szkice, refleksje* [Conversations, essays, reflections]. Ed. I. Grzenkowicz. Kraków: PWM, 1982.
Tarnawska-Kaczorowska K. *Świat liryki wokalno—instrumentalnej T. Bairda* [The world of lyricism in TB's vocal-instrumental works]. Kraków: PWM, 1982.
—————— "T. Baird—glosses to a biography." *Music in Poland* 38, No. 1-2 (1983), pp. 5–14.
Nikol'skaja I. "O ewolucji stylu T. Bairda" [On the evolution of TB's style]. *M* No. 1-2 (1984), pp. 19–47. With summary in English.
Stanilewicz-Kamionka M. "T. Baird: dokumentacja twórczości" [Dokumentation of his work]. *M* No. 1–2 (1984), pp. 145–189.
Tadeusz Baird—sztuka dźwięku, sztuka słowa [TB—art of sound, art of the word: materials of a symposium]. Ed. K. Tarnawska-Kaczorowska. Warszawa: Sekcja Muzykologów ZKP, 1984.

BLOCH Augustyn

Cegiella J. "Augustyn Bloch." *Szkice* . . . , pp. 140–150.
Zieliński T. A. " 'Espressioni' per soprano ed orchestra A. Blocha." *RM* No. 5 (1961).
Schiller H. " 'Dialoghi' A. Blocha." *RM* No. 22 (1966), p. 6.
Michalski G. "O twórczości A. Blocha" [On the works of AB. An article in the program for Bloch's *Very Sleeping Beauty*]. Warsaw: Teatr Wielki, 1974.

BUJARSKI Zbigniew

Zieliński T.A. " 'Contraria' Z. Bujarskiego." *Spotkania* . . . , pp. 163–165.
Meyer K. "Z. Bujarski—a sketch to a portrait." *PM* No. 3 (1980), pp. 28–34.
Tarnawska.****

DOBROWOLSKI Andrzej

Pilarski B. "Kilka uwag" [A few remarks]. *PK* No. 20 (1955).
f. " 'Studia' na obój, trąbke, fagot i kontrabas pizzicato A. Dobrowolskiego." *RM* No. 22 (1961).

[author unknown] [about Symphony No. 1]: *PM* No. 2/3 (1969), p. 31.
——— [about "Amar"]: *PM* No. 4 (1971), p. 6.
Zieliński T. A. " 'Passacaglia' i 'Muzyka No. 6' A. Dobrowolskiego." *RM* No. 15 (1985), pp. 3–4.

GÓRECKI Henryk Mikolaj

Pociej B. " 'Epitafium' H. Góreckiego" [Epitaph]. *RM* No. 6 (1959).
Pociej B. " 'Zderzenia' H. Góreckiego" [Scontri—Collisions]. *RM* No. 18 (1960).
Markiewicz L. "O 'Zderzeniach,' radości i katastrofizmie" [About 'Collisions,' joy and catastrophy]. *RM* No. 21 (1960).
Gorczycka M. " 'Diagramy' H. Góreckiego." *RM* No. 21 (1961).
Markiewicz L. "Rozmowa z H. Góreckim" [Conversation with HG]. *RM* No. 17 (1962).
——— " 'Choros I' H. Góreckiego." *RM* No. 21 (1964), p. 8.
——— " 'Elementy' H. Góreckiego." *RM* No. 17 (1965).
Pociej B. "Opis—analyza—interpretacja: na materiale 'Elementi' i 'Canti strumentali' H. Góreckiego" [Description—analysis—interpretation: on material of 'Elementi' and 'Canti strumentali' by HG]. *Res Facta* No. 4 (1970).
——— "Kosmos, tradycja, brzmienie. O II symfonii Kopernikowskiej HM Góreckiego" [Cosmos, tradition, sound. II Symphony by HMG]. *RM* No. 15 (1973).
Gąsiorowska M. "Symfonia pieśni żalosnych" [III Symphony of Lamentation Songs]. *RM* No. 3 (1978).
Droba K. "Droga do sensu tragicznego" [The path to a sense of tragedy: the works of HMG]. *RM* No. 15 (1978), pp. 3–4.
Pociej B. "The music of Górecki." *PP* No. 12 (1972), pp. 20–27. "The music of depth: the work of HMG." Ibid., No. 9 (1978), pp. 38–43.
Gąsiorowska M. "Czas zatrzymany H. Góreckiego" [The stopped time of HMG]. *RM* No. 25 (1983), pp. 3–4.
Droba K. "The music of H.M. Górecki." *Music in Poland* No. 1 (39) (1984), pp. 27–36. With a list of works.
Droba K. *Twórczość Henryka Góreckiego* [The works of HG]. Kraków: PWM.

KILAR Wojciech

Marek T. "Piękny start kompozytorki" [A wonderful composer's start]. *PK* No. 31 (1955).

Pociej B. " 'Herbsttag' W. Kilara." *RM* No. 21 (1961).
Markiewicz L. " 'Riff 62' W. Kilara." *RM* No. 2 (1963).
Markiewicz L. "Wojciech Kilar: en nutida Komponist." *Nutida musik* IX/ 1-2 (1965–66).
Zieliński T. A. " 'Générique' W. Kilara." *Spotkania* . . . , pp. 145–147.
———— " 'Training 68' W. Kilara." Ibid., pp. 170–173.
Cegiella J. "Wojciech Kilar." *Szkice* . . . , pp. 70–84.
Marek T. " 'Bogurodzica' by Wojciech Kilar," *PM* No. 1 (1977), pp. 19–24.

KISIELEWSKI Stefan

Z. L. "O dwóch nowych symfoniach polskich" [On 2 new Polish Symphonies]. *PK* No. 4 (1952).
Pilarski B. "Kilka uwag" [Few remarks]. *PK* No. 20 (1955).
Hordyński J. "Stefan Kisielewski." *ZL* No. 13 (1961).
Kisielewski S. "O moim komponowaniu i myśleniu" [On my composing and thinking.] *RM* No. 21 (1961).
Pociej B. Kisiel jako kompozytor [S. K. as composer]. *TP* No. 15 (1984), p. 7; *RM* No. 10 (1984), p. 18.

KNAPIK Eugeniusz

Rychlik J. "E. Knapika poemat slowno-muzyczny 'Tak, jak na brzegu morza' " [E.K.'s vocal-instrument poem 'On the sea shore']. *Z problemów muzyki wspólczesnej.* Kraków: PWSM, 1978, pp. 75–86.
Pociej B. "Ze śląskiej szkoly" [From the silesian school: E.K.] *Zeszyty Muzyczne Pro Sinfonika* II st., 1979/80, No. 5, pp. 334–337.

KOTOŃSKI Wlodzimierz

Zieliński T.A. " 'Concerto' i 'Trio' W. Kotońskiego." *RM* No. 21 (1961).
Zieliński T.A. " 'Kwintet dęty [Wind quintet]; 'A battere'; 'Pour quatre' W. Kotońskiego." *Spotkania* . . . , pp. 159–163, 173–176.
Cegiella J. "Wlodzimierz Kotoński." *Szkice* . . . , pp. 85–103.

KRAUZE Zygmunt

Krauze Z. "Polish music in my repertory." *PM* No. 2, 1968, pp. 29–32.
Michalski G. "Z.K.'s 'Folk Music.' " *PM* No. 1 (1973).

———— "Piece for Orchestra No. 1." *PM* No. 2 (1970); *PM* No. 1 (1971).
Kaczyński T. " 'Kwartet smyczkowy' Z. Krauze" [String Quartet ZK]. *RM* No. 17 (1965).
Gąsiorowska M. "Koncert fortepianowy Z. Krauzego" [Z.K.'s Piano Concerto]. *RM* No. 11, 1979, pp. 6–7.

LUTOSLAWSKI Witold

Jarociński S., editor. *Witold Lutoslawski. Materialy do monografi* [Materials for a monograph]. Kraków: PWM, 1967.
Kaczyński T. *Rozmowy z Witoldem Lutoslawskim* [Conversations with WL]. Kraków: PWM, 1972.
Pociej B. *Lutoslawski a wartość muzyki* [L. and the value of music]. Kraków: PWM, 1976.
Zieliński T. "Droga twórcza W. Lutoslawskiego" [The creative path of WL]. In: *Spotkania* . . . , pp. 38–68.
———— " 'Preludia i fuga' W. Lutoslawskiego." Ibid., pp. 189–196.
Cegiella J. "Witold Lutoslawski." In: *Szkice* . . . , pp. 5–17.
Lissa Z. " 'Mala suita' and 'Tryptyk' W. Lutoslawskiego" [Little Suite and Silesian Triptych WL]. *M* No. 5/6 (1952).
———— " 'Koncert na orkiestre' W. Lutoslawskiego." *SM* V (1956).
Pilarski B. "W. Lutoslawski odpowiada na pytania" [WL answers questions: interview]. *RM* No. 7 (1958).
Shiller H. " 'Kwartet smyczkowy' W. Lutoslawskiego" [String Quartet]. *Res Facta* No. 2 (1968).
Lutoslawski W. "Uwagi o sposobie wykonywania mego kwartetu smyczkowego" [Remarks on the method of performing of my String Quartet]. *RM* No. 17 (1965).
Piotrowska M. "Aleatoryzm W. Lutoslawskiego na tle genezy tego kierunku w muzyce wspólczesnej" [The aleatorism of WL against a background of the origins of this tendency in contemporary music]. *M* XIV, No. 3 (1969), pp. 67–86.
Blaszkiewicz T. *Aleatoryzm w twórczości W. Lutoslawskiego* [The aleatorism in Lutoslawski's work]. Gdańsk: PWSM, 1973.
Witold Lutoslawski—prezentacje, interpretacje, konfrontacje [Presentations, interpretations, confrontrations: materials of a Symposium]. Ed. K. Tarnawska—Kaczorowska. Warszawa: Sekcja Muzykologów ZKP, 1985.
Witold Lutoslawski—sesja naukowa poświęcona twórczości kompozytora [Papers of a session devoted to his works, Cracow 1980]. Ed. L. Polony. Kraków: Akademia Muzyczna, 1985.

Studia nad twórczością W. Lutoslawskiego [Studies on works by WL]. Ed. K. Meyer. Kraków: *PWM*, 1985.
Tarnawska-Kaczorowska K. *Witold Lutoslawski. Myśl i kreacja* [WL. Conception and realization]. Kraków: *AKM*, 1983.
Stanilewicz-Kamionka M. *Katalog tematyczny dziel W. Lutoslawskiego* [Thematic catalog of WL's works]. Kraków: PWM, 1985.

Western and non-Polish books and periodicals on Lutoslawski

Jarociński S. "The Music of W. Lutoslawski." *PP* 1 (Oct. 1958), pp. 29–34.
Cowie E. "Mobiles of Sound." *Music and Musicians* 20 (Oct. 1971), pp. 34–40.
Nordwall O. "Förtecking över W. Lutoslawskis viktigaste verk 1934–64" [Catalog of WL's principal works 1934–64]. *Nutida Musik* 8 (1964–5), pp. 128–129.
Lutoslawski. Ed. Ove Nordwall. Stockholm: W. Hansen, 1968.
Lutoslawski W. "About the Element of Chance in Music." In: *Three Aspects of New Music*. Stockholm: Nordiska Musikförlaget, 1968.
Thomas A. "A Deep Resonance: Lutoslawski's Troix Poèmes d'Henri Michaux.'" *Soundings* No. 1 (Autumn 1970), pp. 58–70.
Brennecke W. " 'Die Trauer Musik' von W. Lutoslawski." In: *Festschrift für F. Blume zum 70. Geburtstag*. Ed. A. A. Abert and W. Pfannkuch. Kassel: Bärenreiter, 1963, pp. 60–73.
Shaltuper J. "O stil'e Lutoslawskogo 60. godov" [On Lutoslawski's style of the 60's]. *Problemy muzykal'noj nauki*, v. 3. Moskva: Sovietskij Kompozitor, 1975, pp. 238–279.
Kaczyński T. *Gespräche mit W. Lutoslawski*. Mit einem Anhang: Neun Stunden bei Lutoslawski von Balint Andras Varga. Leipzig: Verlag Reclam, 1976. Reclams Universal-Bibliothek 619.
Maciejewski B. M. *Twelve Polish Composers*. London: Allergo Press, 1976, pp. 36–56.
Nikol'skaia I. "Traurnaia muzyka W. Lutoslawskogo i problemy zvukovysotnoj organizacji v muzykie XX vieka" [The "Musique funèbre" of WL and the problems of pitch organization in 20th century music]. In: *Muzyka i sovremennost'* No. 10, Ed. D. Frishman. Moskva: Muzyka, 1976, pp. 187–206.
Rappoport L. *Witold Lutoslawski*. Moskva: Muzyka, 1976.
——— "Niekotoryje osobennosti orkestrovoj polifonii W. Lutoslawskogo" [Some features of orchestral polyphony of WL]. In: *Polyphonia*, Ed. K. Yužak. Moskva: Muzyka, 1975.

Schonberg H. C. "Music: A Century in Polish Perspective" [Cello Conterto]. *NY Times*, 1 October 1976, sec. 3, p. 16.
Marek T. "W. Lutoslawski: 'Mi-Parti.' " *PM* 12, No. 2 (1977), pp. 3–4.
Couchoud J.P. *La musique polonaise et W. Lutoslawski*. Paris: Stock, 1981. Collection "Musique."
Stucky S. *Lutoslawski and His Music*. London: Cambridge Univ. Press, 1981. (See the Bibliography).
Helman Z. "Intellekt and Phantasie in der Musik von W. Lutoslawski." *Musicologie Sbornik pro hudebni vědu a kritiku* [Prague], v. 18 (1982).
Bálint András Varga. Lutoslawski Profile. London: Chester Music, 1976.

LUCIUK Juliusz

Zieliński T.A. " 'Szkic symp. No. 4' J. Luciuka" [Symphonic Sketch No. 4]. *RM* No. 11 (1961).
Zieliński T.A. " 'Muzyka fortepianowa' J. Luciuka" [Piano music]. *Spotkania* . . . , pp. 165–169.

MACIEJEWSKI Roman

Kański J. " 'Requiem' R. Maciejewskiego." *RM* No. 21 (1960).
Cegiella J. "Roman Maciejewski." *Szkice* . . . , pp. 161–178.

MAKLAKIEWICZ Jan

Mycielski Z. " 'Pieśni japońskie' Maklakiewicza" [Japanese Songs]. *RM* No. 18 (1947).
Żulawski W. " 'Zlota kaczka' Maklakiewicza w Operze Śląskiej" [Golden Duck]. *NK* No. 32 (1951).
T.M. "Zlota kaczka." *M* No. 9 (1951).
[author unk.] "Jan Maklakiewicz." *PM* No. 3/4 (1954).

MALAWSKI Artur

Mycielski Z. "Prawykonanie 'Drugiej symfonii' Malawskiego" [Premiere of II Symphony]. *PK* No. 18 (1956).

Mycielski Z. "Artur Malawski (1904–1957)." *PK* No. 2 (1958).
Bacewicz G., Baird T., Rowicki W., Baranowski M. "Wspominając A. Malawskiego" [In memory of AM]. *RM* No. 6 (1958).
Pociej B. " 'II Sympfonia' A. Malawskiego." *RM* No. 6 (1958).
Schäffer B. "Artur Malawski." *RM* No. 6 (1958).
Stankiewicz A. "Folklor góralski w 'Wierchach' A. Malawskiego" [Goralski folklore in the ballet 'Mountain Tops']. *M* IX/4 (1962).
Gorczycka M. " 'Trio fortepianowe' A. Malawskiego." *M* IX/4 (1962).
Artur Malawski. Zycie i twórczość [AM. His life and works]. Ed. B. Schäffer. Kraków: PWM, 1969.

MATUSZCZAK Bernadetta

Schiller H. " 'Romeo and Juliet' by B.M." *PM* No. 4 (1969), pp. 18–20.
Z. Bargielski, S. Behr, L. Ciuciura, B. Matuszczak, K. Meyer: "Pytania i odpowiedzi" [Interviews]. *Res Facta* No. 5 (1971).
"Composer's workshop: B.M.'s 'The Raptures of Heloise,' " an opera. *PM* No. 4 (1974), pp. 24–27.

MEYER Krzysztof

Walaciński A. "I kwartet smyczkowy Meyera." *RM* No. 17 (1965).
Marek T. Composer's Workshop K.M. *PM* No. 1 (1971).
Michalski G. "Symfonie K. Meyera." *RM* No. 18 (1971).
Rappoport L. "Symfonie K. Meyera." *M* XX/1 (1975).
Zieliński T.A. "Kwartety K. Meyera." *RM* No. 15 (1976).
Cegiella J. "Krzysztof Meyer." *Szkice* . . . , pp. 39–46.
Osborn N. "Second String Quartet." *Music and Letters* No. 1 (1979).
Welanyk S. "24 Preludia K.M." [24 Preludes]. *RM* No. 14 (1979).
Polony L. "Koncert wiolonczelowy K.M." [Cello Concerto]. *RM* No. 15 (1982).
Podhajski M. "Symfonie Krzysztofa Meyera—problemy formy i ekspresji" [The symphonies of K. Meyer: problems of forms and expression]. In: *Zeszyty Naukowe* No. 15, Gdańsk: PWSM, 1976, pp. 111–124.
Lesle L. "Neue Werke von K.M. in Hamburg." *Das Orchester* No. 2 (1983).

Polony L. "K. M.: Symfonia polska." [Polish Symphony]. *RM* No. 13 (1983).
Zieliński T. "K.M.: V. Symfonia." *RM* No. 18 (1983).
Gojowy D. " 'Gracze' Szostakowicza i Meyera." [Gamblers]. *RM* No. 16 (1983).
Szczepańska-Malinowska L. " 'Gracze'—zamiast recenzji." *RM* No. 23 (1983).
Lesle L. Krzysztof Meyer—Komponistenportrait. *Neue Zeitschrift für Musik* No. 6 (1981), pp. 572–575.
Assmann K. "Neue Literatur für Streichquartette." *Neue Musikzeitung* XII 83/I 84.

MOSZUMAŃSKA-NAZAR Krystyna

"Composer's workshop: K. M.–N." *PM* No. 2 (1974), pp. 10–13.
Schiller H. " 'Muzyka na smyczki' K. Moszumańskiej-Nazarowej" [Music for Strings]. *RM* No. 22 (1963).
Tarnawska.****
Mizerska-Golonek E. " 'Madonny polskie' K. M.–N." [" 'Polish Madonnas' by K. M.–N.: selected problems of vocal texture"]. *Muzyka instrumentalno-wokalna kompozytorów krakowskich*. Kraków: PWSM, 1979.

MYCIELSKI Zygmunt (1907–1987)

"Mycielski-laureatem ZKP" [ZM—prize-winner of ZKP]. *M* No. 5/6 (1954).
Zieliński T.A. "Z. Mycielski o swoim nowym utworze" [ZM about his new work: II Symphony]. *RM* No. 11 (1961).
"Composer's workshop: Z. M." *PM* No. 4 (1977), pp. 15–19.
Pocej B. "Muzyka i mądrość" ["Music and wisdom: on musical writings by Z.M."] *TP* No. 34 (1977), p. 3.
Rudziński W. "Z.M. at 75." *PM* No. 1/2 (1983), p. 12–15.

PACIORKIEWICZ Tadeusz

Mazur K. "O utworach T. Paciorkiewicza." [On works of TP]. *RM* No. 2 (1962).

Marek T. "Koncert współczesnej polskiej muzyki kameralnej" [Concert of contemporary Polish chamber music: Sonata for violin and piano]. *M* No. 11/12 (1954).
jol. " 'Ciężar ziemi' T. Paciorkiewicza" [Weight of the Earth—Cycle of Songs for Soprano and Orch.]. *RM* No. 21 (1961).

PALESTER Roman+

Schäffer B. "Muzyka Romana Palestra" [The music of RP]. *Kierunki* No. 17 (1959), p. 10.
Kaczyński T. "Trzydzieści pięć lat muzyki" [35 years of music: RP]. *RM* No. 20 (1964), pp. 5–7.
Helman Z. "Powrót Marsjasza" [Marsias' return: the music of RP]. *RM* No. 19 (1983), pp. 11–14.

PANUFNIK Andrzej+

Mycielski Z. " 'I Symfonia' Panufnika." *RM* No. 6 (1945).
Wrobel F. "Z zagadnień muzyki ćwierćtonowej (na marginesie 'Kolysanki' A. Panufnika) [Problems of 1/4-tone music in 'Lullaby' AP]. *RM* No. 18 (1948).
Haubenstock R. "A. Panufnik. 'Uwertura tragiczna' " [Tragic Overture]. *RM* No. 21 (1948).
Jarociński S. "Andrzej Panufnik." *PK* No. 15 (1953).
Bristiger M. "Rozwazania bez hagiografii nad twórczością A. Panufnika" [Meditations without hagiography: on works of AP]. *PK* No. 10 (1954).
Panufnik A. *Impulse and design in my music*. London: Boosey and Hawkes, 1972.
Bowen M. "Panufnik at 60." *Music and Musicians* No. 1 (1974–75), pp. 20–24.
Walsh S. "The music of A. Panufnik." *Tempo* No. 111 (1974), pp. 7–14.
Macdonald C. "O muzyce A. Panufnika" [On AP's music]. *RM* No. 20 (1983), pp. 3–7.

PENDERECKI Krzysztof

Lisicki K. *Szkice o Krzysztofie Pendereckim* [Sketches of KP]. Warszawa: "Pax," 1973.

Erhardt L. *Spotkania z K. Pendereckim* [Encounters with KP]. Kraków: PWM, 1975.

Zieliński T.A. "Świat dźwiękowy K. Pendereckiego" [The sonoric world of KP]. *Spotkania* . . . , pp. 68–82.

―――― " 'Fluorescencje' K. Pendereckiego." Ibid., pp. 152–159.

―――― " 'Utrenia' K. Pendereckiego." Ibid., pp. 176–182.

Schiller H. "Z warsztatu mlodych" [From the workshop of youth] (Strofy, Emanacje, Psalmy Dawida). *RM* No. 13 (1959).

―――― "Po prawykonaniu 'Wymiarów czasu i ciszy' K. Pendereckiego" [After the premiere of 'Dimensions']. *RM* No. 21 (1960).

Wallek-Walewski M. "W kręgu poszukiwań materialowych" [In search of materials] (Strofy, Wymiary . . . , Anaklasis, Emanacje). *RM* No. 17 (1960).

Zieliński T. "Nowy utwory K. Pendereckiego" [New works KP] (Anaklasis, Tren, Psalm). *RM* No. 12 (1961).

―――― "Wspólczesny kompozytor a tradycja. Rozmowa z K. Pendereckim" [The contemporary composer and tradition. Interview with KP]. *RM* No. 12 (1963).

Mycielski Z. " 'Dies irae' Pendereckiego—oratorium pamięci zamordowanych w Oświęcimiu" [Dies irae—oratorio in memory of the victims of Auschwitz]. *RM* No. 14 (1967).

Zieliński T. "Technika operowania instrumentami smyczkowymi w utworach K. Pendereckiego" [Technique of the use of string instruments in KP's works]. *M* XIII/1 (1968).

Nordwall T. "K. Penderecki—studium notacji i instrumentacji" [KP: study of notation and instrumentation]. *Res Facta* No. 2 (1968).

Kaczyński T. "Do 'Kosmogonii' Pendereckiego dobieranie klucza" [Finding the key to Cosmogony]. *Wspólczesność*, 26 June 1971.

Bilica K. " 'Ofiarom Hiroszymy' Tren K. Pendereckiego. Proba analizy jednego z aspektów utworu" [An attempt to analyze one of the aspects of Threnody]. *M* No. 2 (1974).

Rychlik J. "Punktualizm we wczesnej twórczości K. Pendereckiego" [Pointillism in early work KP]. *M* No. 2(81) (1976).

Droba K. "Hierarchia czynników formalnych w twórczości K. Pendereckiego (na przykladzie 'Polimorfii')" [Hierarchy of formal factors in KP's work: modelled on Polimorfia]. Ibid.

Koncepcja, notacja, realizacja w twórczości Krzyszstofa Pendereckiego [Conception, notation, realization in the works of Penderecki: a selection of materials of a seminar in Cracow, 1975]. Kraków, PWSM: PWM, 1976.

Swiercz T. *Technika choralna w dzielach wokalno-instrumentalnych Krzysztofa Pendereckiego* [Choral technique in the vocal-instrumental works by

Penderecki]. Gdańsk: PWSM, 1976. With summaries in English and Russian.

Współczesność i tradycja w muzyce Krzysztofa Pendereckiego [The present and the tradition: selected materials of the 2nd seminar in Cracow devoted to the works of Penderecki, 1980]. Kraków: Akademia Muzyczna, 1983.

Chlopicka R., Szwajgier K., editors. *Studia nad twórczośią Krzysztofa Pendereckiego* [Study of the work of KP]. Kraków: PWM.

Western and non-Polish Books and Periodicals

Erhardt L. *Contemporary Music in Poland* (transl. by Tarska E.). Warsaw: PWM (Polonia Publishing House), 1966.

Jarociński S., editor. *Polish Music*. Warsaw: PWN, 1965.

Schwinger W. *Penderecki: Begegnungen, Lebensdaten, Werkkommentare.* Stuttgart: Deutsche Verlagsantalt, 1979.

Robinson R. *Krzysztof Penderecki. A Guide to His Works.* Prestige Publications. Princeton, New Jersey, 1983.

Ivaškin A. *Krzysztof Penderecki—monografičeskij očerk* [KP—a monograph]. Moskva: Sovetskij Kompozitor, 1983.

Robinson R., Winold A. *A Study of the Penderecki St. Luke Passion.* Celle: Moeck, 1983.

Zieliński T.A. "Der einsame Weg des K. Penderecki." *Melos* XXIX (Oct. 1962), pp. 318–323.

Pociej B. "K. Penderecki: en traditionell kompositor." *Nutida Musik* VIII/1-2 (1965–66).

Dibelius U. "Polische Avantgarde." *Melos* XXXIV (Jan. 1967), p. 7–.

Orga A. "Penderecki: composer of martyrdom," *Music and Musicians* XVIII (Sept. 1969), pp. 34–38.

Patton H. "Penderecki, Composer for the Last Judgment." *Chicagoland and FM Guide* (Apr. 1969).

Schonberg H.C. "Penderecki's Aggressive Modernism." *New York Times* (March 7, 1969), p. 30.

Fleming S. "Musician of the Month, K. Penderecki." *Hi Fi/Musical America* XXV (Dec. 1975).

Cook E. "Penderecki: the Polish question—and others." (Interview). *Music Journal* XXXV (Feb. 1977), pp. 8–10.

Felder D. and Schneider M. "An Interview with K. Penderecki." *The Composer* VIII (1976–77), pp. 8–20.

Grzenkowicz I. "Conversations with K. Penderecki." *PM* XII, No. 3 (1977), pp. 24–30; No. 4 (1977), pp. 10–14.

Erhardt L. "A Glance at Contemporary Music in Poland." *PM* XII, Nos. 1–2 (1979), pp. 22–24.
Nikol'skaja I. "Derzajuščij chudožnik" [The bold artist]. *Sovetskaia Muzyka* (1984), No. 1, pp. 109–113.

PERKOWSKI Piotr

Szeligowski T. " 'Swantewit' Perkowskiego na scenie poznańskiej" [Production of ballet 'Swantewit' in Poznań]. *RM* No. 15/16 (1948).
Marek T. "Nowa polska kantata" [New Polish cantata]. *PK* No. 11 (1953).
Kański J. "Nowy balet polski: 'Klementyna.' " *RM* No. 1 (1970).
Cegiella J. "Piotr Perkowski." *Szkice* . . . , pp. 104–114.

RUDZIŃSKI Witold

Marek T. " 'Janko muzykant'—nowa polska opera" [New Polish Opera: Janko the Fiddler]. *PK* No. 27 (1953).
Kański J. 'Komendant Paryża.' *RM* No. 10/11 (1960).
Hordyński J. "Witold Rudziński" [Interview]. *ŻL* No. 50 (1960).
Olkuśnik J. "Nowe utwory W. Rudzińskiego. 'Deux portraits des femmes,' 'Dach świata' "[New works of WR]. *RM* No. 14 (1961).
Mycielski Z. "Nad 'Odprawą' W. Rudzińskiego" [About 'The Dismissal of the Greek Envoys']. *RM* No. 2 (1967), p. 3.
"Rudziński W. 'The Shulamite.' " *PM* No. 2 (1966); No. 1 (1971); No. 3 (1974).

RUDZIŃSKI Zbigniew

Zieliński T. " 'Contra fidem' Z. Rudzińskiego i 'Choros I' H. Góreckiego." *Spotkania* . . . , pp. 150–152.
Kaczyński T. " 'Moments musicaux' Z. Rudzińskiego." *RM* No. 12 (1966).
"Piano Sonata by Z. R." *PM* No. 3 (1976), pp. 19–23.
"Rudziński Z. 'Moments musicaux,' 'Music at Night,' 'Requiem,' 'Symphony.' " *PM* No. 2 (1968); No. 2 (1971); No. 1 (1972); No. 4 (1974).
Grzenkowicz I. "Mannequins" [opera by Z. R.] *PM* No. 1/2 (1983), pp. 3–11.

SCHÄFFER Boguslaw

Wysocki T. [Interviews with B. Schäffer]: *RM* No. 17/18 (1959); Nos. 18, 19 (1960).
Wachowicz Z. "Muzyka B. Schäffera." *RM* No. 19 (1960).
Pociej B. " 'Tertium datur' B. Schäffera." *RM* No. 21 (1960).
Markiewicz L. "Propozycje czy zagadki?" [Phrases or puzzles?]. *RM* No. 1 (1961).
Schäffer B. "O pewnym analityku, czyli who is who" [On the true analyst, or who is who] (Answer on the article above). *RM* No. 4 (1961).
Zieliński T. " 'Kody' b. Schäffera" [Codes BS]. *RM* No. 21 (1961).
Pociej B. " 'Muzyka ipsa' B. Schäffera." *RM* No. 7 (1963).
——— "O twórczości B. Schäffera" [On the works of BS.] *M* IX/3–4 (1964).
Mycielski Z. " 'Scultura' B. Schäffera" [On the works of BS]. RM No. 19 (1969).
Cegiella J. "Boguslaw Schäffer." *Szkice* . . . , pp. 47–59.
Pociej B. "Composer's Workshop: B. Schäffer." *PM* XII (1969).
"Schäffer: 'Action,' 'Concerto for Tape,' 'Collage and Form,' 'Configurations,' 'Encounters,' 'Monodrama,' etc." *PM* No. 1 (1969); No. 2 (1971).
Bednarcik O. "Graficky prvek w dile B. Schäffera." *Opus Musicum* [Czechoslovakia], III (1971).
Michalski G. *Koncert poswięcony twórczości B. Schäffera* [Concert dedicated to the works of BS]. Warsaw: National PO Publication, 1971.
Hodor J. and Pociej B. *Boguslaw Schäffer and His Music.* Glasgow, 1974.
Karkoschka E. "Über B. Schäffer und einige Kriterien musikalischer Qualität." *Melos/NZM*, II (1976).

SEROCKI Kazimierz

Lissa Z. " 'Koncert romantyczny' K. Serockiego." *M* No. 2 (1951).
Erhardt L. "Grupa 49" [Group 49]. *PK* No. 25 (1953).
Marek T. "Grupa 49." *M* Nos. 5–6 (1954).
Broszkiewicz J. "Cena ludzkiej prawdy" [The value of human integrity: II Symphony]. *PK* No. 26 (1954).
Schiller H. "K. Serocki: 'Sinfonietta na 2 orkiestry smyczkowe." *RM* No. 3 (1958).
Derewecka-Falkowska E. " 'Oczy powietrza' K. Serockiego." *RM* No. 18 (1960).

Gorczycka M. "Wobec nowych utworów: na marginesie 'Musique en relief' W. Kotońskiego i 'Epizodów' K. Serockiego" [On new works: on the problem of Episodes KS]. *RM* No. 21 (1960).
Erhardt L. "K. Serocki—laureat nagrody ministra Kultury i Sztuki za rok 1963" [Serocki was named Artist-Laureate in 1963 by the Polish Ministry of Culture]. *RM* No. 19 (1963).
Markiewicz L. " 'Freski symfoniczne' Serockiego." *RM* No. 21 (1964).
Zieliński T. " 'Continuum' K. Serockiego." *Spotkania* . . . , pp. 182–189.
Gawrońska B. "Organizacja tworzywa muzycznego w twórczości Kazimierza Serockiego" [The organization of musical material in the work of KS]. *Muzyka* No. 2 (1981), pp. 23–45. With a summary in English.
Zieliński A. "Kazimierz Serocki (1922–1981)." *PM* No. 1–2 (1981), pp. 3–13.
Michalski G. "The glittering music of Kazimierz Serocki." *Music in Poland* No. 1–2(38) (1983), pp. 15–19.
Davis L. "Serocki's spatial sonoristics." *Tempo, a Quarterly Review of Modern Music* No. 145 (June 1983).
Zieliński T. A. *O twórczości Kazimierza Serockiego* [On the work of K. Serocki]. Kraków: PWM, 1985.

SIKORSKI Kazimierz

Cegiella J. "Kazimierz Sikorski." *Szkice* . . . pp. 31–38.
Żulawski W. "K. Sikorski." *NK* No. 1 (1950).
Marek T. "Nowa symfonia K. Sikorskiego" [III Symphony]. *PK* No. 42 (1954).
Feicht H. "K. Sikorski Jako teoretik propedeutyki i kompozycji" [KS as a theoretician of propaedeutics and compositions]. *SM* v.V (1956).
Schiller H. " 'III Symfonia' K. Sikorskiego." *RM* No. 5 (1958).
Mazur K. " 'Koncert polifoniczny' K. Sikorskiego." *RM* No. 22 (1966).

SIKORSKI Tomasz

Kaczyński T. " 'Antyfony' T. Sikorskiego." *RM* No. 22 (1963).
Kaczyński T. " 'Concerto breve' T. Sikorskiego." *RM* No. 17 (1965).
Jaroszewicz J. " 'Sequenza I' T. Sikorskiego." *RM* No. 22 (1966).

SKROWACZEWSKI Stanislaw

Wydrzyński A. "Stanislaw Skrowaczewski." *PK* No. 30 (1953).
Koszewski A. " 'Kantata pokoju' S. Skrowaczewskiego." [Cantata of peace] *M* No. 5/6 (1954).
Marek T. "Koncert współczesnej polskiej muzyki kameralnej" [Concert of contemporary Polish chamber music: VI Sonata for Piano]. *M* No. 11/12 (1954).
Pilarski B. " 'Muzyka nocą' S. Skrowaczewskiego" [Night Music]. *PK* No. 1 (1956).
Polska Współczesna Kultura Muzyczna 1944–1964. Kraków: PWM, 1967. (Index of works by Skrowaczewski on p. 447).
Ewen D. *Musicians since 1900*. New York, 1978.

STACHOWSKI Marek

Malecka T. " 'Neusis II' M. Stachowskiego." *M* No. 1 (1978). Tarnawska.

SZABELSKI Boleslaw

Lissa Z. " 'III Symfonia' B. Szabelskiego." *M* No. 1 (1956).
Pociej B. " 'IV Symfonia' B. Szabelskiego." *RM* No. 19 (1958).
Markiewicz L. " 'Trzy sonety' na orkiestre B. Szabelskiego" [Three Sonnets]. *RM* No. 8 (1959).
Zieliński T. " 'Sonety' B. Szabelskiego." *Spotkania* . . . , pp. 143–145.
Pociej B. " 'Wiersze' B. Szabelskiego" [Verses BS]. *RM* No. 21 (1961).
Markiewicz L. "Stare i nowe w muzyce B. Szabelskiego" [The old and new in music BS]. *RM* No. 18 (1962).
Wachowicz Z. "Stare i nowe w tworczości B. Szabelskiego" [The old and new in the works of BS]. *M* IX/3–4 (1964).
Markiewicz L. "Ostatnie utwory B. Szabelskiego" [Last works of BS]. *Res Facta* No. 3 (1969).
Markiewicz L. "Boleslaw Szabelski on his 70th birthday." *PM* No. 1 (1967) (Text also in German).
Pociej B. "The power of symphonic language [of B. Szabelski]." *PP* No. 5 (1975).
Kisielewski S. "The two faces of B. Szabelski." *PM* No. 4 (1978).
Zieliński T. "Boleslaw Szabelski (1896–1979). *Wychowanie Muzyczne w Szkole* No. 1 (1980).
Cegiella J. "Boleslaw Szabelski." *Szkice* . . . , pp. 189–197.

SZALONEK Witold

"Witold Szalonek o Darmstadzie i 'Wyznaniach' " [WS about Darmstadt and "Confessions." (Interview). *RM* No. 22 (1960).
Schiller H. " 'Concertino' W. Szalonka." *RM* No. 22 (1963).
Markiewicz L. " 'Les sons' W. Szalonka." *RM* No. 17 (1965).
Gabryś R. "Nad utworem W. Szalonka 'Proporzioni' " [About 'Proporzioni' by WS]. *RM* No. 17 (1969).
Kaczyński T. " 'Monologhi' Szalonka." *RM* No. 4 (1969).
Kondracki M. "W. Szalonek: 1+1+1+1 per 1–4 strumenti ad arco." *RM* No. 14 (1970).

SZELIGOWSKI Tadeusz

Marek T. "Tadeusz Szeligowski." *M* No. 5 (1950).
Brandstaetter R. "Bunt żaków" [Opera "The Students' Revolt"]. *M* No. 2 (1951).
Lissa Z. " 'Bunt żaków' T. Szeligowskiego." Kraków: PWM, 1957.
Kański J. " 'Krakatuk' T. Szeliogowskiego." *RM* No. 14 (1957).
────── " 'Mazepa' T. Szeligowskiego." *RM* No. 3 (1959).
Weber J. "Mówi T. Szeligowski" [Interview]. *RM* No. 3 (1959).
Mycielski Z. "T. Szeligowski 15.IX.1896–10.I.1963." *RM* No. 4 (1963).
Krassowski J., editor. *Tadeusz Szeligowski. W 10 rocznice smierci kompozytora* [Materials from the musicological session on 10th anniversary of composer's death]. Gdańsk: PWSM, 1973.

ŚWIDER Józef

Marek T. "Piękny start kompozytorski" [A wonderful composer's start]. *PK* No. 31 (1955).
Markiewicz L. " 'Concertino da camera' J. Świdra." *RM* No. 2 (1963).
Markiewicz L. "Zur polnischen Uraufführung der Oper 'Wit Stwosz' von J. Ś." *Musik and Gesellschaft* No. 1 (1975), p. 15.
Wybraniec E. "Forte czy piano" [The works by J. Ś.] *Poglądy* No. 6 (1981).

TURSKI Zbigniew

Mycielski Z. "Zloty medal olimpijski za 'Symfonie' Z. Turskiego" [Olympic Gold medicla for the Symphony No. 2 ZT]. *O* No. 29 (1948).

Mycielski Z. " 'III Symfonia' Z. Turskiego." *PK* No. 12 (1956).
Hordynski J. "Z. Turski" [Interview]. *ŻL* No. 2 (1961).
Frydrychowicz B. " 'Sinfonia da camera' Z. Turskiego, 'Allegro de Voiron' M. Spisaka." *RM* No. 21 (1961).
Cegiella J. "Z. Turski." *Szkice* . . . , pp. 179–188.

TWARDOWSKI Romuald

Mycielski Z. " 'Cyrano' Twardowskiego w Bytomiu." *RM* No. 23 (1963).
Kolińska K. "Z wizytą u R. Twardowskiego" [Interview]. *ŻŚ* No. 12 (1963).
Cegiella J. "R. Twardowski." *Szkice* . . . , pp. 125–139.

WIECHOWICZ Stanislaw

Rutkowski B. "S. Wiechowicz." *Muzyka Polska* No. 2 (1939).
Chomiński J. "Zagadnienie folkloru w tworczości współczesnych kompozytorów polskich" [Folkloric Problems in the works of Contemporary Polish Composers]. *M* Nos. 5–6 (1951).
Prosnak J. "S. Wiechowicz. Zyciorys i twórczość chóralna" [Biography and Choral Works]. *ŻŚ* No. 10 (1954).
Chomiński J. " 'Kujawiak-ballada' S. Wiechowicza." *SM* V (1956).
Pociej B. "S. Wiechowicz." *PK* No. 7 (1956).
Schiller H. "S. Wiecowicz—kompozytor i pedagog" [Composer and Teacher]. *RM* No. 12 (1960).
Kaczyński T. " 'List do Marc Chagalla' S. Wiechowicza." *RM* No. 21 (1961).
Kisielewski S. "S. Wiechowicz. 1893–1963." *RM* No. 12 (1963).
Mrygoń A. *Stanislaw Wiechowicz*. Cz. I: *Dzialalność*. Cz. II: *Twórczość* [P.I: Activity; P. II: Art]. Kraków: PWM, 1982.

WISZNIEWSKI Zbigniew

Derewecka E. "Opera radiowe ('Neffru')" [Radio-operas: Neffru]. *RM* No. 21 (1960).
Pociej B. " 'Trio' Z. Wiszniewskiego." *RM* No. 22 (1963).
Malinowski W. " 'Tristia' Z. Wiszniewskiego." *RM* No. 5 (1966).

WOYTOWICZ Boleslaw

Mycielski Z. " 'II Symfonia' Woytowicza." *RM* No. 6 (1946).
——— " 'Kwartet' Woytowicza." *RM* No. 11 (1947).
Woytowicz B. "Wypowiedź na temat wlasnej techniki kompozytorskiej" [Statements about the composer's own technique]. *Kwartalnik Muzyczny* No. 24 (1948), p. 141.
Lissa Z. "Trzy rozmowy z. B. Woytowiczem" [Three conversations with BW]. *Kuźnica* No. 3 (1949).
Rudziński W. "Kantata 'Prorok' B. Woytowicza."*M* No. 5/6 (1954).
Wilkowska-Chomińska K. " 'Etiudy fortepianowe' B. Woytowicza." *SM* V (1956).

Footnotes for Bibliography

*Abbreviations used: M: Muzyka; NK: Nowa Kultura; O: Odrodzenie; PK: Przegląd Kulturalny; PM: Polish Music; PP: Polish Perspectives; PWM: Polskie Wydawnictwo Muzyczne; PWN: Polskie Wydawnictwo Naukowe; PWSM: Państwowa Wyzsza Szkola Muzyczna; SM: Studia Muzykologiczne; TP: Tygodnik Powszechny; WL: Wydawnictwo Literackie; ZKP: Związek Kompozytorów Polskich; ŻL: Życie Literackie; ŻŚ: Życie Śpiewacze.

**Future references to this book will be designated as *Spotkania* . . .

***Future references to this book will be designated as *Szkice* . . .

****Future references to this article will be designated as Tarnawska.

Index

Aeschylus, 168, 171
aleatory music, 69, 78, 82, 142
   "aleatory without aleatory", 110, 114
   aleatorism limited, 82, 180
Alshvang, Arnold, 41
Aragon, Louis, 168, 169
Asafiev, Boris, 41
Aubris, P., 30
Augustyn, Roman, 114, 115, 194

Bacewicz, Grażyna, xi, xii, 17, 18, 21, 25, 26, 27–29, 45, 60, 68, 104–111
   Adventures of King Arthur, 50
   Cello Concerto No. 2, 105
   Concerto for Orchestra, 106, 107–108, 109, 110, 111
   Concerto for String Orchestra, 27–28, 45, 107
   Concerto for Two Pianos, 110
   Contradizione, 105, 108, 109
   From Peasant to King, 17–18
   In una parte, 105, 110
   Music for Strings, Trumpets and Percussion, 29, 60, 106, 107
   Musica sinfonica, 105, 106, 107
   Overture for Orchestra, 27
   Pensieri notturni, 104, 106–107, 108, 109
   String Quartet No. 6, 60
   Symphony No. 2, 27
   Symphony No. 3, 21, 27
   Symphony No. 4, 21, 27
   Viola Concerto, 105
   Violin Concerto No. 3, 27
   Violin Concerto No. 7, 105, 110
Bach, J. S., 28, 93, 155, 156, 157, 159, 163
Baird, Tadeusz, x, xiii, 2, 5, 7, 8, 18, 21, 25, 26, 27, 29–31, 44, 51, 54–58, 94, 104, 111–117, 194
   Colas Breugnon, 19, 25, 30
   Concerto for Orchestra, 29, 30–31
   Concerto lugubre, 114, 117
   Egzorta, 54, 56–58
   Elegeia, 114
   Epiphany Music, 54, 56
   Erotics, 54
   Espressioni Varianti, 54, 56
   Five Songs (to the words by H. Poświatowska), 114
   Four Essays, 45, 54, 55–56
   Four Love Sonnets (W. Shakespeare), 30, 114
   Goethe-Briefe, 104, 114, 116–117
   Piano Concerto, 29
   Psychodrama, 114, 115–116
   Songs of the Trouvères, 30
   Sinfonietta, 29
   Symphony No. 1, 21, 29
   Symphony No. 2, 21, 29–30

Tomorrow, 94–96, 114, 115, 194
Variations Without a Theme, 54, 56
Bargielski, Zbigniew, 99
Baroque style, 25, 30, 37, 97, 156, 182
Bartók, Béla, x, 29, 37, 60, 62, 72, 97, 104, 106, 107, 109, 111
Beethoven, Ludwig van, 138, 165
Berg, Alban, 54, 95, 112, 113, 141
Bielawski, Ludwik, xiii
Bilica, Krzysztof, 196
Bloch, Augustyn, 98–99, 194
  Ayelet (Mystery-Opera), 98–99
  Awaiting, 98
  Gilgamesh, 98
  Very Sleeping Beauty, 98, 99
Boguslawski, Edward, 104
Borodin, Alexander, 28
Borowski, Tadeusz, 1, 15
Boulanger, Nadia, 27, 134, 137
Boulez, Pierre, 45, 58, 62, 66
Brahms, Johannes, 138
Brandstaetter, Roman, 12
Bratny, Roman, 1
Brockes, B., 157
Broniewski, Wladyslaw, 168, 169
Bruckner, Anton, ix, 24, 25, 31
Bruno, Giordano, 174
Büchner, Georg, 99
Bujarski, Zbigniew, 52, 69, 104
Bukowski, Ryszard, 103
Bunsz, F., 41
Bussotti, Sylvano, 78
Bystroń, Jan, 10

Cage, John, 45, 78
Carroll, Lewis, 99
Cegiella, Janusz, 194
Cholopova, Valentina, 42, 83, 92
Chomiński, Józef M., xiii, 8, 41, 42, 53, 54, 58, 90, 91, 194
Chopin, Frederick, xi, xiii, 7, 40, 91, 113
F. Chopin Society (Towarzystwo im. F. Chopina, TIFC), 40
Chybiński, Adolf, xiii
"club music", 2
Conrad, Joseph, 94, 97
Copernicus, Nicolaus, 121, 124, 174
Cusa, Nicolaus de, 174
Czerwieński, Bruno, 3
Czyż, Henryk, 7

Dallapiccola, Luigi, 45, 168
Darmstadt School, 64, 74
Davis, Lyn, 196
Dąbrowski, Florian, 7
Dąbrowski, Jaroslaw, 16
Debussy, Claude, ix, x
Denisov, Edison, 69
Dobrowolski, Andrzej, 7, 8, 26, 50
dodecaphonic technique, xiii, 53, 68, 78, 150
  ("serial dodecaphony", 53–68)
Droba, Krzysztof, 77, 90, 92, 126, 133, 194, 195
Drobner, Meczyslaw, 12, 42
Dygacz, Adolf, 127, 131
Dziewulska, Maria, 5

Eliot, T. S., 101
Erenberg, G., 3
Erhardt, Ludwik, 75, 90, 91, 155, 169, 174, 175, 196

Fiszer, Edward, 4
Fitelberg Composers' Competition, xiii
folkloric Polish trend, xii, 5, 7, 8, 10, 19, 20–21, 33, 36, 37, 38

Gagarin, Yuri, 174, 177
Galczyński, Konstanty Ildefons, 5, 58, 145
Gąsiorowska, Maria, 129, 131, 133, 195
Glenn, John, 174, 177
Globokar, Vinko, 78
Goethe, Johann Wolfgang von, 97
Goluj, Tadeusz, 1
Gomólka, Mikolaj, 125
Gomulka, Wladyslaw, xi
Górecki, Henryk Mikolaj, 45, 51, 62, 63–65, 69, 76–78, 104, 117–133, 134
  Ad Matrem, 78, 104, 117–120, 131
  Amen, 117
  Concerto for 5 Instruments, 63
  Epitaphium, 63
  Genesis, 48, 76, 77, 126
  Muzyka Staropolska, 77, 117
  Refrain, 76, 126
  Scontri, 64–65
  Symphony No.1, 63
  Symphony No.2, 78, 117, 121–126, 131
  Symphony No.3, 117, 126–133
  Two Sacred Songs, 117

Index   245

Gradstein, Alfred, 3, 4, 5
"Group 49", 2, 29, 31, 41
Gruszczyński, K., 4

Hadyna, Stanislaw, 5
Hindemith, Paul, 37, 121
Hoffman, E. Theodor, 42
Hogarth, A. D., 94, 194
Honegger, Arthur, 23, 29, 36, 45, 57, 95, 123, 150, 157, 168
Huxley, Aldous, 94, 158

Ives, Charles E., 45
Iwaszkiewicz, Jaroslaw, 21, 94, 97

Jarociński, Stefan, xiii, 2, 92
Jarzębski, Adam, 26

Kabalewski, Dmitri, 29
Kaczyński, Tadeusz, 92, 149, 194, 196
Kancheli, Givi, 69
Karlowicz, Meczyslaw, x, 9, 21
Kawalerowicz, Jerzy, 94
Kiesewetter, Tomasz, 18, 19
Kijowski, Andrzej, 196
Kilar, Wojciech, 45, 52, 104
Kisielewski, Stefan, xi, 25, 51
Kochanowski, Jan, 48, 73, 96, 158
Koffler, Józef, 53
Kohoutek, Ctirad, 82, 91, 92
Kolaczkowska, G., 4, 5
Kolberg, Oscar, xiii, 5, 43
Kondracki, Michal, x
Konopnicka, Maria, 7
Kord, Kazimierz, 82
Kościuszko Foundation, 121
Koszewski, Andrzej, 25
Kotoński, Wlodzimierz, 19, 45, 51, 104
Kraszewski, J., 99
Krauze, Zygmunt, 46, 69, 78–82, 104
    Aus Aller Welt Stammende, 82
    Folk Music, 79–82
    Piano Concerto, 82
    Piece for Orchestra: No.1–79, No.2—79
Krenz, Jan, 2, 5, 7, 21, 26
Krzanowski, Andrzej, 78
Kurpiński, Karol, 3

Lachman, Waclaw, 7
Lagów Lubuskie, composers' conference at, 1–2

Lebkowski, M., 5
Lenartowicz, Teofil, 7
Lem, Stanislaw, 101
Leonardo da Vinci, 174
Ligęza, Józef, xiii, 5, 10
Lissa, Zofia, xiii, 42
Lobaczewska, Stefania, xiii
Luciuk, Juliusz, 49, 99
Lucretius Titus Carus, 174
Lutoslawski, Witold, xi, xii, xiii, xv, 4, 5, 6, 7, 18, 21, 25, 34–38, 41, 51, 62–63, 82–89, 104, 111, 123, 124, 139, 140, 141, 147, 174, 178–192
    Cello Concerto, 180, 182, 186
    Concerto for Orchestra, 36–38, 178
    Espaces du sommeil, Les, 104
    Jeux vénitiens, 48, 82, 178, 180
    Little Suite, 10, 36, 45
    Livre pour orchestre, 83, 180, 181–182, 184
    Musique funèbre, 45, 48, 62–63, 189
    Paroles tissées, 83, 147
    Preludes and Fugue, 180, 182–192
    Silesian Triptych, 7, 9, 10–11, 33, 36
    String Quartet, 82, 84, 178, 180, 190
    Symphony No.1, 21, 23, 35–36
    Symphony No.2, 83, 180–181, 182, 184, 188
    Trois Poèmes d'Henri Michaux, xiv, 48, 83, 84–89, 139, 178, 180
    Three Postludes, 178
Lysogor Songs (collection of the 15th century), 128

Mahler, Gustav, 25, 29, 30, 31, 112, 117, 134, 138, 141, 150, 189
Maklakiewicz, Jan, x, xi, 4, 5, 7, 8, 16, 17, 18, 26, 27
    Cagliostro in Warsaw, 16
    The Golden Duck, 17
Malawski, Artur, x, xi, 7, 8, 18, 19
    Wierchy (The Mountain Tops), 8
Malinowski, Wladyslaw, 68, 91
Marek, Tadeusz, 16, 17, 21, 31, 42
mass-song, 2, 3–5
Matuszczak, Bernadetta, 101
Mazel, Lev, 41
"Mazowsze" (ensemble), xiii, 5
Mérimée, Prosper, 103
Messiaen, Olivier, 45, 69, 137, 138

Meyer, Krzysztof, 101, 104, 133–141, 195, 196
  Cyberiada, 101
  Gamblers, 140, 195
  String Quartets Nos. 5, 6, 139, 141
  Symphony No. 1, 134–136, 140
  Symphony No. 2, 136–137
  Symphony No. 3, 136, 137–139
  Symphony No. 5, 141
  Symphony No. 6, 141
Miaskovsky, Nikolaj, 23
Michalski, Grzegorz, 138, 195
Mickiewicz, Adam, xi, 7, 113
Miechow Monastery Antiphonarium, 124
Milhaud, Darius, 57, 168
Mlodziejowski, Jerzy, x, 7
Mlynarski, Emil, 40
Moniuszko, Stanislaw, xiii, 11, 15
Moussorgsky, Modest, 13
Munk, Andrzej, 1
Muradeli, Vano, 11
Musicologists', First International Congress of, xiii
"Muzyka", the magazine, xii
Mycielski, Zygmunt, xi, 8, 19, 45

Natanson, Tadeusz, 103
neo-baroque, 25
neo-classicism, x, xi, xii, 24, 25, 27, 29, 35, 36, 53, 55, 93, 96, 111, 112, 134, 145, 165
neo-impressionism, 67
neo-romanticism, 113
new-Viennese school, 45, 55, 72, 78 (post-webernism), 113, 190
Niżyńska, Krystyna, 42
Nikolskaya, Irina, 194
Nono, Luigi, 45, 168
Norwid, Cyprian, 103, 113
Nowowiejski, Feliks, 11

Obrecht, Jacob, 155
Ochlewski, Tadeusz, xiii
Olearczyk, Edward, 3, 4, 5
Orff, Karl, 96
Or-Ot (collection of tales), 17
Ovid (Publius Ovidius Naso), 174, 176

Paciorkiewicz, Tadeusz, 5, 7, 26, 48
Palester, Roman, 45
Palestrina, Giovanni, P., 30

Panufnik, Andrzej, 6, 18, 20, 24, 26, 35
  Lullaby, 20
  Nocturne for Orchestra, 25
  Sinfonia Rustica, 20
  Symphony of Peace, 21
  Tragic Overture, 21
Pärt, Arvo, 134
Parun, Vesna, 114
Pękiel, Bartlomiej, 48
Penderecki, Krzysztof, xiii, xv, 46, 51, 64–68, 71–76, 91, 93, 104, 134, 139, 154–178, 194
  Anaklasis, 72, 74, 154, 167, 177
  Canon for 2 String Orch., 72, 154
  Cosmogony, 75, 104, 121, 125, 154, 173–178
  Devils of Loudun, The, 93–94, 158, 194
  Dies Irae, 139, 154, 168–173
  Dimensions of Time and Silence, 66–68, 154
  Emanations, 64, 66, 72, 154
  Fluorescences, 72, 75, 154, 167, 172, 177
  Magnificat, 104, 154, 168
  Natura Sonoris, De, No.1—72, 154
                       No.2—154
  Polymorphia, 72, 154, 167
  Psalms of David, 72, 154, 158
  Stabat Mater, xiv, 48, 154
  St. Luke Passion, xiv, 48, 94, 139, 154–167, 168, 169, 178
  String Quartet No.1, 154
  Strophes, 48, 66, 72
  Threnody, 48, 71, 72, 73–74, 154, 167
  Utrenya, 94, 154, 168
Penherski, Zbigniew, 52, 69–70, 99, 103
  Quartet, 69–70
  Peryn's Twilight, 99
Perkowski, Piotr, xi, xii, 7, 16, 26
  Swantewit, 16–17
Picander, 157
Picasso, Pablo, 119, 168
Polish colorism, 68, 91
Polish postwar music divisions into periods, xii
Polish Renaissance, xiii, 26, 45, 48, 77, 96
Polish romantic tradition, xi, 113
Polskie Wydawnictwo Muzyczne (PWM), xiii, 35

Poradowski, Stefan, x
Poświatowska, Halina, 114
Poulenc, Francis, 29, 102
Poźniak, Wlodzimierz, x
Prokofiev, Sergei, 10, 21, 23, 27, 29, 31, 35, 36, 72, 90, 97, 123
Prosnak, Antoni, 91
Prószyński, Stanislaw, 18, 48
Przyboś, Julian, 58
Puccini, Giacomo, 15, 97
Pushkin, Alexander, 7, 9
Pythagor, 176

Ravel, Maurice, x, 29, 97
Regamey, Konstanty, 53
Reger, Max, ix
Rey, Jan, 17
Rimsky-Korsakov, Nikolai, 9
Rizos, J., 102
Rolland, Romain, 19, 30 (*Colas Breugnon*)
Roussel, Albert, 27
Różewicz, Tadeusz, 1, 142, 144, 146, 168, 169
Różycki, Ludomir, 11, 16
Ruch'evskaya, Ekatherine, 86, 92
"Ruch Muzyczny" (magazine), xii
Rudziński, Witold, x, xii, 4, 7, 12, 48, 49, 96
    Johnny, The Musician, 15–16
    The Dismissal of the Greek Envoys, 48, 96
Rudziński, Zbigniew, 48, 52, 69, 104
Rychlik, Józef, 66, 90
Rytel, Piotr, 12, 16, 19
    Andrew of Chelmno, 16

Satie, Eric, 79
Schäffer, Boguslaw, xiii, 46, 50, 51, 54, 64, 101–103
    Missa elettronica, 103
    Monodram, 102
Scheller, Max, 126, 195
Schoenberg, Arnold, 45, 53, 57, 95, 102, 168
Schubert, Franz, 112
Schütz, Heinrich, 155, 156
Scriabin, Alexander, x, 121, 124
Seferis, J., 102
serial technique, 53, 90; see also: dodecaphonic technique, serial dodecaphony

Serocki, Kazimierz, 2, 4, 5, 6, 7, 18, 19, 26, 31–34, 44, 46, 52, 54, 58–60, 69, 78, 104, 142–149, 196
    Ad libitum, 142
    A piacere, 78, 142
    Continuum, 142
    Dramatic Story, 144, 148–149
    Episodes, 60
    Eyes of the Air, 58, 59, 144
    Fantasia elegiaca, 144
    Forte i piano, 142
    Heart of the Night, 58, 144
    Impromptu Fantasque, 144
    Musica concertante, 58, 59
    Niobe, 104, 142, 145–146
    Phantasmagoria, 144
    Poems (Poetry), 142, 146–148
    Symphonic Frescoes, 142
    Symphony No. 1, 31–32
    Symphony No. 2, 32–34
    Swinging Music, 142
    Three Kurpiowski Melodies, 31
Shakespeare, William, 30, 56, 114
Shostakovich, Dmitri, 11, 21, 23, 29, 31, 32, 36, 123, 134, 138, 140, 141, 150, 189, 195
Sienkewicz, Henryk, 15, 16
Sikorski, Kazimierz, xii, 3, 5, 19, 25, 26, 27, 42, 45
    Symphony No.3, 25–26, 37
Sikorski, Tomasz, 52, 69, 70, 104
    Holzwege, 70
Sito, Jerzy, S., 95
Six, Les, 29, 31, 41, 45
Skierkowski, Wladyslaw, 5, 127
Skorik, Michail, 90
Skrebkov, Sergei, 41
Skrowaczewski, Stanislaw, 7, 8, 19, 24, 49
"Śląsk" (vocal ensemble), xiii, 5
Slonimski, Sergei, 91
Slowacki, Juliusz, xi, 113
Sobieski, Jadwiga and Marian, xiii
Society of Young Polish Musicians, the (SMMP), xi
Sokhor, Arnold, 41
sonorism, xiii, 66, 68–69, 80, 144, 165
    sonorism reduced (or limited), 64, 77, 121, 126, 129, 133
Sophocles, 66, 174, 177
Spisak, Michal, 25, 26

Stachowski, Marek, 104
Stęszewski, Jan, 79
Stockhausen, Karlheinz, 45, 79, 108, 109, 142
Strauss, Richard, ix, x, 44, 97
Stravinsky, Igor, x, 17, 35, 36, 37, 45, 60, 66, 72, 96, 107, 111, 112, 137, 159, 163
Strumiłło, A., 41
Stucky, Steven, 35, 42, 43, 196
Święcicki, W., 3
Świerzyński, Adam, 7, 26
Świder, Józef, 103
Swinarski, Artur, 17
Swinarski, Konrad, 1
Sygietyński, Tadeusz, 3, 4, 5
Szabelski, Bolesław, xi, xii, 7, 18, 19, 25, 37, 45, 52, 60–61, 150–154
  Aphorisms "9", 60, 61
  Symphony No.5, 150–154
  Three Sonnets, 60, 61
  Verses, 60
Szalonek, Witold, 46, 51, 69, 104
Szeligowski, Tadeusz, xi, 5, 7, 8, 12, 15, 26, 42, 48, 49
  The Students' Rebellion, 12–15
Szpilman, Władysław, 3, 4
Szymanowski, Karol, x, xiii, 6, 8, 9, 16, 17, 21, 23, 27, 36, 68, 91, 112, 113, 133

Tananaeva, Ludmila, 42, 91
Taneiev, Sergei, 9
Taraeva, Galina, 42
Tishchenko, Boris, 134
Turska, Irena, 18
Turski, Zbigniew, 4, 7, 18, 26, 49
  Symphony No.2 (Olympic), 21, 23–24
  Warsaw Legend, 18
Tuwim, Julian, 9, 137, 139
Twardowski, Romuald, 48, 49, 94, 97–98 (ballets, operas), 104
  Lord Jim, 97–98, 104

Urbański, Kazimierz, 78
Urgacz, T., 4, 5
Ustwolska, Halina, 134
U Thant, 173

Valéry, Paul, 137, 168
Varèse, Edgar, 45, 69, 72

Wacław from Szamotuły, 26, 77
Wagner, Richard, ix, x, 117
Wajda, Andrzej, 1, 41, 94
Walentynowicz, Władysław, 12
Wallek-Walewski, Bolesław, 11
Waryński, L., 3
Warsaw Autumn Festival (Warszawska Jesień), xiii, 3, 44–45
Warsaw Opera, 8, 194
Warsaw Philharmonic, 40
Wasita, R., 196
Webern, Anton, 55, 58, 61, 62, 90–91, 109, 150
Whiting, George, 94
Wiechowicz, Stanisław, x, xii, 5, 6, 7, 19, 136
  Ballada-Kujawiak, 5
  Carols, 6
  On a Clay Vase, 6
Wiłkomirski, Kazimierz, 18, 26
Winkler, K., 4
Wisłocki, Stanisław, 19, 26
Wiszniewski, Zbigniew, 50
Witkiewicz, Stanisław Ignacy, 99
Wojciechowski, A., 22
Wolski, 7
Woytowicz, Bolesław, 7, 9, 18, 21, 35
  The Prophet, 9–10
  The Warsaw Symphony, 22–23
Wróblewski, Andrzej, 1, 41
Wygodzki, Stanisław, 4, 15
Wyspiański, Stanisław, 113

Yarustowsky, Boris, 42
Young Poland, ix, x, xiii, 9, 40, 45, 58
Young Polish Musicians, Society (Stowarzyszenie Młodych Muzyków Polaków, SMMP), xi
Yujak, Kiroline, 90

Zieliński, Tadeusz, 27, 42, 61, 75, 90, 91, 108, 113, 116, 144, 194, 196
Zukkerman, Victor, 41
Związek Kompozytorów Polskich (ZKP: Polish Composers' Union), xii, xiii, xv, 2, 3, 35